THE CAMBRIDGE COMPANION TO
GABRIEL GARCÍA MÁRQUEZ

Gabriel García Márquez is Latin America's most internationally famous and successful author, and a winner of the Nobel Prize. His oeuvre of great modern novels includes *One Hundred Years of Solitude* and *Love in the Time of Cholera*. His name has become closely associated with magical realism, a phenomenon that has been immensely influential in world literature. This companion includes new and probing readings of all of García Márquez's works by leading international specialists. His life in Colombia, the context of Latin American history and culture, key themes in his works and their critical reception are explored in detail. Written for students and readers of García Márquez, the companion is accessible for non-Spanish speakers and features a chronology and a guide to further reading. This insightful and lively book will provide an invaluable framework for the further study and enjoyment of this major figure in world literature.

PHILIP SWANSON is Hughes Professor of Spanish at the University of Sheffield.

A complete list of books in the series is at the back of this book

THE CAMBRIDGE COMPANION TO GABRIEL GARCÍA MÁRQUEZ

EDITED BY
PHILIP SWANSON

CAMBRIDGE UNIVERSITY PRESS
Cambridge, New York, Melbourne, Madrid, Cape Town, Singapore,
São Paulo, Delhi, Dubai, Tokyo

Cambridge University Press
The Edinburgh Building, Cambridge CB2 8RU, UK

Published in the United States of America by Cambridge University Press, New York

www.cambridge.org
Information on this title: www.cambridge.org/9780521687102

First published 2010

Printed in the United Kingdom at the University Press, Cambridge

A catalogue record for this publication is available from the British Library

Library of Congress Cataloguing in Publication data
The Cambridge companion to Gabriel García Márquez / [edited by] Philip Swanson.
p. cm. – (Cambridge companions to literature)
Includes bibliographical references.
ISBN 978-0-521-86749-8 (hardback)
1. Garcma Marquez, Gabriel, 1928–Criticism and interpretation. I. Swanson,
Philip, 1959– II. Title. III. Series.
PQ8180.17.A73Z6155 2010
863'.64–dc22
2010014789

ISBN 978-0-521-86749-8 Hardback
ISBN 978-0-521-68710-2 Paperback

CONTENTS

Notes on contributors page vii
Acknowledgements x
Chronology xi

Introduction 1
PHILIP SWANSON

1 Gabriel García Márquez: life and times 7
GENE H. BELL-VILLADA

2 The critical reception of García Márquez 25
DONALD SHAW

3 Before *One Hundred Years of Solitude*: the early novels 41
ROBIN FIDDIAN

4 *One Hundred Years of Solitude* 57
PHILIP SWANSON

5 An eco-critical reading of *One Hundred Years of Solitude* 64
RAYMOND L. WILLIAMS

6 *The Autumn of the Patriarch* 78
STEVEN BOLDY

7 *The General in His Labyrinth* 94
GERALD MARTIN

8 García Márquez's novels of love 113
MARK I. MILLINGTON

9 García Márquez's short stories 129
STEPHEN HART

10 García Márquez's non-fiction works 144
ROBERT L. SIMS

11 García Márquez and film 160
CLAIRE TAYLOR

12 García Márquez, magical realism and world literature 179
MICHAEL BELL

Further reading 196
Index 201

CONTRIBUTORS

PASCALE BAKER, of the University of Sheffield, is completing a thesis on the representation of banditry in the literature of Mexico and the US Southwest.

MICHAEL BELL took his BA and Ph.D. (external) from University College London. He taught in France, Germany, Canada and the USA before moving to the University of Warwick where he is Professor in the Department of English and Comparative Literary Studies. He is also a founding member, and current Director, of the University's Centre for Research in Philosophy, Literature and the Arts. He has written books and essays on topics including primitivism, sentimentalism, mythopoeia and education, ranging across several European literatures from the Enlightenment to modernity, and often with an emphasis on the relations between literary and philosophical thought.

GENE H. BELL-VILLADA is Professor of Romance Languages at Williams College. He is the author of *García Márquez: The Man and His Work* (1990, currently in its sixth printing) and *Borges and His Fiction: A Guide to His Mind and Art* (1981, revised edition 1999). His *Art for Art's Sake and Literary Life* (1996) was a finalist for the 1997 National Book Critics Circle Award and has been translated into Serbian and Chinese. Bell-Villada has also published a novel, a book of stories and, most recently, a memoir, *Overseas American: Growing up Gringo in the Tropics* (2005).

STEVEN BOLDY is Reader in Latin American Literature at the University of Cambridge and previously taught at Liverpool and Tulane. He has published articles on Rulfo, Carpentier and others, and books on Julio Cortázar and Carlos Fuentes. He is at present working on a volume on Borges.

ROBIN FIDDIAN is Professor of Hispanic Studies at Oxford University and Fellow of Wadham College, Oxford. His most recent monographs include *The Novels of Fernando del Paso* (2000) and *García Márquez: Los funerales de la mamá grande* (2006). Professor Fiddian also edited *García Márquez* in the Modern Literatures in Perspective series published by Longman (1995) and *Postcolonial Perspectives on the Cultures of Latin America and Lusophone Africa* (2000).

STEPHEN HART is Professor of Hispanic Studies at University College London. He has published widely on Latin American film and literature, including *Latin American Cultural Studies* (2003), *A Companion to Latin American Film* (2004) and *A Companion to Latin American Literature* (2007). He is currently writing a book on Gabriel García Márquez for Reaktion Books. An authority on César Vallejo, he has directed and produced a docudrama based on the poet's life and work, *Traspié entre 46 estrellas* (2006), and in 2003 he published, with Juan Fló, *Autógrafos olvidados,* an edition of the fifty-two handwritten manuscripts of early versions of Vallejo's later poems discovered in Montevideo. He is General Editor of Tamesis and founder-director of the Centre of César Vallejo Studies.

GERALD MARTIN is Andrew W. Mellon Professor Emeritus of Modern Languages at the University of Pittsburgh and Senior Professor in Caribbean Studies at London Metropolitan University. His research focuses on twentieth-century Latin American narrative, on which he has published extensively. He is known in particular for his work on Miguel Ángel Asturias and Gabriel García Márquez. His *Gabriel García Márquez: A Life* appeared in 2008.

MARK I. MILLINGTON took his Ph.D. at the University of Cambridge and has taught at the University of Nottingham since 1980, where he currently holds a chair in Latin American studies. His research has concentrated on twentieth-century Latin American prose fiction and on debates concerned with cultural difference. He has published books and articles on numerous authors, in particular Onetti, García Márquez, Gallegos, Borges, Vargas Llosa and Monterroso. He has recently published a book entitled *Hombres in/visibles: La representación de la masculinidad en la literatura latinoamericana, 1920–1980* (2007).

DONALD SHAW graduated MA from the University of Manchester in 1954 and obtained his Ph.D. from Trinity College Dublin. He later taught in Glasgow and Edinburgh before moving to the University of Virginia, where he is Brown Forman Professor of Spanish American Literature. He has published numerous books on nineteenth-century Spanish literature, the Generation of 1898 and modern Spanish American fiction and poetry.

ROBERT L. SIMS is the Coordinator of Spanish Studies at Virginia Commonwealth University. He was a Fulbright scholar in 1987, 1988 and 1992 in Colombia, where he taught courses in Latin American literature. He served in the Peace Corps between 1968 and 1970. Dr Sims received his Ph.D. at the University of Wisconsin-Madison in 1973. He wrote his dissertation on 'The Use of Myth in Claude Simon and Gabriel García Márquez'. He specialises in the theory and function of myth in modern literature, the modern French and Latin American novel, the structuralist study of literary texts, dialogic criticism, reader-response criticism, narratology, deconstruction and the critical writings of Mikhail Bakhtin, the image of Christopher Columbus in modern literature, the New Latin American Historical Novel, and postmodernism/postcolonialism in Latin America.

PHILIP SWANSON is Hughes Professor of Spanish at the University of Sheffield. He has published extensively on Latin American literature, including various books on the New Novel, José Donoso and Gabriel García Márquez. His most recent books are *Latin American Fiction* (2005) and the edited volume *The Companion to Latin American Studies* (2003). He is currently working on the postmodern detective in Latin America, on attitudes to Isabel Allende and on a project on representations of Latin America. Professor Swanson has taught in a number of universities in Europe and in the USA. He is currently President of the Association of Hispanists of Great Britain and Ireland.

CLAIRE TAYLOR is Lecturer in Hispanic Studies at the University of Liverpool. Her research interests include Latin American women's writing, postcolonial theory in a Latin American context, and Latin American cyberculture. She has published a number of articles on these topics, as well as the monograph *Bodies and Texts: Configurations of Identity in the Works of Griselda Gambaro, Albalucía Ángel and Laura Esquivel* (2003).

RAYMOND L. WILLIAMS is Professor of Latin American Literature at the University of California, Riverside. He has published articles and books on the modern fiction of Latin America, and his books include *Gabriel García Márquez* (1984) and *The Colombian Novel, 1844–1987* (1991). His most recent book is *The Latin American Novel, 1945–Present* (2007).

ACKNOWLEDGEMENTS

I would like to thank all the contributors for their knowledge, insight and, in many cases, patience. I would also like to thank Linda Bree and Maartje Scheltens of Cambridge University Press, and Kaarina Hollo and David Shepherd of the University of Sheffield, for their much-appreciated practical support.

CHRONOLOGY

1927	Gabriel García Márquez born 6 March at 9 a.m. in Aracataca, northern Colombia.
1938–46	School in Barranquilla, Sucre, Zipaquirá.
1947	Joins National University of Colombia in Bogotá and starts to study law. Publishes his first story 'The Third Resignation' ('La tercera resignación') in *El Espectador,* 13 September.
1948	Moves to Cartagena de Indias on the Caribbean coast and becomes a journalist on *El Universal.*
1949	Moves to Barranquilla. Gives up studies and works as a journalist for *El Heraldo* and *El Nacional* from 1950 to 1953.
1950	Moves to Bogotá and works as a journalist for *El Espectador.*
1955	Travels to Europe. First novel, *Leaf Storm* (*La hojarasca*), is published.
1956–7	Lives in Paris and works on *No One Writes to the Colonel* (*El coronel no tiene quien le escriba*). Returns to Latin America December 1957 to take a job with the magazine *Momento* in Caracas, Venezuela.
1958	Publishes *No One Writes to the Colonel.* Marries his wife, Mercedes.
1959–61	Following the Cuban Revolution, works for Prensa Latina in Bogotá, Havana and New York. In 1961, moves to Mexico and wins the Esso Prize for *In Evil Hour* (*La mala hora*) in Colombia.
1962	Publishes *Big Mama's Funeral* (*Los funerales de la mamá grande*).

1967	Publishes *One Hundred Years of Solitude* (*Cien años de soledad*). The novel is an immediate success. Moves to Barcelona.
1972	Wins the prestigious Rómulo Gallegos Prize. Publishes *Innocent Eréndira and Other Stories* (*La increíble y triste historia de la cándida Eréndira y de su abuela desalmada*).
1975	Publishes *The Autumn of the Patriarch* (*El otoño del patriarca*). Moves back to Latin America to live mainly in Mexico and also Colombia.
1981	Publishes *Chronicle of a Death Foretold* (*Crónica de una muerte anunciada*).
1982	Wins the Nobel Prize for Literature.
1985	Publishes *Love in the Time of Cholera* (*El amor en los tiempos del cólera*).
1986	Inauguration of the Foundation for New Latin American Cinema in Havana and the nearby International School for Film and Television.
1987	Release of film version of *Chronicle of a Death Foretold.*
1989	Publishes *The General in His Labyrinth* (*El general en su laberinto*).
1992	Publishes *Strange Pilgrims* (*Doce cuentos peregrinos*).
1993	Publishes *Of Love and Other Demons* (*Del amor y otros demonios*).
1994	Premiere of play, *Diatribe of Love against a Seated Man* (*Diatriba de amor contra un hombre sentado*) in Buenos Aires.
1996	Publishes the documentary narrative *News of a Kidnapping* (*Noticia de un secuestro*).
2001	Publishes the memoir *Living to Tell the Tale* (*Vivir para contarla*).
2004	Publishes *Memories of My Melancholy Whores* (*Memorias de mis putas tristes*).
2007	Publication of anniversary edition of *Cien años de soledad* by the Real Academia Española. Release of film version of *Love in the Time of Cholera.*

PHILIP SWANSON

Introduction

Gabriel García Márquez is much more than a writer: he has become something of an icon in his native Colombia and throughout Latin America, as well as a darling of the chattering classes throughout the world. The towering success of his 1967 novel, *One Hundred Years of Solitude* (*Cien años de soledad*), the wide popular appeal of his best-selling *Love in the Time of Cholera* (*El amor en los tiempos del cólera* [1985]), his Nobel Prize triumph in 1982 and his general association with the assiduously promoted Latin American New Novel and the marketing of the related phenomenon of magical realism – all of these factors were key in his national and international projection as the voice of Colombian, Latin American and even 'Third-World' identity alongside his identification with a new type of globally influential tropical, exotic, fantastic literature. By the middle of the first decade of the twenty-first century, his status as icon was solidified by a number of big 'events': the fortieth anniversary of the publication of *One Hundred Years of Solitude* and the much-hyped publication by the Real Academia Española and the Asociación de Academias de la Lengua Española of a special commemorative edition (including a reprinted essay by Mario Vargas Llosa, which helped generate more publicity as it fuelled press speculation of a possible end to the rift between the two writers prompted famously by a bout of fisticuffs outside a Mexican cinema in 1976); the appearance of what has been widely touted as García Márquez's 'last' novel in 2004, coming out in English translation in 2005 under the title of *Memories of My Melancholy Whores;* and the much-anticipated arrival in 2002 (2004 in English) of the first – and, many think, only – volume of the author's memoirs, *Living to Tell the Tale* (*Vivir para contarla*). A spicy appetiser for this culmination of a cult had begun at the turn of the new century, when a hoax message purported (falsely) to be from García Márquez began to appear on websites all over the world in 2000 in which the author had allegedly penned a gushing public farewell to life in the face of a supposedly terminal cancer. Email messages proliferated around the globe as aficionados shared in this bogus authorial lament.

In a sense, then, at the time of writing, the consolidation of García Márquez's reputation has turned him into a myth as much as a real-life celebrity, a curiously fitting achievement, perhaps, for a writer so closely identified in the public imagination with the paradoxical notion of magical realism. This mythification is not without significance. In the Colombian context, for example, some commentators have noted a tendency to blame the fragmentation and violence that has wracked the country since Independence – unlike the cases of Brazil, Argentina, Chile or Mexico – on 'the lack of a founding national myth'.[1] As Daniel Pécaut has suggested, 'Colombia invented its only myth: that its entire history has been violence'.[2] It is probably true that the varied physical geography of Colombia – in which the region has been made up, since the arrival of the Spaniards, of diverse and dispersed population pockets – has led to what are often perceived as ineffective national structures and the proliferation of groups operating outside the conventional parameters of the state. Indeed the fundamental Liberal–Conservative tension which was at the heart of the civil conflict that took off in the late nineteenth century (and which provides the background to much of García Márquez's work) has its roots in the divide between centralism and localism and the consequent failure of a unifying project.[3] This, of course, is a modern manifestation of the civilisation-versus-barbarism dichotomy first predicted in 1845 by Argentina's Domingo Faustino Sarmiento in his seminal work *Facundo,* in which the future statesman expressed his anxiety about the ability of urban patches of orderly society to tame the vast and unruly interior in the post-Independence period.[4] The result in Colombia has been civil war, political compromise that alienated non-participants in the main parties from the state, ongoing conflict (known simply as *la violencia* or 'the violence'), the rise of guerrilla groups, paramilitaries, cartels and armed bands linked to drug trafficking and, more generally today, the pervasive presence of private security. Yet, interestingly, if the image of modern-day Colombia is tied up for many with notions of a drugs trade fired by urban capitalism and guerrilla- or paramilitary-fuelled conflict, the image created by iconic Garciamarquian fictions is often rather the opposite.

His prose fiction generally concentrates on the past (most notably the late nineteenth century and early twentieth century in *One Hundred Years of Solitude* and *Love in the Time of Cholera*) and pays relatively little attention to *la violencia* (save, for example, tangentially in an early novella, *No One Writes to the Colonel* [*El coronel no tiene quien le escriba* (1957)] or more directly in a minor and fairly atypical novel such as *In Evil Hour* [*La mala hora* (1962 and 1966)]). Indeed, the author's central creation, the timeless somnolent backwater town of Macondo in which much of his fiction is set, has generated an international Colombian archetype that is in many ways jarringly at odds with this harsh reality.[5] García Márquez's iconicity is, then, remarkably problematic. His adoption as national symbol, as with many icons, perhaps involves an emptying of real significance. A curious indicator of this is the Centro Cultural Gabriel García Márquez which opened in the centre of Bogotá in 2007. Not only was the Centre funded by Mexico's Fondo de Cultura Económica, it is decorated outside with a series of pictures of García Márquez bearing the quotation from him: 'La patria amada aunque distante' ('The homeland is loved even though one is far away from it'). This inadvertently projects García Márquez (whose main base is now Mexico) as central to Colombian national identity yet peculiarly absent from it. It echoes the experience of the visitor to Cartagena de Indias (the city most associated with García Márquez, especially since the publication of *Love in the Time of Cholera*). Here tour guides and carriage riders will possessively point out the home of Gabo, the casually adopted nickname suggesting the degree of affectionate regional and national identification with the writer. However, as they gesture to the rather flash and inaccessible property hidden behind high walls, they are also likely to comment that he is hardly ever there (and rumours circulate in early 2008 that it is to be put up for sale). Meantime the waiting staff of the local restaurant, Patios de Macondo, proudly offer dishes such as 'hierbas del último Buendía', 'pechuga de Pietro Crespi', 'langostinos en salsa Amaranta' or 'filete de róbalo en cocina de Ursula' (all containing references to characters from *One Hundred Years of Solitude*), accompanied on their tables by the nationally popular chilli sauce, McKondo. However, at least on the occasion of my visit, there were no Colombians to be seen dining there, and the assembled British, Italian, Dutch and German diners were serenaded by excruciatingly poor singers attempting to rehash clichéd tourist fodder (there was even an unsightly scrap between some of the waiters for the additional tip prompted by my request for a copy of the menu). The idea of a romantic projection of Colombia is, nonetheless, important for the country, as the major official nation-branding exercise 'Colombia es pasión' ('Colombia is Passion') clearly demonstrates.[6] In a sense, the timeless romance associated with García Márquez and his fictional fantasies is preferable as a national myth to other less palatable realities.

The tension between myth and reality is carried on into the relationship between literature and reality in García Márquez. The Colombian author has a long history of political pronouncements and activities. Especially memorable to many was his impassioned Third-Worldist speech on the occasion of his winning of the Nobel Prize, delivered in showman style in a white 'liqui liqui' (the formal national dress for men). He has also become a particular favourite of the Left, in part because of his apparent close friendship with Cuba's Fidel Castro. Of course, he is also a friend of former Conservative President Belisario Betancur and has some good relations with rightist Liberal President Álvaro Uribe. And he has not followed through on all his popular declarations – not least his claim after the publication of his (extremely ambiguous) dictatorship novel *The Autumn of the Patriach* (*El otoño del patriarca*) in 1975 that he would not publish another novel until after the fall of the Chilean dictator General Augusto Pinochet. (*Chronicle of a Death Foretold* [*Crónica de una muerte anunciada* (1981)] appeared some eight years before Pinochet's eventual withdrawal from power after the 1989 elections.) In any case, some might feel that there is a certain unreality anyway in the maintenance of a species of pan-Latin American internationalism inspired by the Cuban Revolution in an era of globalisation and neoliberalism. Most striking, of course, is the lack of congruence between the author's sometime external political stance and the sceptical and often seemingly nihilistic content of his literary writings.

Readings of García Márquez's fiction often lurch uncomfortably between claims of radical politics and suggestions of metaphysical malaise or the reality-busting freeplay of the literary imagination. When the colonel at the end of *No One Writes to the Colonel* says that he and his wife are going to have to eat shit to survive, is he expressing the political defiance of an irrepressible underclass or revealing the hopeless futility of his world-view? When the final Buendía is wiped off the face of the earth at the end of *One Hundred Years of Solitude,* is this an image of Revolution or of absolute pessimism (or even of the realisation that this is no more than a work of fiction which will inevitably end in a blank space of nothingness)? Does the ribaldly exaggerated and often sympathetic portrayal of the dictator in *The Autumn of the Patriarch* undermine political criticism or subtly bring out the people's dangerous susceptibility to the populist strongman? Is the ending of *Love in the Time of Cholera,* in which an elderly couple defy the odds and find love, a positive subversion of bourgeois rationalism or a flight from reality into fantasy, the unreal or wishful thinking? The point is that García Márquez's literary works are supremely ambiguous and often irreducible in terms of conventional patterns of interpretation. This creates a conflict in approaches to García Márquez between what some might broadly call 'traditional' criticism (often associated with notions such as the 'universal' or the 'literary') and, equally broadly, 'political' criticism – a divide which has become especially acute in Latin Americanism since the 1980s. However, this tension is unavoidably present in the literature itself, which is always constructed around an unresolved relationship between the local and the universal, the political and the existential, the literary world and the external world, the magical and the real. An acceptance of the existence of this tension rather than a drive towards its resolution is perhaps a necessary starting point for an appreciation of García Márquez's fictional universe. Whatever one's position, its spectre is certainly a presence behind virtually all of the contributions in the present volume.

The readings which follow here represent, then, a range of enthusiasms and reactions which do ample justice to the myriad possibilities presented by García Márquez, while attempting to provide a framework within which usefully to approach the man and his work. The essays begin with an authoritative account by Gene H. Bell-Villada of García Márquez's life and times, after which long-standing Latin American literary critic, Donald Shaw, offers a survey of the critical reception of García Márquez which thoroughly documents the tensions alluded to above. Our author's earlier fiction is examined by Robin Fiddian: though he recognises the refusal to cancel difference in García Márquez's writing, he draws attention to an emerging moral and political agenda in his work, ultimately from a postcolonial perspective. The editor then offers a brief survey of the key tensions in García Márquez's most famous work *One Hundred Years of Solitude.* My intention here is to cover the main bases in terms of possible readings and to bring out the different and, depending on perspective, sometimes complementary or conflicting threads that characterise the Garciamarquian canon through the filter of this his most celebrated novel. This chapter is complemented by a new approach from the well-established García Márquez critic, Raymond L. Williams: he takes a somewhat specialised revisionary approach to this seminal text, updating critical approaches to the novel by situating it in the context of eco-criticism as well as in the context of important selected predecessor novels. *The Autumn of the Patriarch* is, without question, the Colombian's most difficult novel, and Steven Boldy, while acknowledging its powerfully political content, does justice to the at-times-overwhelming complexity and irreducibilty of the text. Gerald Martin considers what some would regard as the last great novel by García Márquez and the closest he has come to writing a historical fiction rooted in reality, *The General in His Labyrinth* (*El general en su laberinto* [1989]). This compelling account of the events leading up to the final days of the great Latin American Independence hero Simón Bolívar is situated by Martin organically in the context of García Márquez's earlier works, and he ultimately sees Bolívar himself as an embodiment of the author's own everyday Latin American character-heroes, as they struggle with their hopes, dreams, failures and occasional triumphs. Of course, as the earlier allusions to romance suggest, García Márquez is as much a novelist of love as of anything else, and what one might term the love novels are grouped together in Mark I. Millington's chapter which explores the complexity and contradictory nature of love in García Márquez – rebellious, spirited, but limited and strangely solitary. Also considered is García Márquez's considerable body of short fiction: Stephen Hart analyses the development of a characteristic style in an evolving corpus of short stories and also brings out their political dimension alongside their suggestiveness. García Márquez's massive contribution to journalism as well as his other non-fiction writings (including biography) are forensically examined by Robert L. Sims, while, in a further acknowledgement of the author's appeal beyond his own literary work, Claire Taylor provides a wide-ranging account of García Márquez's relationship to film and other media, particularly his role in the production of cinema. The final chapter seeks to emphasise the global significance of García Márquez and focuses on his relationship to world literature, especially via a study of *One Hundred Years of Solitude.* This probing essay by Michael Bell invites the reader to revisit the notion of magical realism and addresses head-on the issue of the tensions and ambiguities referred to earlier. In some ways, it resolves the dilemma and brings the various strands together, elaborating a persuasive argument that history and memory are revived through imaginative literary language and that literature is itself the main means of establishing a kind of national allegory. In the end, public persona and literary phenomenon exist side by side in the figure of 'Gabriel García Márquez', and that figure has an ongoing life of its own in the psyche and imagination of Colombian, Latin American and world readers and citizens.

NOTES

1. Pécaut is quoted from *Revista Estrategia* (Bogotá), 15 November 1996, in Marco Palacios, *Between Legitimacy and Violence: A History of Colombia, 1875–2002,* Durham, NC: Duke University Press, 2006, p. 261. Palacios's book is one of the best available introductions to Colombian history.
2. Pécaut, *Revista Estrategia,* p. 261.
3. Though, in the Colombian context, García Márquez sometimes reinforces this sense of division in his distinction between the capital and the Caribbean, his Caribbean version of Colombian identity has become something of an iconic romantic projection of national identity. The anxiety about division and the utopian urge to unity is played out in and probably explains his fascination with the Liberator Simón Bolívar, whose pan-American ideals collapse into the realisation that 'La América es ingobernable' ('Latin America is ungovernable' [my translation]) and chaos is inevitable: Gabriel García Márquez, *El general en su laberinto,* Madrid: Mondadori, 1989, p. 259.
4. For more on the civilisation and barbarism debate, see my 'Civilization and Barbarism' in Philip Swanson (ed.), *The Companion to Latin American Studies,* London: Arnold, 2003, pp. 69–85.
5. See Palacios, *Between Legitimacy and Violence,* p. 242.
6. See www.colombiaespasion.com.

1

GENE H. BELL-VILLADA

Gabriel García Márquez: life and times

Gabriel García Márquez was born on 7 March 1927 in the dusty small town of Aracataca, some 80 kilometres (50 miles) from Colombia's Caribbean shore.[1] For some decades hence, and for reasons unknown, he had mistakenly given his birth date as 1928.

Owing to family conflicts, 'Gabito' (his childhood nickname) was at first raised by his maternal grandparents, Colonel Nicolás Márquez and Tranquilina Iguarán. The grandfather was an imposing figure. A hero on the Liberal side in Colombia's 1899–1902 civil war, he was also a natty dresser with fine manners, who served a term as Aracataca's mayor. In addition, he was an excellent paternal surrogate, teaching the boy to use the dictionary, telling him war stories and leading him by the hand hither and yon about town.

For his first nine years, Gabito grew up in a loving household, surrounded by aunts who encouraged his curiosity and storytelling bent. They filled his mind with much of the folklore and family lore that eventually enriched his fiction. In Aracataca he attended the local Montessori school, learning to see and examine with discipline. It was the only elementary institution that he would recall with great affection.

At age nine, Gabito went to live with his parents in the town of Sincé. (Grandpa Nicolás passed away a short while later.) The boy scarcely knew the couple. His birth, in fact, had been the culmination of a long chain of events. His father, Gabriel Eligio García, was a medical-school dropout who had then become a telegraph operator, and finally ended up in his calling of homeopathic pharmacist. A newcomer to Aracataca in 1924, he had from the outset taken a fancy to the town beauty, Luisa Santiaga Márquez, daughter of the Colonel. He wooed her with serenades. She reciprocated after some resistance. Her mother and father, however, doggedly opposed the courtship, in great measure because the young suitor was poor, illegitimate and a Conservative. Colonel Márquez did everything in his power to separate the starry-eyed pair, even sending Luisa off for a spell in distant

Valledupar. But a wily Gabriel Eligio, using his knowledge of the telegraph network, always managed to make secret contact with his sweetheart.

Luisa's parents in time resigned themselves to the situation, and the lovebirds were wedded in June 1926. Gabriel Eligio nonetheless resented his in-laws and refused to live in Aracataca, 'ese moridero de pobres' ('that charnel-house for the poor').[2] As a concession, however, he sent his young wife to have their first-born in her home town, where the child then spent his early years. Their strange courtship would serve as basis for the adolescent *amour* of Florentino Ariza and Fermina Daza in the novel *Love in the Time of Cholera* (*El amor en los tiempos del cólera*).

Though Gabito had at last settled in with his immediate kin and five siblings, his father–son tie, it seems, was not a happy one. Gabriel Eligio felt that the Colonel had 'spoiled' the child and saw the boy's love of telling tales as mere 'lying'. Meanwhile, Gabito was started on what would be nearly three decades of nomadism, due initially to his father's incessant pursuit of homeopathic, money-making schemes. In two years the family of eight transferred to Barranquilla, on the Caribbean coast, later moving once again to Sucre, a small, inland river port that serves as the model for the nameless 'town' in several of the author's classic stories and in *Chronicle of a Death Foretold* (*Crónica de una muerte anunciada*).

The family, still growing at the rate of roughly one baby per year, stayed in Sucre for twelve years, though in 1940 Gabito was sent back to Barranquilla to study at a Jesuit boarding school. In 1943 he received a full scholarship at the Liceo de Zipaquirá, a prestigious secular academy located in a beautiful, neo-Castilian town an hour's train ride from the capital. Gabito now saw his family only during holidays, usually needing to get reacquainted with his siblings as well as to meet a brand new tot. In one of those summer vacations he met a neighbour, an exotic-looking thirteen-year-old girl of Egyptian descent named Mercedes Barcha, to whom he proposed marriage on their very first encounter. Mercedes did not take him seriously at first; yet they did in fact wed thirteen years later.

In his personal columns and interviews, the great novelist often assumes an anti-academic stance. It must be said, though, that Gabito was a top pupil who got the highest marks and very much impressed his teachers. At school he was so unathletic and shy that his peers dubbed him 'el viejo' ('the old man'). Meanwhile he read vast amounts on his own, devouring *The Arabian Nights,* Grimm's fairy tales and Dumas's novels by age ten. His own verse efforts in student magazines had faculty members detecting in them a budding literary genius.

Gabito's four years at Zipaquirá were his first direct experience of Andean Colombia and its vast contrasts with his own world. At the time, getting there from the northern region was a long journey that required over a week of river and rail travel. The chill and thin air at 3,000 metres above sea level, moreover, came as an initial shock to the tropically raised youngster.

These geographic differences bear a close look. Gabo (as he now became known) heralds from Caribbean Colombia, where the heat is a constant presence, and the physical and human atmosphere resembles that of the Antilles. The inhabitants, as do other Caribbean Hispanics, drop their final 's' in speech, and also demonstrate the breezy informality that one finds among Dominicans and Cubans. Last but not least, the African background in northern Colombia is ubiquitous and can be seen in the local peoples' many shades of dark-skin pigmentation. African place names pepper the local maps, and African drumming can fill the sultry evening air.

Caribbean Colombia includes the gorgeously well-preserved, old colonial city of Cartagena (once a centre of the African slave trade), the historically rich and varied port of Barranquilla, the holiday-resort culture of Santa Marta (the town where Independence leader Simón Bolívar died), and the frontier town of Riohacha on the desert of La Guajira, where descendants of the indigenous Wayrúu (hence 'Guajiro') peoples constitute a majority. In addition there are inland settlements such as Ciénaga (where a 1928 massacre of banana workers took place), and, of course, Aracataca and Sucre, Gabo's first hometowns. These localities, suitably reimagined, would serve as settings for most of the author's work.

Northern Colombians are known as *costeños* ('coastals'), a label they wear with some pride. They thereby distinguish themselves from the denizens of highland Bogotá, who are referred to casually as *cachacos*. The latter term, though technically neutral, in certain contexts can convey scorn. In the *costeño* world-view, *cachacos* are stuffy, arrogant, cold and overly concerned with power and prestige. The prejudice reflects the fact that Bogotanos regard themselves as speaking the most correct Spanish in the hemisphere; moreover, official rhetoric praises their city as 'the Athens of South America' ('la Atenas sudamericana'). Bogotá natives do in fact tend to be more formal and rule-bound than their coastal compatriots. And while the indigenous legacy there is demographically present in local, copper-skinned *mestizaje* ('race-mixing'), African traces among the highland population are rare. The *costeño/cachaco* dichotomy is but an instance of the age-old split between provinces and capital city, a pattern one finds in almost every country.

Following graduation from the Liceo in 1946, Gabo matriculated as a law student at the Universidad Nacional in Bogotá. His interest in the law was nil; he enrolled merely to please his father, who wanted the elder child to learn a saleable trade and eventually help support the ten other offspring. Gabo, however, took his law studies less than seriously, having other plans.

Since his teens he had been writing both poetry and fiction. His dramatic discovery of Franz Kafka had opened his eyes to the potential of non-realistic narrative. And by sheer luck he had published in the literary supplement of *El Espectador* two youthful stories – 'La tercera resignación' ('The Third Resignation') and 'Eva está dentro de su gato' ('Eva Is Inside Her Cat') – that earned him the esteem of his classmates and of Eduardo Zalamea Borda, a novelist and the nation's leading book critic. Still uncertain as to his direction, Gabo was nevertheless launched as a writer. Meanwhile he hung around literary cafés and immersed himself in the European and Spanish literary classics.

Gabo's life would take a horrific turn on 9 April 1948, when the fiery, charismatic Liberal Party leader Jorge Eliécer Gaitán was assassinated point-blank in front of a Bogotá café. The brutal murder sparked a vast, apocalyptic riot in which untold thousands of enraged Liberal sympathisers took to the city's streets, burning, smashing and looting whatever they could lay their hands on. Among the accidental casualties was Gabo's rooming house, where his books and manuscripts were reduced to ashes.

The event, known as *el nueve de abril* in Colombia and as *el bogotazo* ('the Bogotá crash') in other countries, was of enormous significance. It signalled the arrival, in the capital, of *la violencia,* a destructive, undeclared, almost hidden civil war that had been raging between Liberal and Conservative forces in portions of the countryside since 1946. The conflict had now spread visibly. In addition, even as a radical populist insurgency within the Liberal ranks had been decapitated, at the same time left-wing revolutionary juntas sprouted in many a small town. Though the alleged assassin was trampled to death by an angry mob, to this day serious doubts remain as to his culpability. In time, the growing turmoil would lead to a military coup by General Gustavo Rojas Pinilla in 1953.

In the wake of mass chaos, the Universidad Nacional temporarily shut its doors, and Gabo's social life in Bogotá was up in smoke. He promptly took a flight back to the northern coast (the region was scarcely affected by *la violencia*) and duly enrolled at the Universidad de Cartagena's law school. Soon thereafter he found employment in that venerable city, writing a six-days-per-week personal column for *El Universal,* a new daily. Despite the meagre wages, he thoroughly enjoyed the scribbling for hire and all but stopped attending his law courses. In time, he began the process of rediscovering his *costeño* roots, absorbing whatever he could of the geography, folklore and peoples of Caribbean Colombia.

Within a year, Gabo met a group of bright, young literati who lived in Barranquilla. The cenacle's reigning spirit, an ageing Catalan émigré bookseller by the name of Ramón Vinyes, knew intimately the Euro-American modernist legacy. With near-missionary zeal he had been introducing his eager disciples to the work of, among others, Joyce, Woolf, Camus, Melville, Dos Passos, Hemingway and, especially, Faulkner. Gabo, the twenty-something journalist-cum-law-school-dropout, was warmly welcomed into the zestful Barranquilla fold and would spend many a night sitting around in their company, discussing literature and its myriad possibilities over drinks at bars and brothels. Three within the group – Álvaro Cepeda, Alfonso Fuenmayor and Germán Vargas – became the author's closest, lifelong friends. He had their first names immortalised via a trio of roistering characters towards the end of *Cien años de soledad* (*One Hundred Years of Solitude*), while Master Vinyes is reimagined as 'el sabio catalán' ('the wise Catalonian').

Through their good offices, Gabo soon landed a job at *El Heraldo* of Barranquilla, the coastal region's largest news daily. Duties were roughly the same as at *El Universal* but at slightly higher pay. He also published more stories in *El Espectador.* These abstractly Kafkaesque and uncharacteristic juvenilia would later be gathered in the collection *Ojos de perro azul* (*Eyes of a Blue Dog*). Meanwhile, some time since his return north he had begun work on a massive family saga called simply *La casa* (*The House*), a preliminary draft, with many of the same characters, for *One Hundred Years of Solitude.* Contemporaries who did read the manuscript concur that Gabito's narrative resources were still in the developing stages and that the result was naive and raw.

In time, the apprentice focused his materials, and now at every spare moment in the newsroom or in his cheap hotel he laboured with craftsmanlike attention on a brief novel that would become *La hojarasca* (*Leaf Storm*). Gabo's troubles as a writer, however, had scarcely begun. A more or less final version of the manuscript, ready in 1950, was rejected outright by the prestigious Losada firm in Buenos Aires; a letter from Guillermo de Torre (brother-in-law of Jorge Luis Borges) informed the aspiring novice that his narrative gifts were slight and suggested that he try some other field. Not until 1955 did the book see the light of day, from a tiny, fly-by-night operation whose owner-publisher then simply vanished, leaving the author and his friends to dispose of the 1,000 printed copies. Though in both form and content the book owes an obvious debt to William Faulkner's *As I Lay Dying* (a dead body, a coffin, a quarrel over the burial, the shifting points of view), it is a worthy first novel in which many of García Márquez's settings and themes are clearly delineated and in place.

In 1954, Gabo accepted an invitation by *El Espectador* to join their team as a staff writer, and he moved once again to the capital. The prestigious Bogotá daily was also the nation's oldest, and in its highly professional milieu García Márquez truly blossomed as a journalist, penning editorials and film reviews and doing investigative reports that earned him a national reputation. One of those reports was a series of interviews with the hapless seaman Luis Alejandro Velasco, who had gone mysteriously overboard off a Colombian destroyer in the Gulf of Mexico, surviving on a raft for ten days until reaching the Colombian shore. The highly vivid account would be gathered fifteen years hence in the short volume *Relato de un náufrago* (*The Story of a Shipwrecked Sailor*). During his *Espectador* years the author also published his first genuinely mature story, 'Un día después del sábado' ('One Day after Saturday'). Written in his distinctively ironic voice, and with the near-magic of a rain of dead birds, it won a local prize.

The series about the sailor implied that the navy ship had been illegally overloaded, causing some tension with the military regime. So, in the summer of 1956, the newspaper sent Gabo abroad as their first European correspondent. His opening assignment was in Geneva, to cover a 'Big Four' summit, and thence to the Vatican, where Pope Pius XII was suffering from an alarming case of hiccoughs. While in Rome the writer took classes at the Centro Sperimentale di Cinema, withdrawing two months later when he found the curriculum too academic for his needs. Next stop was Paris, where soon after his arrival he found out that *El Espectador* had been shut down by the dictatorship. The editors sent him money for airfare; he chose instead to pocket the cash and stay on, working full-time on his fiction.

Over the next two years García Márquez began work on *La mala hora* (*In Evil Hour*), completed the manuscript of *El coronel no tiene quien le escriba* (*No One Writes to the Colonel*) and finished most of the now-classic tales that comprise *Los funerales de la mamá grande* (*Big Mama's Funeral*). Economically, however, it turned out to be Gabo's worst period ever. Dependent exclusively on occasional freelance fees, he was able to stay in his Paris garret thanks solely to the generosity of the hotel-keeper couple. And he literally went hungry, much as does the unfortunate colonel in his short novel. To supplement his slight income, García Márquez returned empty bottles and even begged for his metro fare. Some of his misadventures on the old Continent he would later fictionalise in the story collection *Doce cuentos peregrinos* (*Strange Pilgrims*).

What yanked Gabo out of the trap of Bohemian poverty was an offer in December 1957, through his friend Plinio Apuleyo Mendoza, of an editing job at *Momento,* an illustrated glossy in Venezuela. A grateful Gabo was soon Caracas-bound, and the final years of the decade would be chock-full of new experiences for him. In 1958 he witnessed at first hand the fall of the brutal, US-supported dictatorship of General Marcos Pérez Jiménez. The event planted in his mind the seeds for a possible novel about a Latin

American despot. Meanwhile, *No One Writes to the Colonel* ran in a small Bogotá magazine but would not see book form until 1962. (The novelette, about a retired military man who finds himself without any economic means except a fighting cock, is one of Gabo's more tender and humane works.) In March 1958, García Márquez made a lightning decision and flew to Barranquilla to marry his sweetheart Mercedes, thirteen years after his youthful proposal. Their first son Rodrigo would be born in August 1959.

The triumph of Fidel Castro's guerrillas in Cuba earlier that year prompted an invitation to numerous journalists to come and witness the military trials of General Batista's more bloodthirsty henchmen. The initiative, aimed at countering the negative coverage of the tribunals in the US press, was the beginning of Gabo's extended ties with Cuba. A few months later, he and Plinio Mendoza returned to Bogotá and set up the branch office of Prensa Latina, the official agency of Castro's revolution.

By 1960, García Márquez was in Havana itself, learning the ins and outs of the news organisation. And in 1961 he was running the agency's branch in New York, amid death threats phoned in by right-wing Cuban exiles on the one hand and sectarian intrigues by old-guard, pre-Castro Communists on the other. The latter elements resented Prensa Latina's youngish director, a new-left type from Argentina named Jorge Massetti, and they were in the process of elbowing him out of the job. In solidarity with his boss, the writer resigned after six months. Soon Gabo, Mercedes and little Rodrigo were aboard Greyhound buses, travelling south through Faulkner country and the US gulf states. On occasion they were denied lodging by racist hotel clerks and managers who saw them as Mexicans.

The threesome's ultimate destination was Mexico City, then and now a leading culture and media centre in Latin America. Again through friends, Gabo secured employment as an editor at two gossip sheets and later worked at the local branch of an American advertising agency. Within a year he began fulfilling another of his dreams: writing movie scripts. (The Mexican industry back then was a commanding presence in the Hispanic world.) Eventually, though, he became disillusioned at being a mere cog in the machine whose words could be mangled beyond recognition. In the meantime, the manuscript of *In Evil Hour* won the prestigious literary award, the Esso Prize; the book was issued by a Madrid publisher, who had purged Gabo's spicy dialogue of its colloquialisms and, to boot, replaced all uses of South American *ustedes* with Peninsular-pure *vosotros*! The author promptly repudiated this edition. (The novel, about a town resembling Sucre that is thrown into turmoil when lampoons start appearing mysteriously on people's doors, is probably Gabo's weakest.) In April 1962, Gabo and Mercedes' second son, Gonzalo, was born.

Other than the transitional short story 'El mar del tiempo perdido' ('The Sea of Lost Time'), between 1962 and mid-1965 García Márquez wrote no fiction. Office routines, film scripts and family duties were crowding his life, and he complained regularly about being blocked and having nothing to say. How that drought ended is one of literature's astounding legends. In the summer of 1965, Gabo was in his white Opel, driving his wife and two sons to Acapulco. Then, all of a sudden, he saw in his mind's eye the shape of the family saga that he had spent so many years attempting to write; he now could have recited the opening chapter line by line. Thereupon he made a U-turn and asked Mercedes to take charge of the family finances while he wrote this big novel.

And write he did: eight hours per day in his home study. The author had originally given himself a deadline of six months; the composition process took nearly a year and a half. By then Mercedes had sold or pawned everything, and the family was $10,000 in debt – in 1967 dollars. When the book was ready for mailing off to Editorial Sudamericana in Buenos Aires, the couple at first did not even have enough money to pay the full postage.

The volume, of course, was *One Hundred Years of Solitude* (*Cien años de soledad*). Public reception of the book next became equally legendary. Selected chapters had already been serialised in prestigious literary journals across the continent; editors and subsequent commentators concurred in that they were faced with a singular masterpiece. Reviews of the entire novel were absolutely and unreservedly glowing, yet no surprise there – Gabo himself had expected it to achieve critical success. What absolutely no one had foreseen for this elaborate and complex work were the sales. The initial printing of 10,000 copies sold out within a month, and in Buenos Aires alone. The publisher could scarcely keep up with paper and printing orders. Throughout the Hispanic world, even among non-intellectuals, people in halls and buses were *talking* about it. The rest, as the phrase goes, is history. *One Hundred Years of Solitude* has since had sales of tens of millions of copies in several dozen languages. Consensus regards it as the great novel of Latin America and a world classic besides.

From a historical perspective, *One Hundred Years of Solitude* is several things at once. It soon became widely regarded as the signature work of what is known as the Boom ('el boom') of the Latin American novel.[3] In the two decades that preceded its publication, Spanish American authors had started publishing works of fiction that were comparable technically and stylistically to the Euro-American modernist classics, and that moreover possessed acknowledged staying power. By early 1967, Julio Cortázar (Argentina), Juan Rulfo and Carlos Fuentes (Mexico), Alejo Carpentier (Cuba), Juan Carlos Onetti (Uruguay) and Mario Vargas Llosa (Peru) were recognised literary artists. Indeed, years before García Márquez's masterpiece had seen the light of day, Rulfo's *Pedro Páramo* (1953) and Carpentier's *Los pasos perdidos* (*The Lost Steps* [1953]) enjoyed canonical standing in Latin America, and Cortázar's unique experiment *Rayuela* (*Hopscotch* [1963]) had caused something of a sensation both in the original and in translation. Prior to these novels, Borges's short stories had been enjoying the status of an international cult.

The Boom, in sum, was one of those rare moments in history, an explosion of exceptional literary creativity analogous to such other moments as the flourishing of Elizabethan drama or the rise of the Russian novel. What was new about the Boom – its high artistic quality aside – was its application of European and US modernist techniques in narrating Latin America's realities.

Before the Boom, the Hispanic continent could boast some fine poets (among them José Martí, Pablo Neruda, César Vallejo and Nicolás Guillén). The overall panorama of the novel, by contrast, was far from satisfactory. Nineteenth-century Latin American novelists had more or less slavishly imitated the French realists. Early in the twentieth century, in a spirit of nationalism, writers like Rómulo Gallegos and José E. Rivera had tried overtly to convey the minute details of Spanish-American rural life, resorting too often to dialect lexicon and local colour. The Mexican Revolution (1910–17) showed cultural promise and generated some quality fiction – notably Maríano Azuela's *Los de abajo* (*The Underdogs* [1916]) and Martín Luis Guzmán's *El águila y la serpiente* (*The Eagle and the Serpent* [1928]) – but these works were not readily accessible without some previous knowledge of events and people in the home country.

The Boom and Gabo's masterwork, then, showed that it was possible to tell of Latin America, its ordinary concerns and tragic struggles, via means other than those of straight, nineteenth-century realism and naturalism. The element in the saga of Macondo that did break new ground was what is now called magical realism. Granted, Latin American literature has had its history of non-realist narrative dating back to the ingenious short fictions of Rubén Darío and Leopoldo Lugones (both of them poets). And in the two decades before the appearance of *One Hundred Years of Solitude*, the stories of Borges and Cortázar had established the Fantastic as a specific genre with distinctive traits all its own. When we read those Argentines' tales, however, some 'hesitation' (in Todorov's revealing word) often arises as to how the plot is ultimately to be construed.[4] Does Juan Dahlmann, in Borges's 'El Sur' ('The South'), really ride a train through the Pampas to his death, or is it all delirium in the hospital room? Does the narrator in Cortázar's 'Carta a una señorita en París' ('Letter to a Young Lady in Paris') really vomit bunnies, or is he actually lying, maybe mad? There is no final answer. By contrast, in the magical-realist procedure crystallised by García Márquez, no doubt exists as to the nature of the events. A priest levitates; a girl rises to heaven; and that is simply that.

García Márquez did not invent magical realism. Actually, Rulfo's *Pedro Páramo,* with its narrating ghosts, already qualifies to some degree as 'magical realist'. The term itself, like so many critical categories, is a bit of retrospective shorthand that simply designates a certain way of telling stories. Nevertheless, *One Hundred Years of Solitude* provides probably the clearest, liveliest, most extensive use of the resource in modern literature. Magical-minded novelists and film-makers around the globe have taken their artistic cue from García Márquez. As with Joyce in *Ulysses* and Kafka in his short stories and *The Trial,* Gabo in *One Hundred Years of Solitude* expanded for all time the horizons of prose narrative.

The pop-star fame brought by *One Hundred Years of Solitude* was to complicate Gabo's life beyond measure. The constant telephone calls, the unannounced visits by strangers and solicitors, the importunings by journalists, the offers of sex and the requests for support from this or that cause all made it impossible for the author to maintain his writing routines, let alone live in privacy and peace his life as spouse and father.

And so, late in 1967, García Márquez and his family all moved to Barcelona, Spain, where the author could live in relative seclusion yet also find himself within a Spanish-speaking milieu. Moreover, the Franco dictatorship was relaxing its grip on the Catalan area, and the proximity of France meant an easier circulation of ideas. Gabo's long-range project was to write the novel about a Caribbean dictator that had been on his mental drawing board since 1958. Meanwhile, he also composed the stories gathered in *La increíble y triste historia de la cándida Eréndira y de su abuela desalmada* (*The Incredible and Sad Tale of Innocent Eréndira and her Heartless Grandmother* [1972]).

The volume's title novella – known to many simply as 'Eréndira' – and the shorter pieces have a notable feature in common: they all take place in villages on or near Colombia's Atlantic shore. Gabo was hence moving his sights away from inland Macondo to a landscape dominated by the sea. To a certain extent, then, they are practice pieces for the novel-in-progress about a tyrant (though also very beautiful narratives in their own right). One story, 'El último viaje del buque fantasma' ('The Last Voyage of the Ghost Ship') even inaugurates the serpentine prose that would be the stylistic hallmark of that much-awaited work.

García Márquez had hoped to complete the novel in a year. The creative labours instead stretched over seven. Public expectation was thus at a high pitch when *El otoño del patriarca* (*The Autumn of the Patriarch*) came out in 1975, to initial sales of half a million copies. Many Gabo fans, however, were disappointed, having looked forward to a return visit to Macondo as well as another straightforward reading experience. The author thwarted such hopes by putting the Buendía clan solidly behind him. Moreover, with its six chapters consisting of a single paragraph each, and a final chapter comprised of just one sentence, the newer book proved to be one of the most difficult novels ever written, on a par with Faulkner's most experimental opuses. The author had clearly set out to make this volume different and in no way to repeat himself. Despite its daunting obstacles, though, over time *The Autumn of the Patriarch* has established itself as another among Gabo's several masterpieces and arguably *the* novel of Latin American dictatorship.

García Márquez and his kin now returned to Mexico City, where he purchased a house in the Pedregal San Ángel district. There he settled into an occupational routine that he had maintained and even expanded in the wake of his global fame: journalism. The chosen topic may have been Vietnam, Chile, the Middle East or music, but he kept up regular contact with a medium that he felt very much at home in and that he spoke of with affection as 'the best in the world'. These pieces appeared in newspapers and magazines throughout the Hispanic realm and in foreign translations as well.

With the growing insurgency of the Sandinista guerrillas against the tyranny of Nicaragua's General Anastasio Somoza in the late 1970s, and the bloody, US-sponsored wars in Central America that followed, Gabo's news reports now became openly committed 'advocacy journalism', as the phrase goes. As a result he emerged as a more visible figure on the international left.

This brings us to the issue of the author's political views. García Márquez makes no secret of being a socialist, and his friendship with Fidel Castro is public knowledge. It must be noted first of all that there is nothing particularly unusual about Gabo's stance; indeed, a considerable majority of Latin America's writers and intellectuals frankly hold views such as his. García Márquez's opinions simply happen to be in the limelight. Gabo, we have seen, grew up in abject poverty, and his initiation into Western capitalism was the local memory of United Fruit Company abuses and of the military reprisals against strikers in 1928. In addition he has taken his hits from right-wing dictatorships and spent years on the US immigration blacklist as a subversive. Moreover, to conservative carpers who begrudge Gabo his accidental riches, it should be pointed out that he gives generously to progressive causes and also utilises portions of his wealth to finance quality journalism in Colombia and elsewhere.

Nevertheless, García Márquez has always acknowledged the positive cultural, political and technical achievements of North Atlantic civilisation. And in the 1990s he complemented his Fidelista ties with a personal friendship with President Bill Clinton. Clinton's favourite novel happens to be *One Hundred Years of Solitude,* and during his White House term he removed the novelist from the immigration blacklist, allowing him easier access to US institutions.

In 1981, 2 million copies of García Márquez's short novel, *Crónica de una muerte anunciada* (*Chronicle of a Death Foretold*) were released by publishers in Argentina, Colombia, Mexico and Spain. The work takes as its topic a terrible, real-life honour killing that occurred in Sucre in 1951. Gabito knew each one of the parties involved (including the murder victim), and he already then wanted to write about the horrendous deed, which had shaken up the entire community. Yet he also found himself constrained by his acquaintance with all of the players and by the sheer magnitude of the event. The novel, published thirty years after the bloody episode, transmogrifies it into a love story, further enriching it with religious and ritualistic details. *Chronicle of a Death Foretold,* it bears noting, contains very little magic and is probably the one major book by Gabo that is not leavened with humour.

Since 1968, the author had been accumulating international awards aplenty. His 1982 Nobel Prize, however, came almost unexpectedly, inasmuch as there were several more senior Hispanic authors who deserved the prize. In response to the announcement, street celebrations arose in Mexico and Colombia, and dailies ran headlines such as 'Gabo Nobel de Literatura'. The ceremony in Stockholm, with its Colombian dance and music troupes, was reportedly the most festive in the history of the award. García Márquez himself wore a native, white linen, high-collared suit; his acceptance speech, 'The Solitude of Latin America', about the continent's troubled history, has become a small classic.

A Nobel Prize can sometimes spell the kiss of death for a writer. García Márquez, by contrast, continued to grow as an artist. Late in 1985 his new novel, *El amor en los tiempos del cólera* (*Love in the Time of Cholera*) came out, with the usual transatlantic fanfare and millions of copies printed. Set in a traditional town that closely resembles Cartagena, it is also a traditional work of fiction that both revives and parodies its nineteenth-century narrative models. In addition, in a kind of first in literary history, the eponymous amour is postponed during adolescence and not at last fulfilled until the couple are in their seventies – passion in old age. The book highlighted what had hitherto only been acknowledged: that García Márquez is one of the great novelists of romantic love and affiliated sentiments.

This side of the author was to manifest itself in other art forms when he embarked on a series of six films, produced by Spanish National Television under the umbrella title *Amores difíciles* (rendered as *Dangerous Loves*). The scripts were penned by Gabo; five Latin American cineastes and one Spaniard were assigned the directing tasks. Issued in 1989, the cycle screened largely at art houses and museums. Some of the titles – notably *Milagro en Roma* (*Miracle in Rome*) – soon evolved into classics in their own right. The series rubric is especially fitting for the film *Yo soy la que buscas* (*I'm the One You're Looking For*), a disturbing account of a rape victim who obsessively seeks her violator and ends up falling in love with him.

Around this time Gabo wrote his only play, *Diatriba de amor contra un hombre sentado* (*A Diatribe of Love against a Seated Man* – still not translated into English at the time of writing). The format is unusual: a passionate, hour-long monologue delivered by a Caribbean housewife in which she raves at her silent, newspaper-reading husband and reminisces about different moments in their marriage. The play recalls similar experiments in monologue such as Strindberg's *The Stronger* and Cocteau's *La voix humaine;* it premiered in Buenos Aires in 1994.

García Márquez took a new path as a novelist with *El general en su laberinto* (*The General in His Labyrinth* [1989]). The work depicts the final few weeks in the life of liberator Simón Bolívar as he sails down the Magdalena river with hopes of exile in Europe but instead meets his premature death, at age forty-six, near Santa Marta. Writing the book required some courage on the part of the author. The myth of Bolívar is solidly entrenched in South American lore. Schoolchildren are taught to worship him; the indoctrination is further reinforced by the countless statues, streets, parks, the Venezuelan currency and a nation-state bearing his name. García Márquez thus assumed some risk when he chose to 'humanise' the General and portray him not as a frozen monument but as a broken man whose hopes have been dashed – and who mouths obscenities and even has a sex life too.

Rigorously built on hundreds of volumes of historiography, *The General in His Labyrinth* is by far the most fact-based of García Márquez's fictions. As a result there is none of his celebrated magic here, and (except in some of the dialogues) precious little of his wry humour. This difference perhaps makes *The General in His Labyrinth* a book that impresses us with its detailed reconstructions of an entire time and place but that, for these very reasons, lacks the imaginative leaps and smiling ironies for which the Colombian fabulist is most admired.

Sometime in the late 1980s García Márquez started telling reporters he was drafting a memoir about his early experiences as a Latin American living in Europe. The book that did come out in 1992, *Doce cuentos peregrinos*

(*Strange Pilgrims*), fits this description only in part. Its dozen tales portray fictive Lain Americans, expatriates of various ages and both sexes, who find themselves coping in sundry ways with the curious, alien customs of the Old World. The settings are rich and varied – among them Geneva, Vienna, Barcelona, an Italian isle, Madrid and, of course, Paris. A few of the pieces – 'La santa' ('The Saint'), 'Maria dos Prazeres', 'El rastro de tu sangre en la nieve' ('The Trace of Your Blood in the Snow') – can be counted among the most moving fictions ever written by García Márquez, who continues as a master of the short form. One of them, 'The Saint', is a reworking of Gabo's own film script for *Miracle in Rome,* yet with an entirely different and realistic finale. A brand-new feature of this book is the author's 'Prologue' in which he explains the volume's contents.

The Colombian's capacity for renewal and surprise became again manifest in 1994 with his spare yet luminous novel, *Del amor y otros demonios* (*Of Love and Other Demons*). The title's second half hints from the outset at the García Márquez known for his grasp of the irrational, magical, 'demoniacal' powers of love. Much of the book, on the other hand, is a new departure within Gabo's total oeuvre, focusing on worlds that lie outside his immediate experiential ken: slavery, Spanish colonialism, African culture and clerical-monastic life. Whereas Bolívar in *The General* is already a modern figure, the universe of *Of Love and Other Demons* is uncompromisingly archaic.

The setting once again is Cartagena, the former slave port and 'museum city' whose colonial architecture and atmosphere serve as the ideal backdrop for a novel with action unfolding from around 1750 to 1780. Both plot and dramatis personae are unique, with its thirteen-year-old, Rapunzel-blonde-haired daughter of slaveholding aristocrats, who is unloved by her progenitors, raised by slaves in their stead, and eventually confined to a convent. In time, a learned priest falls in love with her, visiting her in secret. The feeling grows mutual; the outcome for both turns tragic.

Of Love and Other Demons vividly captures and conveys the day-to-day repressive limits of Iberian colonialism as well as the beauties of the Afro-Hispanic folk and their folklore, not to mention the attractions, mixed consolations and sheer dangers of illicit romance. Once readers overcome the special hurdles posed by the remote subject matter, *Of Love and Other Demons* comes through as among the Colombian author's most masterfully conceived and constructed works.

Drug-trafficking and its attendant violence, unfortunately, are for what Colombia is most known across the globe. This 'narcoreality' is also a grim fact that ordinary Colombians live with day by day. García Márquez's despair at the state of his homeland and his journalistic passions found their natural outlet in *News of a Kidnapping* (*Noticia de un secuestro* [1995]), his lengthiest and most substantial work of non-fiction thus far. The book puts Gabo's best reporting skills to work in recounting the ordeal experienced by nine women and one man when they are seized successively in broad daylight, on Bogotá streets, by drug-cartel paramilitaries. The victims are held cooped up for about a year within small, windowless rooms, and with masked armed guards and the threat of death ever present.

García Márquez applies his narrative crafts to the full in this strictly factual account, placing the horrific kidnapping matter in the odd-numbered chapters, and, in the even-numbered ones, depicting the largely fruitless government efforts at resolving the crisis. A high point in the text comes when the most notorious trafficker of them all, Pablo Escobar, appears on the page, to almost electrifying effect. Though evil and lawless, Escobar cannot but amaze us with his tactical and organising genius and even his prose style; and García Márquez draws him in-the-round as he would a villain in a novel. On a related note, the ruses and tricks that Gabo utilised in order to obtain his data are in themselves fascinating and bear a close look.[5] Of all of Gabo's writings, *News of a Kidnapping* is especially painful to read, inasmuch as the entirety of the text tells of real people who have endured genuine suffering.

As García Márquez entered his sixties in 1987, his role as public figure took on a new cast. He had always been called upon to support worthy enterprises, but now his actions carried greater weight. And so in 1988, with Argentine film-maker Fernando Birri, he helped found, near Havana, the Escuela Internacional de Cine y Televisión (International School of Film and Television). Cuba, of course, has an unusually advanced, high-quality cinema industry, and the Escuela inevitably gains from access to that technical infrastructure. It also enjoys considerable prestige abroad, drawing visits from such figures as the US film-makers Steven Spielberg and Francis Ford Coppola.

Yet another of García Márquez's pedagogical activities has to do with training Latin American journalists, offering workshops in which young reporters can improve their craft, notably at the Fundación para un Nuevo Periodismo Iberoamericano (Foundation for a New Latin American Journalism). The centre, located in Cartagena, is supported in part by UNESCO and the Inter-American Development Bank. Gabo himself has helped launch various print-media ventures, and in 1999 he used his own money to purchase the Colombian edition of the Spanish weekly *Cambio*.

Since the onset of his sudden wealth and fame, García Márquez has resided in a number of places, with houses or apartments in Barcelona, Paris and Mexico City. In the 1990s, however, he had an entire ochre-coloured house with a large terrace designed and built for himself, from the ground up, in Cartagena. He now became part of that city's daily life once again, going out on late-afternoon strolls and chatting with strangers who approached him on the street. In addition, President Clinton's lifting of the unfortunate US travel restrictions on the author meant that Gabo could visit North America frequently, giving talks at major universities and visiting his own son Rodrigo, who works in film in California.

Old age and its rack of infirmities gave García Márquez a rude shock in 1999, when he was diagnosed with lymphatic cancer. High-level treatments in both Bogotá and Los Angeles fortunately saved his life, and he has been in remission since. The following year, though, Gabo's illness produced a rather bizarre consequence: under his byline, a purported farewell to life, in which the author invoked God and talked of being a rag doll, started appearing on the Internet in several languages. Entitled 'The Puppet', it listed the things the speaker would do had he more time left. (A brief sample: 'I would enjoy a good chocolate ice cream.') Only after millions worldwide had read the swooning adieu did García Márquez publicly repudiate the lament as a complete hoax and utterly *'cursi'* ('corny', 'pretentious').

There was a positive result to García Márquez's ailment. Feeling the itch to record his life story while there was still time, he now embarked on writing his memoirs. *Vivir para contarla* (*Living to Tell the Tale*), the first in what he announced would be a three-volume project, appeared in 2002. Two million copies were sold in the first six months, and journalists reported touching instances of its eager readers being publicly moved. The volume vividly captures the difficulties of Gabo's childhood, the battles with poverty and for his writerly vocation, and his early apprenticeship and literary friends. One is struck by the sheer amount of proper names immediately recognisable to us from his fiction, including the madam in Sucre whose resonant name he retained in *Chronicle of a Death Foretold*. The author also has some amazing, eyewitness-based insinuations regarding the assassination of Gaitán. The book ends inconclusively with Gabo's arrival in Europe in 1955.

When the slim volume *Memorias de mis putas tristes* (*Memories of My Melancholy Whores*) came out in 2004, many Gabo fans probably jumped at the book, believing it the sequel to the memoirs. But the joke was on them – this *Memories* is fiction. The prank goes beyond that; the contents are not at all what the outrageous handle suggests. The central *amour* in the book is non-sexual and chaste, and involves a fourteen-year-old virgin who is always asleep. The narrator, a nameless, exquisitely cultured, somewhat jaded newspaper man, is a ninety-year-old bachelor without friends, who lives in his ancestral mansion in, one infers, the coastal city of Barranquilla. At various points he reminisces about his late kin and bedmates past. The entire action takes place well before 1960, further enhancing the sense of worlds long gone. Despite the whores in the title, the Colombian author here gives us another magical love tale, filled with unexpected twists and subtle surprises.

Few authors in our time have attained the cultural influence of García Márquez. For a presence of this magnitude, one needs to look back to nineteenth-century grand masters like Dickens or Hugo. The very idea of magical realism has become a potent symbol for alternative ways of novel-writing. Commercially successful works of magical realism *lite* such as Isabel Allende's *The House of the Spirits* and Laura Esquivel's *Like Water for Chocolate* simply could not have existed without the example set by García Márquez.[6] His renovating effects can also be seen in the work of the US magical fabulists Robert Coover, John Nichols and William Kennedy. Finally, the Colombian has demonstrated that romantic love and family life can still be the stuff of great fiction. And, in an unusual development, in 2004, *One Hundred Years of Solitude* was the featured title in Oprah Winfrey's TV book club.

García Márquez's sway can even be detected at the level of daily language. Formulas on the order of 'X Years of Solitude' (or 'of Y'), or 'Love in the Time of X', or 'Chronicle of an X Foretold' serve as templates for press headlines the world over. And in the Spanish-speaking world, lesser-known titles as well as specific phrases from the author's work are commonly echoed by newspapers, much as occurs with Shakespeare and the Bible in English.

As of this writing, no one knows what García Márquez will give us next. Volumes II and III of his memoirs are yearned for by millions. And yet in recent interviews he has proudly boasted of producing absolutely nothing in 2005 and of feeling much relief at the fact. Whatever his current claims, it is to be hoped, at the time of writing, that Gabo has many years (his parents, after all, died in their nineties) and more books still ahead.

NOTES

1. This biographical sketch builds upon the information provided in the following volumes: Óscar Collazos, *García Márquez: La soledad y la gloria – Su vida y su obra,* Barcelona: Plaza y Janés, 1983; Gabriel García Márquez, *El olor de la guayaba, Conversaciones con Plinio Apuleyo Mendoza,* Barcelona: Bruguera, 1982; Gabriel García Márquez, *Vivir para contarla,* Barcelona: Mondadori, 2002; Jacques Gilard, the 'Prólogos' to each of the four volumes he has edited of García Márquez's *Obra Periodística,* 4 vols., Barcelona: Bruguera, 1981–3; Stephen Minta, *Gabriel García Márquez: Writer of Colombia,* London: Jonathan Cape, 1987; Dasso Saldívar, *García Márquez: El viaje a la semilla – La biografía,* Madrid: Alfaguara, 1997; Mario Vargas Llosa, *García Márquez: Historia de un deicidio,* Barcelona and Caracas: Seix Barral/

Monte Ávila, 1971. There are also the countless interviews, particularly those gathered in Alfonso Rentería Mantilla (ed.), *García Márquez habla de García Márquez,* Bogotá: Rentería Mantilla Ltda., 1979; and in Gene H. Bell-Villada, *Conversations with Gabriel García Márquez,* Jackson, MS: University Press of Mississippi, 2006. The memoir by García Márquez and the biography by Saldívar, one should note, have greatly expanded our knowledge of the Colombian author's early life.

2. Saldívar, *García Márquez,* p. 87.
3. For a fuller discussion of the Boom and related issues, see, for example, Philip Swanson, *Latin American Fiction,* Oxford: Blackwell, 2005, or Efraín Kristal (ed.), *The Cambridge Companion to the Latin American Novel,* Cambridge: Cambridge University Press, 2005.
4. Tzvetan Todorov, *The Fantastic: A Structural Approach to a Literary Genre,* trans. Richard Howard, Ithaca, NY: Cornell University Press, 1975, pp. 25–30.
5. See Susana Cato's interview with the author, 'Gabo Changes Jobs', in Gene H. Bell-Villada (ed.), *Conversations,* pp. 184–90, especially pp. 185–6.
6. For more on post-Boom reactions to García Márquez, see sources in note 3 above, or Stephen M. Hart and Wen-chin Ouyang (eds.), *A Companion to Magical Realism,* Woodbridge: Tamesis, 2005.

2

DONALD SHAW

The critical reception of García Márquez

Serious criticism of Gabriel García Márquez began in the late 1960s, with a particular breakthrough in 1967, the year of *One Hundred Years of Solitude* (*Cien años de soledad*). Before that critical date, however, Volkening, Loveluck and Harss (who is said to have introduced the term 'Boom') had already recognised that a potentially important new figure had emerged in Spanish American fiction. Early criticism of the Boom tended to approach early Boom fiction from standpoints associated with readings of older regional novels by writers such as Ricardo Güiraldes and Rómulo Gallegos in the 1920s. Thus Volkening begins by lamenting the tendency to relate contemporary Spanish American fiction to European and North American models (Joyce, Faulkner) and demanding that the '*criollo* (i.e. Spanish American) author' be evaluated on his own terms.[1] He goes on to suggest that García Márquez (before *One Hundred Years of Solitude,* of course) continues the creative pattern of the regional novel but with 'new means of expression'.[2] At the same time, however, like Ángel Rama in the following year, he emphasises the 'dry realism' of García Márquez's style and his tone of social protest. This was not how much future criticism would develop. Loveluck, on the other hand, immediately emphasises García Márquez's newness and associates it right away with 'overcoming outworn nativist and costumbrist formulae'.[3] It is noteworthy that at this point the idea of the Boom had not yet gelled, and Loveluck places García Márquez correctly alongside Carlos Fuentes, José Donoso and Mario Vargas Llosa, but allows Rosario Castellanos, Enrique Lafourcade and David Viñas to get into the act. What is ground-breaking about Loveluck's article is his recognition that the renovation of modern Spanish American fiction began around 1950, being in large measure due to the very influences Volkening deplored, and that García Márquez was part of it. The same year, Harss published *Los nuestros* (*Into the Mainstream* [1967]), the first book-length study in both English and Spanish which saw the Boom writers as a group, including Carpentier, Onetti, Cortázar, Rulfo, Fuentes, García Márquez and Vargas

Llosa. In his chapter on García Márquez he at once emphasises the latter's 'team sense', that is to say, his sense of belonging to what the English text calls 'that somewhat loosely knit group of young internationalists, all under forty – Fuentes, Vargas Llosa – whose work is changing the face of our literature'.[4] The importance of this book, which at once went into several editions, can hardly be overestimated. It put the Boom on the map both in North and South America. The second feature of it which is relevant is that Harss instantly recognised that a central theme of García Márquez's presentation of Macondo both before and in *One Hundred Years of Solitude* is his pessimistic vision of the 'moral gangrene' that characterises its inhabitants.[5] In addition, Harss mentions another important feature of García Márquez's work, the strength of character of his women figures in contrast to the weakness and instability of the men.[6] A shortcoming of Harss's approach is that although he foregrounds García Márquez's humour (and, interestingly, García Márquez's distrust of it at this stage), he does not set it against his pessimism.[7] To Vargas Llosa's subsequent mention of García Márquez's reading of Rabelais, Harss adds Joyce, Virginia Woolf, Kafka and Faulkner. The influence of Hemingway had still to be recognised.

The 1967 article by Tomás Eloy Martínez marked the beginning of the consecration of García Márquez as the foremost novelist of the Boom. Martínez linked García Márquez with Cortázar, Vargas Llosa, Onetti and Carpentier, as well as (still) with the regional novel, in order to assert that *One Hundred Years of Solitude* summed up better than any of their novels the various currents present at that time in Spanish American fiction. Seeing Macondo as it would always be seen subsequently, as microcosmic, Martínez asserted that *One Hundred Years of Solitude* is 'a meticulous metaphor of all Latin American life'.[8] For the first time we begin to see García Márquez not just as another new novelist but as the potential leader of the New Novel in Spanish America. This position was endorsed in the same year by Emanuel Carballo who hailed García Márquez as 'the first of his team mates to write a masterpiece'.[9] Carballo's article is significant also because it is one of the first, if not the first, to raise the important question of the dichotomy of hope and despair in García Márquez's world-view. This is an issue which has still not been entirely resolved.

Other leading Spanish American critics, including Mario Benedetti (1967) and Julio Ortega now took up the song.[10] But, in parallel, the idea of the Boom itself as a movement began to take shape. In 1969, the already famous Mexican novelist Carlos Fuentes published his immensely influential *La nueva novela hispanoamericana*.[11] In it he stressed the division between the novel of the decade of the 1960s (the key decade of the Boom) and the earlier regionalist fiction, as well as suggesting that Spain had an equivalent novelist to those we think of as Boom novelists, in Juan Goytisolo. This was a suggestion which was to have important reverberations in Spain, where Fuentes's essay was soon to be followed by another by a leading Spanish figure, Ricardo Gullón.[12] But now Emir Rodríguez Monegal entered the scene he was soon to dominate. He and Vargas Llosa broke out of Latin America and published in English, in *Books Abroad* (1970), two important articles that strongly reinforced critical interest in the Boom outside the continent of its birth.[13] The consequences were to be far-reaching as the North American and European academic Establishments took note. Neither of these two articles uses the word 'Boom', though it was already accepted as the name of the new movement, and neither of them presents García Márquez in the leadership role. Both of them, however, make similar points, all of which would affect the mainstream of García Márquez criticism. They were: first, that the old regionalist novel was now obsolete and its themes replaced by a new emphasis on the wider human condition; second, that a qualitative leap in narrative technique had taken place; third, that observed reality was now flanked by created, imaginary, reality; and fourth, that language had assumed central importance in the new novel. From now on, criticism of García Márquez would be inseparable from criticism of the Boom and vice versa.

Gullón's essay, at that time the longest to date on García Márquez, deals almost exclusively with *One Hundred Years of Solitude* and signals the beginning of analytic criticism of it. Much that we find later in Vargas Llosa, Maturo and other critics who concentrate on technique is prefigured by Gullón. The main thrust of his essay, however, suggests that whereas other novelists lose themselves in the complexities of technical experimentalism, García Márquez avoids this fate, his novel being dominated by an 'imperturbable' narrative tone which treats realistic and fabulous episodes as if they were exactly alike, carrying the reader along at a fast clip, unchallenged to suspend disbelief. Although he alludes to circularity and the treatment of time in *One Hundred Years of Solitude,* Gullón's chief contribution to understanding the novel's structure is his identification of the biblical subtext which underlies the plot. We miss in this essay any final interpretation of the events described, the possible meaning of the solitude suffered by the Macondinos and their ultimate obliteration. The same is true of Rodríguez Monegal's 1968 article.[14] It establishes once and for all the line of separation between the 'frozen anger' of García Márquez's earlier work and the humour and fantasy of *One Hundred Years of Solitude* and its successors. That line of separation is marked by 'Big Mama's Funeral' ('Los funerales de la mamá grande'). But Rodríguez Monegal's article is characterised by his readiness to emphasise the ultimate solitude of the human individual and the possible fictional nature of all reality as themes in the novel, in parallel with surviving elements of angry social criticism, as though there were no contradiction between them. Still, he does recognise one of the fundamental dualities of the novel, which is at once 'so full of enjoyment, fun and vitality' and one written with 'the saddest, most lonely outlook'.[15] The other crucial duality, first noticed by Angel Rama in his 1964 article, is the permanent ambivalence in García Márquez's outlook which produces an ongoing oscillation between the social and the metaphysical planes in his work.

By the beginning of the 1970s, the critical reception of García Márquez in Spanish America had got off to a fine start with two major collections of early essays: *Nueve asedios a García Márquez* (1969), and *Recopilación de textos sobre Gabriel García Márquez* (1969) with contributions by major critics and fellow writers such as Carlos Fuentes, Vargas Llosa and Reinaldo Arenas. In France, *Le Monde* had taken special notice in 1968. In Spain, critics of the calibre of Gullón and Amorós had saluted *One Hundred Years of Solitude,* and, also in 1968, the prestigious literary review *Indice* had devoted thirteen pages to essays by Spanish, French and English critics. In Italy, important figures including Cesare Segre and Natalia Ginzburg had published reviews of *One Hundred Years of Solitude.* In North America, Ronald Christ had edited a special supplement to *Review* (1971), chiefly with articles translated from the Spanish and reviews by North American, French, German and Portuguese journals. Unquestionably, however, where the critical reception of the Boom and of García Márquez as its most prominent representative was most influential was Spain. There, we recall, García Márquez was living in Barcelona from 1968 to 1975. During this time, apart from giving many interviews, he saw two full-scale books on him: by Miguel Fernández Braso and Óscar Collazos.[16] Dravasa has shown that well before the publication of the second of these books, the impact of García Márquez's presence and the interest generated in Boom fiction by a group of young critics in Barcelona with their magazine *Laye* and the backing of the Seix Barral publishing house had overcome the hostility of prominent figures such as José María Gironella and Alfonso Grosso, and changed the course of modern Spanish fiction.

The year 1970 saw the publication of Óscar Collazos's contribution to a debate with Vargas Llosa and Julio Cortázar which appeared as *Literatura en la revolución y revolución en la literatura* in which he excoriated the Boom writers as suffering from an inferiority complex that produced dependency on European and North American literary culture.[17] This was a view which was to cast a long shadow ahead and produce criticism of García Márquez as a writer too ready to disassociate himself from his social context and from Spanish American 'specificity'. We recall that, at the end of *La nueva novela hispanoamericana,* Carlos Fuentes had suggested that Boom writing might well have an emancipatory and socially progressive effect on the Spanish American reading public. This view has been sharply criticised not only by Collazos but subsequently by Hernán Vidal and also more recently by George Yúdice.[18] Both the last two left-wing critics see the Boom as failing to exert an emancipatory influence and relate Boom narrative technique to capitalist ideology. It is not clear how experimental narrative strategies can reflect a reactionary political outlook, conscious or otherwise. Still, similar views have surfaced specifically with respect to García Márquez, a notable example being Ileana Rodríguez, (1979) who argues that *One Hundred Years of Solitude* is ideologically confused, uncritical of the Buendías, the principal family in Macondo, as the local landowning and socially powerful elite, that it ignores class struggle and material conditions and distorts the role of the gringo banana company. A more extensive Marxist interpretation of the novel is provided by Víctor Farías (1981).[19] Relevant, too, are Jesse Fernández (1984), Lawrence Porter (1986) and Gerald Martin (1987).[20] The other development beginning to break surface in 1970 was the emergence of mythical interpretations of *One Hundred Years of Solitude,* present in Gullón but more explicitly developed by Mejía Duque.[21] This line of approach was to be greatly extended, notably by Arnau, Maturo and Carillo, as we shall see.

At the beginning of the 1970s, the time was obviously ripe for a full-scale authoritative book on García Márquez's work up to that point. This now appeared as Mario Vargas Llosa's *García Márquez: Historia de un deicidio,* still a standard critical text on our author.[22] Its great merit is that it was the first work to deal systematically with the whole of García Márquez's available early work up to and slightly beyond *One Hundred Years of Solitude,* dealing both with content and technique with the insight of an already famous fellow-novelist. Its great demerit is that it fails to face squarely García Márquez's deeply pessimistic portrayal of Spanish America's historical evolution, of which the evolution of Macondo represents a microcosm. This unwillingness to recognise that García Márquez's personal left-wing stance is not entirely compatible with his deeply disenchanted presentation of Spanish America's recent past (what Vargas Llosa calls García Márquez's view of reality as 'essentialist and dominated by fatality') and of the shortcomings of all classes of his fellow Spanish Americans, would henceforth be an important element in criticism of his work and would reverberate for example in Lucila Mena with its lame suggestion at the end that García Márquez's critique is merely intended to prepare the way for some later socio-political renovation.[23] The attempt by Sergio Benvenuto (1971) to attribute the problems of the Macondinos to external factors of underdevelopment, and the suggestion by Josefina Ludmer that the ending of the novel symbolises the end of a period of material and cultural colonialism in Spanish America read unconvincingly both in the light of the rest of the novel and in that of other works by García Márquez.[24] More thought-provoking is Anna Marie Taylor, who, after a rather feeble attempt to relate the novelist's outlook to the decay of capitalism, does correctly insist on a fatalistic and pessimistic interpretation of the ending of the work.[25] By contrast, Wood asserts, without supporting arguments, that in the novel 'despair is dismantled, held up as a superstition, an illusion of destiny'.[26]

As we saw above in reference to Gullón, García Márquez's narrative strategies had already begun to attract critical interest. Vargas Llosa extends this interest, distinguishing among different levels of created reality, remarking on the use of comic exaggeration and enumeration, especially in the watershed work 'Big Mama's Funeral' and suggesting the influence of Rabelais. Another foundational article in this connection, mentioned subsequently in all the bibliographies, is that of Iris Zavala, drawing attention to the use of the chronicles of the conquest of Latin America as sources for García Márquez's most important work.[27]

One of the first critics to develop the 'dark side' of *One Hundred Years of Solitude* and, by extension, García Márquez's outlook generally, was Carmen Arnau.[28] She brings out three of the basic aspects of the novel that cast doubt on a positive interpretation of its contents and, above all, its ending. These are: first, the parodic treatment of Christian themes, especially visible in the presentation of Remedios la Bella, Fernanda del Carpio, Amaranta and the parish priests of Macondo; second, the iron determinism which appears to govern the lives of the Buendías; and third, the role of incest so prominent in the family. All of these were destined to re-emerge frequently in later criticism. The first in particular assumes a special importance in the light of Rodríguez Monegal's division of García Márquez's earlier work into a phase of 'observed' reality and indignation, followed by one of more 'created' reality and humour. It now seemed to some critics that the 'created' reality rests on a mythic basis related to Christian beliefs. We can, in fact, postulate a clear line of development of the mythic approach to *One Hundred Years of Solitude* beginning to take shape, as we have seen, with Gullón and Mejía Duque. It continues with Jara Cuadra and Mejía Duque, where it is suggested that myth plays a positive role in imposing order on reality, and in works by Arnau, Maturo and Carillo.[29] Graciela Maturo insists relentlessly on the primary importance of the mythico-symbolic elements in García Márquez's work as a whole including even, for example, *In Evil Hour* (*La mala hora*), which is seen in universal terms rather than social terms specific to Latin America.[30] Similarly, her approach to *One Hundred Years of Solitude* is predicated on her determination to see José Arcadio Buendía, the patriarch, as a human archetype associated with Christ, Abraham and Moses, the entire novel being seen in abstract symbolic terms of ultimately Christian inspiration. Three years later, Germán Carrillo more cautiously emphasised the idea of a 'Fall' from an Edenic existence into a tragic one as the chief underlying symbol.[31] The whole importance of such approaches lies in the intention to perceive *One Hundred Years of Solitude* as essentially relevant to the whole of (Western) mankind and the modern cultural crisis. What is not quite clear about Carrillo's interpretation is his postulate of a 'final salvation' for the Buendías, which seems to be contradicted by his reference to the tragic irony and final impossibility of the family's (and humankind's) attempt to find a solution to their existential problem.[32] Other such interpretations include subsequently Katalin Kulin (1980), Robert Sims (1981) (the first book to suggest that García Márquez manipulates and at times 'inverts' the mythical elements which he incorporates into his writings) and Michael Palencia-Roth.[33] We should note, however, that mythical approaches to *One Hundred Years of Solitude* have been subjected to sharp criticism by Agustín Seguí.[34] He roundly asserts that 'the similarity between the history of Macondo and the biblical history of mankind is merely a similarity, and as such is quite insufficient to permit talk of myths.'[35]

From this time on, mythical, symbolic and universalist interpretations of *One Hundred Years of Solitude* would find themselves in increasing competition with historical and area-specific interpretations. Among the latter, attention needs to be drawn in particular to Lucila Mena.[36] She correctly emphasises that the novel presents both an interpretation of Colombian (and Spanish American) history and at the same time a questioning of the nature, meaning and object of history. In that sense, *One Hundred Years of Solitude* can be seen as marking the beginning of one branch of the New Historical Novel in Spanish America. Mena's work is significant on the one hand because it rightly emphasises that the mythicisation of history which takes place in the novel points towards condemnation of Macondo, and not towards the biblical notion of history evolving towards an eventual redemption of mankind. On the other hand, her work implies that myth represents an escape from a pattern of historical failure. While Mena attempts to hold a balance between historical (local) and mythical (universal) elements in *One Hundred Years of Solitude,* more recently her work and that of the whole range of critics who have emphasised the latter elements have been challenged by attempts to interpret *One Hundred Years of Solitude* in particular in broadly political and sociological terms. Here we can add reference to Rodríguez's cogent article on an extraordinarily humourless book by Montaner which attempts to treat the novel as if it were a piece of realist fiction.[37] Montaner's conclusion, as far as she has one, is that *One Hundred Years of Solitude* records 'a story as ambiguous as the ambition and exploitation of man by man' (in Latin America).[38] More convincing is José Luis Méndez.[39] His central thesis is that the novel should be understood primarily as a radical critique of the values and way of life of the Macondinos, in which Méndez perceives a reflection of the anachronistic socio-economic and political development of Latin America, as García Márquez remembered it from his childhood. Thus, in Méndez's view, what is necessary above all in interpreting *One Hundred Years of Solitude* is the need to recognise 'the social origin of each structure' which it contains.[40] The whole work is alleged to be nothing more than a metaphorical treatment of the feudalism, the underdevelopment, the oppression and the general backwardness of Latin America. A similar emphasis on the strictly Colombian and Latin American background to the novel can be found in Minta.[41] The reductiveness of this approach hardly needs to be stressed. Its peak can be seen in the polemical attack mounted by Carmenza Kline (2002).[42] The thrust of Kline's books is fiercely opposed to that of those critics, beginning especially with Gullón and Vargas Llosa, who expressly foreground the elements of fantasy in García Márquez. Kline insists on the need to set García Márquez's work consistently in the politico-social context of modern Colombia. She is currently the leading exponent of 'specificity' in García Márquez criticism.

In the same year as Maturo's book, 1972, Josefina Ludmer published her *Cien años de soledad: una interpretación.*[43] The two works mark a kind of crossroads in García Márquez criticism: Maturo's totally interpretative, Ludmer's the first full-scale book to investigate in detail something else: the narrative strategy of *One Hundred Years of Solitude.* Ludmer's book reveals how the entire structure of *One Hundred Years of Solitude* is based on a series of dualities which either parallel each other or contrast with each other, so that the narrative organisation is somehow ludic, game-like, in line with the generally humorous style. This is still the most illuminating book of its kind on García Márquez, though, as we have already noted, there is room for disagreement about Ludmer's interpretation of the ending as a return to unity, with the triumph of the 'mental' characters over the 'physical' ones and the emergence of the proletariat in Maurico Babilonia as a new social force portending a new future for Macondo.

The outburst of critical reactions at the end of the 1960s to the publication of *One Hundred Years of Solitude* can be readily documented in the *Recopilación de textos sobre Gabriel García Márquez,* compiled by Pedro Simón Martínez in 1969 and reissued with additions in 1971.[44] It was these essays, including contributions by future big-name figures such as Fuentes,

Benedetti, Arenas and Vargas Llosa, along with prestigious foreign critics such as Jean Franco and Claude Couffon, which first placed García Márquez in the forefront of the Boom. We notice that many of them reappear in the Giacoman homage volume in 1972 and even the Taurus (Madrid) compilation, edited by Peter Earle in 1981.[45] But it was the full-scale books by Vargas Llosa, Arnau, Maturo, Carillo and others in the 1970s that consolidated García Márquez's reputation as the leader of the new movement. An important turning point came with the first book on García Márquez in English by McMurray in 1977.[46] With this a Latin American author figured for the first time in a well-known series of critical monographs, alongside Saul Bellow, Truman Capote, Gore Vidal and a number of other leading North American writers. It took until the 1990s for Great Britain to catch up, with Michael Bell, who includes García Márquez as the only Latin American in the Macmillan Modern Novelists series, alongside Nabokov, Updike, Naipaul, Spark, Mailer and sundry others.[47] While McMurray's book is largely a descriptive survey, it paved the way for much future criticism in English, or by English-speaking critics, in the form of monographs by figures including Sims, Janes, Williams, Levine, Minta, McNerney, Wood, Hart, Mose and Swanson, in the form of collections of essays such as those edited by Vera-Godwin and Bradley Shaw, McGuirk and Cardwell, Ortega, Bloom and Bell-Villada, or in the form of journal numbers devoted to García Márquez such as the *PEN America* one in 2005.[48] To these must be added the collection of essays in Spanish on *One Hundred Years of Solitude* edited by Francisco Porrata but published in California by the State University at Sacramento's Spanish department, and the bilingual essay collection edited by Megenny and Oyarzún, published by the University of California at Riverside.[49] Meanwhile, much Hispanic criticism has been collected by Cobo Borda and García Nuñez and by Zuluaga Osorio.[50]

The considerable takeover of criticism of García Márquez by North American and British hispanism marks the consecration of García Márquez as a world author. The only article which I have been able to find on the critical reception of García Márquez, by Munday, refers chiefly to reviews of translations of his works into English.[51] Its main points of interest are that not until after the publication of *Love in the Time of Cholera* in 1985 did criticism of García Márquez in the English press emerge from its obsession with a stereotypical image of García Márquez as the author of *One Hundred Years of Solitude,* but that thereafter he was fully accepted as on a par with major Old World writers.

Since the beginning of the 1980s the proliferation of criticism of García Márquez has attained such proportions that it is difficult to survey it systematically. Interest in *One Hundred Years of Solitude* remains central. Here special mention must be made of Porrata's above-mentioned collection of essays, Juan Manuel García Ramos, Michael Wood and Philip Swanson.[52] The fundamental question underlying every attempt to provide a satisfactory reading of the novel is whether in fact it is possible at all 'to provide a coherent interpretation, a logical meaning to the events', as David William Foster put it in 1968.[53] If not, why not? It must be said at once that the vast majority of the existing critical approaches to *One Hundred Years of Solitude* fail to address this question directly enough, with the result that two very perceptive critics agree that little progress has been made on this front. Williamson in 1987 calls the novel, correctly, 'elusive and enigmatic', and Swanson, as recently as 1991, could refer to it as a 'potential minefield'.[54] We have to take account of the fact that both the broadly politico-social and mythical approaches are chiefly descriptive and classificatory, though in both cases they point to interpretative conclusions. The former inevitably tends to see the novel as a 'national allegory' relating it to the central pattern of 'civic' fiction in Latin America whose aim was to raise the level of consciousness of the reader and nudge him or her to withdraw allegiance from the political, social and economic forces responsible for injustice, oppression and underdevelopment. The latter, on the other hand, tends to universalise the thematic thrust of the novel and to see it as ultimately expressing an apocalyptic vision of the human condition, at least in the West. The attraction of the politico-social approach is that it makes it easy to interpret the nature of the 'moral gangrene' afflicting the Macondinos, first recognised by Harss. At this level we can suggest that it reveals a familiar cultural-reformist outlook, in which traditional collective attitudes and outlooks are blamed, alongside objective economic and other forces, for national shortcomings. The problem, however, is that this approach is difficult to conciliate with the mythical approach, which has obvious links with the idea of an ongoing Western cultural crisis which transcends social and economic problems and which is thought to be connected with the collapse of traditional absolutes. But in addition, as, among others, Swanson has signalled, in what is, in my view, the best overall introduction to the novel, *One Hundred Years of Solitude* questions the very nature of reality itself and thus undercuts both a politico-social approach and a mythical one: the idea that all reality may be fictitious leaves us no way to interpret it.[55] For this reason, when I came to publish my analysis of interpretations of *One Hundred Years of Solitude* in 1992, I attempted to suggest that in dealing with the novel the critic now is faced with a series of choices: is the novel concerned ultimately with the nature of reality, or with the human condition generally, or with specifically Latin American problems – with myth, with history, with ultimate 'why' questions, or what? While one may wish to emphasise one approach rather than another, the existence of the remaining approaches and the difficulty of reconciling them with each other must be recognised.

While none of García Márquez's other publications has come near to attracting the degree of critical response enjoyed by *One Hundred Years of Solitude,* the rest of his work, except for the very latest, has attracted much serious attention. His early (and extensive) journalism has been explored by Sims and Williams among others, showing how it prefigures aspects of his later fiction. Thereafter, with respect to García Márquez's fiction before *One Hundred Years of Solitude,* the main emphasis has been on the methods by which he was able to revamp the old novel of protest without losing any of its impact. These range from his innovations in character presentation (Cardwell), to his use of Sophocles's *Antigone* in *Leaf Storm* (Lastra), to his use of monologue in the same novel (Castañeda), to the functions of humour and figurative language in *No One Writes to the Colonel* (*El coronel no tiene quien le escriba*) (Vargas Llosa and Fiddian) and, predictably, to the employment of mythico-symbolic elements (Maturo and Earle).[56] Another fruitful approach has been to trace to the early fiction the origin of major later themes.[57] Many features of the critical reception of the early fiction have been consolidated.[58]

Astonishingly, *The Autumn of the Patriarch* (*El otoño del patriarca*) has so far stimulated no less than six, generally mediocre, short book-length studies on top of more than seventy articles and contributions to books. In synthesis, most of the more serious and thoughtful approaches tend to discuss one or more of three topics: the presentation of dictatorial power, the ambiguous presentation of the Patriarch himself, and aspects of the novel's highly innovative narrative strategy, including the treatment of the narrative voice and the extraordinarily creative use of language. While it is clearly out of the question to discuss this mass of criticism in any detail here, two contributions must be singled out as essential reading. They are Ortega and Labanyi, which together admirably summarise the main critical issues.[59]

In his review of the critical reception of *Chronicle of a Death Foretold* (*Crónica de una muerte anunciada*), Méndez Ramirez concludes that it can be reduced to two basic interpretations: those based on the notion of fatality and those based on collective culpability.[60] Other critics have discussed the novel's formal organisation (for example, Shaw and Olivares), its mythical and symbolic elements (for example, Concha) or have taken a feminist perspective (for example, Ross).[61] Once again there is a fine synthetic overview in Hart's critical guide.[62] Most of the thirty-odd critical contributions on *The General in His Labyrinth* (*El general en su laberinto*) deal either with the work as representing García Márquez's complex contribution to the New Historical Novel (notably Menton) or with his demythologising interpretation of the personality of Bolívar (for example, Boland), but special mention must be made of Rincón, which brings to bear cogently the relevance of the notion of Postmodernist metafiction in this case.[63] The whole question of García Márquez as a modernist or alternatively a post-modernist writer remains open.

Perhaps the greatest surprise recently has been the emergence of *Love in the Time of Cholera* (*El amor en los tiempos del cólera* [1985]) as the chief centre of critical attention after *One Hundred Years of Solitude.* On the one hand, since love was at a discount in Boom fiction, interest has been aroused by García Márquez's treatment of it in this novel, including parodic and ironic elements.[64] On the other hand, his apparent shift towards a technique modelled on that of the great nineteenth-century masters has been examined critically.[65] A handy overall view is offered by Rahy's *A Reader's Guide* (2003).[66] Since no critical consensus has as yet come into being on García Márquez's subsequent works we may here bring these notes to an end.

NOTES

1. E. Volkening, 'Gabriel García Márquez o el trópico desembrujado', *Eco* (Bogotá), 40, 7 April 1963, pp. 275–93; reprinted in Mario Benedetti (ed.), *Nueve asedios a García Márquez,* Santiago: Editora Universitaria, 1969, pp. 147–63.
2. Volkening, 'Gabriel García Márquez'.
3. Juan Loveluck, 'Gabriel García Márquez, narrador colombiano', *Duquesne Hispanic Review,* 5 (1966): 135–54; reprinted in Benedetti, *Nueve asedios*, pp. 52–73.
4. Luis Harss, *Into the Mainstream,* New York: Harper & Row, 1967, p. 311.
5. Harss, *Into the Mainstream,* p. 313.
6. Harss, *Into the Mainstream,* p. 326.
7. Harss, *Into the Mainstream,* p. 326.
8. T. E. Martínez, 'América: la gran novela – Gabriel García Márquez', *Primera Plana,* 5 (234) (1967): 54–5.
9. E. Carballo, 'Gabriel García Márquez, un gran novelista latinoamericano', *Revista de la Universidad de México,* 12 (3) (1967): 10–16; reprinted in Benedetti, *Nueve asedios*, pp. 22–37.
10. Mario Benedetti, 'García Márquez o la vigilia dentro del sueño', in *Letras del continente mestizo,* Montevideo: Arca, 1967, pp. 145–54; reprinted in Benedetti, *Nueve asedios*, pp. 11–21. Julio Ortega, 'Gabriel García Márquez: *Cien años de soledad*', in *La Contemplación y la fiesta,* Lima: Universitaria, 1968, pp. 44–58; reprinted in Benedetti, *Nueve asedios*, pp. 74–88.
11. Carlos Fuentes, *La nueva novela hispanoamericana,* Mexico City: Joaquín Mortiz, 1969.
12. Ricardo Gullón, *García Márquez o el olvidado arte de contar,* Madrid: Taurus, 1970.
13. Emir Rodríguez Monegal, 'The New Latin American Novel', *Books Abroad,* 44 (1970): 45–50; Mario Vargas Llosa, 'The Latin American Novel Today', *Books Abroad,* 44 (1970): 7–16.

14. Emir Rodríguez Monegal, 'Novedad y anacronismo en *Cien años Soledad*', *Revista Nacional de Cultura* (Caracas), 29 (185) (1968): 3–21. Reprinted in Helmy F. Giacoman, *Homenaje a Gabriel García Márquez,* New York: Las Américas, 1972, pp. 15–42.
15. Rodríguez Monegal, 'Novedad y anacronismo', p. 41.
16. Miguel Fernández Braso, *La soledad de Gabriel García Márquez (una conversación infinita),* Barcelona: Planeta, 1972; Oscar Collazos, *García Márquez: la soledad y la gloria – su vida y su obra,* Barcelona: Plaza y Janés, 1983.
17. Óscar Collazos, Mario Vargas Llosa and Julio Cortázar, *Literatura en la revolución y revolución en la literatura,* Mexico City: Siglo XXI, 1970.
18. Hernán Vidal, *Literatura hispanoamericana e ideología liberal: surgimiento y crisis,* Buenos Aires: Hispamérica, 1976; George Yúdice, 'Postmodernity and Transnational Capitalism in Latin America', in George Yúdice, Jean Franco and Juan Flores (eds.), *On Edge: The Crisis of Contemporary Latin American Culture,* Minneapolis, MN: Minnesota University Press, 1992, pp. 1–28.
19. Víctor Farías, *Los manuscritos de Melquíades,* Frankfurt: Vervuert, 1981.
20. Jesse Fernández, 'La ética del trabajo y la acumulación de la riqueza en Cien años de soledad', *Explicación de Textos Literarios,* 12 (2) (1983/4): 29–36; Lawrence Porter, 'The Political Function of Fantasy in Gabriel García Márquez', *The Centennial Review,* 30 (2) (1986): 197–207; Gerald Martin, 'On Magical and Social Realism in *One Hundred Years of Solitude*', in Bernard McGuirk and Richard Cardwell (eds.), *Gabriel García Márquez: New Readings,* Cambridge, Cambridge University Press, 1987, pp. 95–115.
21. Jaime Mejía Duque, *Mito y realidad en Gabriel García Márquez,* Bogotá: Prisma, 1970.
22. Mario Vargas Llosa, *García Márquez: Historia de un deicidio,* Barcelona and Caracas: Seix Barral and Monte Avila, 1971.
23. Vargas Llosa, *García Márquez,* p. 418; Lucila Mena, *La función de la historia en Cien años de soledad,* Barcelona: Plaza y Janés, 1979.
24. Josefia Ludmer, *Cien años de soledad: una interpretación,* Buenos Aires: Editorial Tiempo Contemporáneo, 1972; Sergio Benvenuto, 'Estética como historia', in Pedro Simón Martínez (ed.), *Sobre García Márquez,* Montevideo: Marcha, 1971, pp. 157–65.
25. Anna Marie Taylor, '*Cien años de soledad:* History and the Novel', *Latin American Perspectives,* 2 (3) (1975): 96–112.
26. Michael Wood, *Gabriel García Márquez: One Hundred Years of Solitude,* Cambridge: Cambridge University Press, 1990, p. 7.
27. Iris Zavala, '*Cien años de soledad:* crónica de Indias', *Ínsula,* 25 (286) (1970): 3 and 11.
28. Carmen Arnau, *El mundo mítico de Gabriel García Márquez,* Barcelona: Península, 1971.
29. René Jara Cuadra and Jaime Mejía Duque, *Las claves del mito en García Márquez,* Valparaiso: Ediciones Universitarias, 1972.
30. Graciela Maturo, *Claves simbólicas de Gabriel García Márquez,* Buenos Aires: García Cambeiro, 1972.
31. Germán Carrillo, *La narrativa de Gabriel García Márquez,* Madrid: Castalia, 1975.
32. Carrillo, *La narrativa,* pp. 41 and 89.

33. Robert L. Sims, *The Evolution of Myth in Gabriel García Márquez from* La hojarasca *to* Cien años de soledad, Miami, FL: Universal, 1981; Michael Palencia-Roth, *Gabriel García Márquez: la línea, el círculo y las metamorfosis del mito,* Madrid: Gredos, 1983.
34. Agustín Seguí, *La verdadera historia de Macondo,* Frankfurt: Vervuert Verlag, 1994.
35. Seguí, *La verdadera historia,* p. 146.
36. Mena, *La función de la historia.*
37. Maria E. Montaner, *Guía para la lectura de* Cien años de soledad, Madrid: Castalia, 1987.
38. Montaner, *Guía para la lectura,* p. 186.
39. José L. Méndez, *Cómo leer a García Márquez,* Río Piedras: Universidad de Puerto Rico, 1989.
40. Méndez, *Cómo leer,* p. 113.
41. Stephen Minta, *Gabriel García Márquez: Writer of Colombia,* London: Jonathan Cape, 1987.
42. C. Kline, *Fiction and Reality in the Works of Gabriel García Márquez,* Salamanca: Universidad, 2002.
43. Josefina Ludmer, Cien años de soledad: *una interpretación,* Buenos Aires: Editorial Tiempo Contemporáneo, 1972.
44. Pedro S. Martínez, *Recopilación de textos sobre Gabriel García Márquez,* 2nd edn, Montevideo: Biblioteca de Marcha, 1971.
45. Helmy F. Giacoman, *Homenaje a Gabriel García Márquez,* New York: Las Américas, 1972; Peter Earle (ed.), *Gabriel García Márquez,* Madrid: Taurus, 1982.
46. George McMurray, *Gabriel García Márquez,* New York: Frederick Ungar, 1977.
47. Michael Bell, *Gabriel García Márquez: Solitude and Solidarity,* London: Macmillan, 1993.
48. G. H. Bell-Villada, *García Márquez. The Man and His Work,* Chapel Hill, NC: North Carolina University Press, 1990; H. Bloom, *Gabriel García Márquez,* New York: Chelsea House, 1989; S. Hart, *Gabriel García Márquez,* Crónica de una muerte anunciada, London: Grant & Cutler, 1994; R. Janes, *Gabriel García Márquez: Revolutions in Wonderland,* Columbia, MO: University of Missouri Press, 1981; S. J. Levine, *El espejo hablado,* Caracas: Monte Ávila, 1975; B. McGuirk and R. Cardwell (eds.), *Gabriel García Márquez: New Readings,* Cambridge: Cambridge University Press, 1987; K. McNerney, *Understanding Gabriel García Márquez,* Columbia, SC: South Carolina University Press, 1989; S. Minta, *Gabriel García Márquez: Writer of Colombia,* London and New York: Harper and Cape, 1987; K. Mose, *Defamiliarization in the Work of Gabriel García Márquez,* Lewiston, NY: Mellen, 1989; J. Ortega, *La Contemplación y la fiesta,* Lima: Universitaria, 1968; *PEN America,* special issue on García Márquez, 3 (6) (2005); B. A. Shaw and N. Vera-Godwin (eds.), *Critical Perspectives on Gabriel García Márquez,* Lincoln, NE: Society for Spanish and Spanish American Studies, 1986; R. L. Sims, *The Evolution of Myth in Gabriel García Márquez,* Miami, FL: Universal, 1981; P. Swanson, *Cómo leer a Gabriel García Márquez,* Madrid: Júcar, 1991; R. L. Williams, *Gabriel García Márquez,* Boston, MA: Twayne, 1984; M. Wood, *García*

Márquez: One Hundred Years of Solitude, Cambridge: Cambridge University Press, 1990.

49. F. E. Porrata (ed.), *Explicación de* Cien años de soledad, Sacramento, CA: Department of Spanish and Portuguese, California State University, 1976; Kemy Oyarzún and William W. Megenney (eds.), *Essays on Gabriel García Márquez,* Riverside, CA: University of California, 1984.
50. Juan Cobo Borda and Luis García Núñez (eds.), *Repertorio crítico sobre Gabriel García Márquez,* 2 vols., Bogotá: Instituto Caro y Cuervo, 1995; Osorio C. Zuluaga (ed.), *Anthropos,* 187 (1999) – a special edition on García Márquez.
51. Jeremy Munday, 'The Caribbean Conquers the World? An Analysis of the Reception of García Márquez in translation', *Bulletin of Hispanic Studies,* 75 (1998): 137–44.
52. Porrata, *Explicación;* Juan Manuel García Ramos, *Guía de lectura de Cien años de soledad,* Madrid: Alhambra, 1989; Wood, *Gabriel García Márquez;* Philip Swanson, *Cómo leer a Gabriel García Márquez.*
53. D. W. Foster, 'García Márquez and Solitude', *Américas,* 21 (1969): 36–41; p. 40.
54. Edwin Williamson, 'Magical Realism and the Theme of Incest in *One Hundred Years of Solitude*', in Bernard McGuirk and Richard Cardwell (eds.), *Gabriel García Márquez: New Readings,* Cambridge: Cambridge University Press, 1987, pp. 45–63; p. 45; Swanson, *Cómo leer,* p. 57.
55. Wood disagrees that *One Hundred Years of Solitude* questions the very nature of reality itself: *Gabriel García Márquez,* p. 58.
56. Richard Cardwell, 'Characterization in the Early Fiction of Gabriel García Márquez', in McGuirk and Cardwell, *Gabriel García Márquez,* pp. 5–16; Pedro Lastra, 'La tragedia como fundamento estructural de *La hojarasca*', *Anales de la Universidad de Chile,* 140 (1966): 168–86 (reprinted in Benedetti, *Nueve asedios,* pp. 38–51); B. Castañeda, 'Aproximaciones críticas al monólogo en *La hojarasca*', *Revista Interamericana de Bibliografía,* 47 (1997): 103–17; Vargas Llosa, *García Márquez;* Robin Fiddian, 'Two Aspects of Technique in *El coronel no tiene quien le escriba*', *Neophilologus,* 69 (1985): 386–93; Graciela Maturo, *Claves simbólicas de Gabriel García Márquez,* Buenos Aires: García Cambeiro, 1972; Peter Earle, 'El futuro como espejismo', in Peter Earle (ed.), *Gabriel García Márquez,* Madrid: Taurus, 1982, pp. 81–90.
57. Susan de Carvalho, 'Origins of Social Pessimism in García Márquez: The Night of the Curlews', *Studies in Short Fiction,* 28 (3) (1991): 131–8, on 'Night of the Curlews' and social pessimism; Robin Fiddian, 'The Naked and the Dead: Bodies and Their Meanings in *La hojarasca* by Gabriel García Márquez', *Romance Studies,* 19 (winter 1991): 79–89 on moral gangrene and sexuality in *Leaf Storm* (*La hojarasca*).
58. For example, Harley D. Oberhelman, *Gabriel García Márquez: A Study of the Short Fiction,* Boston, MA: Twayne, 1991, on the short stories up to *Strange Pilgrims;* and J. Box, *Gabriel García Márquez:* El coronel no tiene quien le escriba, London: Grant & Cutler, 1984.
59. Julio Ortega, '*El otoño de patriarca:* texto y cultura', *Hispanic Review,* 46 (4) (1978): 421–46; Jo Labanyi, 'Language and Power in *The Autumn of the Patriarch*', in McGuirk and Cardwell, *Gabriel García Márquez,* pp. 135–49.
60. Ángel Rama, 'García Márquez entre la tragedia y la policial o crónica y pesquisa de la *Crónica de una muerte anunciada*', *Sin Nombre,* 13 (1) (1982): 7–27;

T. Holzapfel and A. Rodríguez, 'García Márquez's *Crónica de una muerte anunciada:* History, Literature and Tradition', in E. Rogers and T. Rogers (eds.), *In Retrospect: Essays on Latin American Literature,* York, SC: Spanish Literature Publishing Corporation, 1987, pp. 170–6. For the first interpretation, R. Predmore, 'El mundo moral de *Crónica de una muerte anunciada*', *Cuadernos Hispanoamericanos,* 390 (1982): 703–12; and Gustavo Pellón, 'Myth, Tragedy and the Scapegoat Ritual in *Crónica de una muerte anunciada*', *Revista Canadiense de Estudios Hispánicos,* 12 (3) (1988): 397–413 for the latter interpretation.

61. D. L. Shaw, '*Chronicle of a Death Foretold:* Narrative Function and Interpretation', in B. A. Shaw and N. Vera-Godwin, *Critical Perspectives on Gabriel García Márquez,* pp. 91–104; J. Olivares, 'García Márquez's *Crónica de una muerte anunciada* as Metafiction', *Contemporary Literature,* 28 (4) (1987): 483–92; J. Concha, 'Entre Kafka y el Evangelio', *Araucaria,* 21 (1983): 105–9; K. Ross, '"La casa de amor es la alternativa": Women in Spanish American Narrative', in *Selected Proceedings,* MIFLIC, Greenville, SC: Furman University Press, 1987, pp. 301–7.
62. Stephen M. Hart, *Gabriel García Márquez:* Crónica de una muerte anunciada, London: Grant & Cutler, 1994.
63. S. Menton, *Latin America's New Historical Novel,* Austin, TX: Texas University Press, 1993; Roy Boland, 'Los más insignes majaderos de este mundo: Simón Bolívar between Christ and Don Quixote in *El general en su laberinto*', *Antípodas,* 4 (1992): 155–65; C. Rincón, 'Metaficción, historia, posmodernismo; a propósito de *El general en su laberinto*', *Nuevo Texto Crítico,* 5 (9/10) (1992): 169–96.
64. For example, Gene H. Bell-Villada, *Gabriel García Márquez: The Man and His Work,* Chapel Hill, NC: University of North Carolina Press, 1990; Mabel Moraña, 'Modernity and Marginality in *Love in the Time of the Cholera*', *Studies in Twentieth Century Literature,* 14 (1) (1990): 27–43; S. Carullo, 'Amor y matrimonio en *El amor en los tiempos del cólera*', in S. Scarlett and H. Wescott (eds.), *Convergencias hispánicas,* Newark, DE: Juan de la Cuesta, 2001, pp. 207–18.
65. For example, Robin Fiddian, 'A Prospective Postscript: A Propos of *Love in the Time of Cholera*', in McGuirk and Cardwell, *Gabriel García Márquez,* pp. 191–205; M. Booker, 'The Dangers of Gullible Reading: Narrative as Seduction in García Márquez's *Love in the Time of Cholera*', *Studies in Twentieth Century Literature,* 17 (2) (1993): 181–95.
66. T. Rahy, *Gabriel García Márquez's* Love in the Time of Cholera*: A Reader's Guide,* New York: Continuum, 2003.

3

ROBIN FIDDIAN

Before *One Hundred Years of Solitude*: the early novels

From the start it is necessary to establish that the three novels gathered under the above rubric were written over a period spanning almost a decade and represent a variety of influences and styles that resist reduction to a single type. According to the author, he began work on *Leaf Storm* (*La hojarasca*) as early as 1950, when he was living in the northern Colombian locations of Sucre and Barranquilla. Although initially rejected by an Argentine publishing house, the novel eventually appeared in Bogotá, in 1955. In the intervening years, García Márquez published a short story, 'Winter' ('El invierno'), which was filleted out of the larger narrative, in December 1952; he subsequently published it again under the revised title of 'Monologue of Isabel Watching It Rain in Macondo' ('Monólogo de Isabel viendo llover en Macondo') in October–November 1955. Together with the slightly earlier story, 'Nabo: The Black Man Who Made the Angels Wait' ('Nabo, el negro que hizo esperar a los ángeles' [1951]), 'Monologue of Isabel' exemplifies the early influence on García Márquez of William Faulkner, whom he first read in 1949 and whose narrative vision, expressed paradigmatically in *As I Lay Dying*, underpins the conception and architecture of *Leaf Storm*.

No One Writes to the Colonel (*El coronel no tiene quien le escriba*, 1958) was penned not in Colombia but in France, where the author was working as a journalist and living in fabled penury, in 1956. The aesthetic imperatives to which García Márquez was now adhering were those of Italian neorealist cinema, on which he wrote a series of journalistic reviews between February 1954 and June 1955, and Ernest Hemingway, whose imprint is recognisable in at least four of the stories included in *Big Mama's Funeral* (*Los funerales de la mamá grande*). Composed in Venezuela and Colombia in 1958, those stories were eventually published along with four others that made up the collection, in 1962. That same year, *In Evil Hour* (*La mala hora*) was awarded the Esso Literary Prize in Bogotá. However, the genesis of García Márquez's third novel can be traced back to the mid-1950s and to the author's time in Paris, when he began writing *In Evil Hour* and almost immediately put it to one side in order to devote himself to *No One Writes to the Colonel.* García Márquez thoroughly revised the text of *In Evil Hour* in 1959, after he had completed the writing of the title story of *Big Mama's Funeral,* back in Colombia. The ghost of the folkloric Big Mama is mentioned in a central section of *In Evil Hour,* introducing an element that moves the novel ever so slightly beyond the aesthetic parameters of *No One Writes to the Colonel.*

The pattern thus described of criss-crossing, postponement and resumption of interrelated projects is enough to dispel any naive assumption of straightforward progression in the author's career as a writer of prose fiction between 1950 and 1962. However, the output of the entire period from 1950 to 1967 can arguably be said to derive from, and to be loosely held together by, a single nucleus and thread, which is the author's conception, as early as 1950, of an ambitious narrative project entitled 'La casa' ('The House'). By the author's own admission, *Leaf Storm* was already an offshoot of that creative impulse, which would continue to find sporadic expression throughout the 1950s before crystallising definitively in *One Hundred Years of Solitude* (1967).

Leaf Storm

In terms of raw narrative content, García Márquez's inaugural novel is interesting on at least three counts: first, it is a novel where very little happens on the immediate plane of events, and all that does happen occurs in a period of no more than half an hour. Second, the minimal storyline is preceded by a block of text, printed in italics and distributed across five paragraphs, providing an account of historical events from around the beginning of the twentieth century, which changed forever the socio-economic order of a small provincial town named Macondo. That change is pictured as a natural catastrophe: a leaf storm, connoting something inevitable and organic, also referred to as an 'avalanche', whose effects are lamented by a narrative voice discoursing in the first-person plural and regretting the loss of patrician status. And third, the narrative is divided into a sequence of eleven chapters comprising a varied number of fragments which range from one in Chapter 9 and two in a majority of chapters, to five in Chapter 11. The fragments alternate between three separate characters who are members of the same family but represent different generations, these being: a grandfather who is a retired colonel, his daughter Isabel who is an evolved version of the young woman in the story 'Monologue of Isabel Watching it Rain in Macondo', and her son, who remains nameless throughout but is nonetheless distinguishable from the two other narrative participants by virtue of a set of personal references and more or less distinctive traits of thought and speech. This complex narrative design is modelled, at least in part, on the layout of Faulkner's *As I Lay Dying,* which the author has explicitly acknowledged as an important source-text for *Leaf Storm* and as a stimulus for him to attempt the task of modernising the novel as a form in his native Colombia.

The story narrated in *Leaf Storm* can be briefly summarised: the former doctor of the town has committed suicide on 12 September 1928, and the colonel, who it turns out was his sole friend in the town, takes it upon himself to ensure that he is buried. This brings the colonel into conflict with the mayor, who represents a widespread resentment towards the doctor but who eventually authorises the sealing of the coffin and its removal to the cemetery. The flimsiness of the action directs attention elsewhere, towards considerations of plot and character involving morality and psychology, and to the thickly textured communal history of Macondo, which is reconstructed, at times laboriously, through the alternating narrative perspectives of the characters.

In essence, the story of the doctor and his relations with the colonel's family and the wider community revolves around issues of class and morality. Twenty-five years after accepting him as a house guest, and notwithstanding serious objections to a sexual liaison that he entered into with the housemaid, Meme, who eventually disappeared, never to be heard of again, the grandfather feels bound to stand firm against the hostility of the pueblo and the shenanigans of its mayor, and ensure that the doctor receives a decent burial. In the wider context of García Márquez's writings, this determination on the part of the colonel, who describes himself in a pithy phrase as 'lame in body and sound in conscience', aligns him with the mother of Carlos Centeno in 'Tuesday Siesta' ('La siesta del martes', the opening story in *Big Mama's Funeral*) who will fight against the apathy and indifference of the parish priest of the town where Carlos was shot, in order to place a bouquet of flowers on her son's unmarked grave.[1] In both cases, an individual who embodies a natural code of morality is pitted against another, representing a strictly institutional branch of the law. The heroic connotations that accrue to the colonel's behaviour and mission in *Leaf Storm* are signalled in the novel's epigraph, taken from *Antigone.* In that canonical play by Sophocles, the eponymous heroine challenges the edict issued by King Creon prohibiting the burial of the corpses of his political enemies which are lying outside the walls of Thebes. Amongst the dead is the corpse of her brother, Polynices, whom Antigone will bury in spite of Creon's ruling, putting blood ties before obedience to the laws of patriarchy and the State.

One of many points of critical debate concerning *Leaf Storm* is the relation between the epigraph and the text of the novel. For Pedro Lastra, the quotation from Sophocles indicated a conscious intent to rewrite an archetypal story.[2] However, according to Dasso Saldívar, when García Márquez wrote the first version of the novel (which Saldívar claims dates from as early as 1949), he had yet to read Sophocles and would not do so until a few years later.[3] García Márquez concurs with his biographer on this point, insisting that he added the epigraph as a homage to Sophocles only after a close friend had exclaimed upon reading the novel, 'This is the myth of Antigone.'[4] Whether we believe García Márquez's version of events or not is a moot point and ultimately immaterial: regardless of questions of borrowing before or after the fact, *Leaf Storm* connects substantively with a powerful archetypal narrative about morality and injustice. In fact, it expands the imaginative possibilities of that narrative, in a gesture that recalls the ambivalent attitude of many twentieth-century authors (including James Joyce, Thomas Mann and Argentina's Leopoldo Marechal) to the pertinence of classical myth in the modern world. Clearly, there is a close structural correspondence between the story of the colonel and the mayor, on the one hand, and Antigone's defiance of Creon on the other. At the same time, the values of the original undergo a transformation as García Márquez revises classical assumptions to do with gender and heroism. In the first respect, the colonel is very much a flawed hero, who uses his daughter as a moral shield and is plainly resented by her; also, he is unwilling to acknowledge the extent to which he allowed himself to be duped by her suitor, Martín, many years before. For her part, Isabel falls far short of the standards of integrity and courage associated with the Greek heroine, Antigone. Yet the collective moral bankruptcy of the pueblo – foreshadowing the conclusion of 'Tuesday Siesta', once more – throws the colonel's greater courage and integrity into relief.

The corruption of the body politic of Macondo is a major focus of the story, set against a richly embroidered social and historical backdrop which provides the blueprint of all subsequent narratives by García Márquez about the town. The corpse of the doctor, who hanged himself, is but one emblem of social decay aggravated by a personal history of isolation and refusal to attend to townsfolk in desperate need of medical care. Another abject body in the story is that of the one-eyed Lucrecia, who routinely exposes herself to a group of young boys, including Isabel's son, each time they come to her window in search of a perverse thrill. Sexual instincts and personal intimacy are degraded in the community, whether in the case of Isabel's broken relationship with Martín, who seems to have had no interest in her happiness and their possible life together, or the 'sterile and tormented' existence of the widow, Rebecca, who also features prominently in the first-written of the stories included in *Big Mama's Funeral,* 'One Day after Saturday' ('Un día después del sábado').[5] Like her, the colonel and Isabel profess attitudes dictated by class and religion, which colour their view of social relations and morality in the stifling world depicted in *Leaf Storm.*

A hallmark of life in Macondo is a widely experienced sense of historical paralysis, reflecting the author's fascination, as intense as that of Virginia Woolf, Marcel Proust or Jorge Luis Borges, with the theme of time. At the beginning of Chapter 5, Isabel muses at length about public and private temporalities ('el tiempo de adentro' and '[el] de afuera' – or inner and outer time) and their moving in and out of synch; in fact, there is scarcely a chapter in which time, memory and relations with the past are not foregrounded, either at the thematic level or in the narrative structure. As a general rule, the colonel's daughter relates to and explains the past in terms of personal experience and landmark events in the life of the family: for example, the death of the colonel's first wife, who died giving birth to Isabel, in 1898; the arrival of the doctor and his admission to the house in 1903; Isabel's marriage to Martín in 1916 and his abandonment of her and her young child three years later; and so on. References to all of these events can be pieced together to form a coherent reconstruction of Isabel's life. Her father provides the narrative with a wider frame of reference that is more properly historical, enabling us to reconstruct the past of Macondo, post-1885, in the wake of a civil war that is mentioned first in the prologue, then at some length in Chapter 2, and patchily thereafter. Three events in particular have shaped the history of Macondo in the twentieth century: first, the arrival of the banana company in 1907, which was a prelude to the invasion of the town by 'la hojarasca' ('riff-raff') and the turning of the existing social order upside down; second, the company's departure in 1915, carrying with it a mass of human detritus ('the rubbish of the rubbish they'd brought us'); and third, the indiscriminate shooting of townsfolk by a band of armed thugs under orders to disrupt political elections, one Sunday in 1918.[6]

We have already noted the effect of the first of these events, seen from the perspective of one of the founders of the town. The other two are important because they are seen to lie at the root of Macondo's present malaise and provide a key to understanding its political paralysis. The reader is assisted in this task by the colonel, who in the very last chapter of *Leaf Storm* attributes Macondo's ruined state to a 'bitter matter of fate' visited upon the town by external forces.[7] Looking back ten years to when elections were violently disrupted, he comments, '[W]hen ruin came down upon us, the collective strength of those who looked for recovery might have been enough for reconstruction. All that was needed was to go out into the fields laid waste by the banana company, clean out the weeds and start again from scratch.'[8] However, the legacy of 'la hojarasca' was so pervasive that it prevented this from happening, and the community never recovered. Assuming a political intention on the part of the author, this diagnosis of a collective paralysis of the will can be read, on one level, as a critique of capitalist exploitation, symbolised by the banana company, and a repudiation of a political system that condones or orders the repression of its own people by violent means. Such a reading is consistent with the stated political philosophy of Gabriel García Márquez and with his public profile. In addition to that critique, the colonel's diagnosis exposes ideological and moral shortcomings in various strata of society, for which the author implies there is no excuse. Macondo is depressed, certainly, because of remorseless outside forces, but the community is also guilty of a repertoire of faults including apathy and defeatism, nostalgia and superstition: in a word, mystification. The high definition of this political message is not generally acknowledged in the criticism written about *Leaf Storm,* which has tended to concentrate on the structural novelty and stylistic interest of the book, regarded quite rightly as a significant landmark in the evolution of the novel in Colombia. However, the moral and political vision that is expressed in *Leaf Storm* is of no lesser importance in an overview of the author's writings and marks it out as a historic precursor of better-known texts and collections that lead up to *One Hundred Years of Solitude.*

No One Writes to the Colonel

Often labelled a 'novella' rather than a novel, *No One Writes to the Colonel* is remarkable for its formal and stylistic economy, which contrasts with the structural contrivance of its predecessor. The book nevertheless owes a lot to *Leaf Storm,* the basic narrative ingredients of which it reprises and takes in new directions. The narrative situation described in *No One Writes to the Colonel* is rooted once more in a small provincial town in northern Colombia at a precise moment in contemporary history (in this case, the end of 1956). Retrospective reference is made to events that had taken place in the national arena a full half-century ago, the legacy of which weighs heavily on the community and on one nuclear family in particular. Their moral and existential dilemmas provide the main source of narrative interest and the focus, from start to finish, of humanistic concerns about justice, love, dignity, hope and the refusal of despair. The addition, to this powerful mix, of resonances of conflict and myth underlines the unmistakable family resemblance between *No One Writes to the Colonel* and *Leaf Storm.* There are, however, significant and crucial differences in both the make-up and the deployment of the narrative ingredients that are carried over into the later text. The family of three is constituted on this occasion by an aged mother and father and their dead son, Agustín, who was murdered by the authorities in a crackdown on political dissidents of the town some nine months before the start of the narrative. Deprived of his earning power and uplifting presence, the parents feel bereft, explaining with genuine pathos, 'We are the orphans of our son.'[9] For all that, Agustín's spirit and political will have been displaced onto his fighting cock, which keeps both qualities alive and takes his place in the domestic sphere, where it is the focus of deep and powerful attachments but also the cause of tension between his parents.

They are the eponymous and anonymous colonel and his wife, a septuagenarian couple of survivors who have been waiting for over half a century for the State to pay the colonel the pension that is his due after fighting, on the losing side, in a civil war (called, in the history books, the 'War of a Thousand Days') that came to an end in 1902. The preposterous amount of time that the colonel has been waiting for a letter from the authorities indicates the absurdity of his situation, which is reminiscent of Kafka and Samuel Beckett amongst others. It also bears witness to a remarkable spirit of endurance and commendable lack of cynicism or despair, conveyed in the early description of the colonel's 'attitude of confident and innocent expectation' and maintained over the period of ten weeks that is covered in *No One Writes to the Colonel*.[10]

Compared with *Leaf Storm*, where a meagre slice of time was allocated to the story, the narrative of *No One Writes to the Colonel* is more capacious, accommodating changes in events and subtle modifications in the couple's relationship and situation. Events in the story are few and are distributed parsimoniously over the seven unnumbered chapters into which the narrative is divided. The main event of the first chapter is a funeral, those of the second, the arrival of a boat bringing mail to the town and the doctor's subversive act of handing a clandestine news-sheet to the colonel. In the third chapter, the colonel visits his lawyer and tells him he wishes to dispense with his services; in the fourth, he takes a clock to Alvaro and returns home with some money, which will provide some temporary financial relief. In the fifth, he visits the toad-like, diabetic entrepreneur, Don Sabas, who raises his expectations by telling him that his fighting cock could command a price of 900 pesos; in the sixth, Don Sabas gives him an advance of 60 pesos. Finally, in the seventh chapter, the town receives the first visit from a travelling circus in ten years, and the colonel recovers the fighting cock from the *gallera* where some of the locals have taken it for training.

These events serve to punctuate what is otherwise an indistinct flow of time and a routine existence consisting in the grim struggle for survival. Initially, the narrative emphasises a prevalent distemper amidst an atmosphere of damp, corruption and death, which affects both the colonel and his wife. Her statement that 'We're rotting alive' encapsulates their position starkly.[11] Over the subsequent chapters, as October gives way, first, to November and then to December, there are perceptible, if short-lived improvements in the couple's financial situation, their health and outlook: an ebb and flow involving crisis and recovery, alternating, and sometimes shared, between husband and wife. For example, the colonel's feeling of well-being at the beginning of Chapter 3 and his renewed determination to pursue his claim with the authorities in Chapter 4 are cruelly undermined by the rains of November, which provoke an emotional crisis in his wife and a relapse in his own health. In Chapter 6, whilst she shows signs of energetic recovery, his fortunes wane, symbolised by his mistaken advice to Alvaro to bet on the number 11 at the casino. With the arrival of December, the colonel recovers his confident and determined outlook, and his wife looks forward to planting roses in the patio. However, she has reached the end of her tether as far as the indulgence of the cock is concerned: in her opinion, the animal is a liability and should be sold. The story ends in stalemate, with the colonel rejecting her argument that the cock may not win its fight, and insisting that they keep it, even if it means that they will have to 'eat shit'.

The prospect of the cockfight and the hope of victory have subtended the story all along, providing it with a perspective on the future which was absent from *Leaf Storm;* with the signal exception of the colonel's wife, the whole town feels a common interest in, and identification with the cock, which embodies their spirit of resistance and hunger for justice. The association of the cock with the political martyr, Agustín, drives and sustains the colonel no less than the motivation of receiving his just financial rewards from a corrupt and dilatory state. Agustín's aura and age (he was born in the spring of 1922 and therefore died aged thirty-three) identify him with another martyr of Western civilisation, who is Jesus Christ, and the story of the colonel's wait overlaps tellingly with the seasonal parameters of the story of Christ. Significantly, the upturn that occurs in the final section of *No One Writes to the Colonel* coincides with the beginning of Advent in the Christian calendar; also, the cockfight is scheduled for 20 January, within the bounds of Epiphany and representing a point in the future on which the people can set their sights and aspirations. The narrative thus acquires a strong archetypal dimension, which is bolstered further by a reference to the Messiah and by the declaration, made early on by the colonel's wife, that 'When I'm well, I can bring back the dead'.[12] Later, the colonel has a vivid sense of being in touch with an almost transcendental life force at the *gallera,* where Agustín had been shot: as he bends down to pick up the cock, he feels 'the warm deep throbbing of the animal' and thinks that 'he had never had such an alive thing in his hands before.'[13] This dense fabric of meanings is reinforced by one other, apparently fortuitous detail, which is the title of the last film that the colonel's wife remembers having seen at the cinema, back in 1931: the film was *La voluntad del muerto,* made in 1930 under the direction of the prolific George Melford for Universal Studios, and known in English by the less felicitous title, *The Cat and the Canary.*

The mythical and spiritual subtext thus described is an important component of *No One Writes to the Colonel* and one that requires careful handling when interpreting its role in the novella. Any attempt to force this story by García Márquez into a Christian straitjacket is ill advised, as it would imply that he is or was a believer, with orthodox views on death and resurrection and a Franciscan approach to poverty, suffering and a second coming. It is perhaps wiser to view *No One Writes to the Colonel* in the light of other texts by the author, which evince a strong and recurrent interest in people's mindsets, including their belief systems, myths and superstitions. Viewed in this light, the motifs of the Messiah and martyrdom, death and resurrection, come across as a credible vehicle for a political message of resistance, hope and renewal: exactly those impulses and aspirations that stir in the minds of the citizens of the town (a town which is not Macondo) on the day that it welcomes the first circus to visit in ten years: 'For a long time the town had laid in a sort of stupor, ravaged by ten years of history. That afternoon ... the people had awakened.'[14]

Tying in with the critique found in *Leaf Storm,* history is figured, here, as a force of destruction and as an anaesthetic. As happened in the earlier novel, the wider community has sunk into a collective stupor, where only a chance event such as the arrival of a circus can shake it awake. The narrative attributes the people's sleepiness in part to the prevailing environment of political violence and repression. Elections were suspended years ago, and the authorities have imposed a regime of curfews, violence and intimidation. Significantly, the musician whose funeral takes place in the opening section of the narrative is reported as being the first person to die of natural causes in the town for many years. Yet, there are individuals of principle and courage who are determined to resist. Agustín was such a man. Others include the doctor and members of the group who gather at the local tailor's shop to read and circulate clandestine news. When there is a news-sheet to circulate, they alert one another by means of a phrase that is coded: 'Escribió Agustín' (literally, 'Agustín has written') fittingly honours the memory of their dead comrade, whose example it paradoxically keeps alive. As a result, the phrase stands in a suggestive relationship with the title of the novella. In point of fact, the colonel has little if any prospect of receiving the long-awaited letter from the authorities confirming his pension, and therefore the statement that 'no one writes to the colonel' is substantively true. Yet in a symbolic sense, the colonel's dead son Agustín writes from beyond the suffocating limits of the town, with news and encouragement for those who oppose the repressive regime. *No One Writes to the Colonel* thus incorporates, and is sustained by, a real and productive ambiguity. On the one hand, the colonel, his wife and countless other citizens suffer hardship, loss and repression, and endure a political and natural climate that exacts a heavy mental and physical toll; in Christian terms that are echoed in the text itself, they live in a fallen world without prospect of justice or redemption. On the other hand, the family and most of the citizens (excepting the unscrupulous capitalist Don Sabas, the policeman who shot Agustín and other members of the security forces) feed off the will and example of Agustín, who caters to their spiritual and political hunger. In the midst of hardship, people find an inner strength that enables them to resist and survive; in Christian terms, they aspire to transcendence and believe in the Resurrection. This profound ambiguity provides a possible explanation for the abiding appeal of the novella, which speaks in equal measure about life and death, corruption and transcendence, as forces that frame and define the very essence of the human condition.

The author's refusal to cancel out opposing terms, and thereby to resolve tension, persists throughout the novella, right down to the colonel's famous, final expletive, 'Shit'. In a suggestive interpretation of bodily motifs in *No One Writes to the Colonel*, René Prieto has viewed the colonel's expletive as providing a fitting climax to a discourse referring throughout to problems with digestion and excreting.[15] Beginning with the colonel's sensation that he has 'fungus and poisonous lilies taking root in his gut', the narrative pays attention to his frequent bouts of intestinal discomfort and identifies the body as the locus of suffering.[16] In addition to this, the body is where the animality of mankind resides, all of which marks the colonel out as organically susceptible and on the same plane as the cock and other animals that are foregrounded in the novella. At the same time, his defiant, one-word answer to his wife's desperate question, 'And meanwhile what do we eat?', is loaded with moral significance.[17] On an earlier occasion, he had taken exception to Alfonso's use of the word 'shit' on the grounds that it was unnecessary swearing.[18] His own recourse to the very same word at the close is a sign, certainly, of frustration and of the transgression of a moral and linguistic barrier. Yet, the narrative makes it clear that there is something undeniably heroic about the colonel's attitude and sensibility at what is a make-or-break moment in his life. Describing him as feeling 'pure, explicit, invincible at the moment when he replied', it stresses the undefiled state of his conscience, determined to persevere and survive.[19] The expletive that he utters at the end of the story is therefore expressive of both physiological *and* moral concerns, and has to be understood with reference to both categories.

There remain two final areas of the novella that require comment. The first concerns the occasional intrusion of dreams and hallucinations into the predominantly realist discourse of the narrative. Examples include the colonel's disturbed perceptions at the dead musician's wake, and his nonchalant admission to his wife that he has been talking in his sleep with the Duke of Marlborough. The narrative voice mimics that manner when it reports that '[the colonel's wife] seemed as if she had the power of walking through the walls. But before twelve she had regained her bulk, her human weight.'[20] Such material briefly qualifies the impression of overall realist objectivity that is conveyed otherwise by García Márquez's prose style.

The second matter is the author's express concern with the theme and fortunes of America or the Americas, vis-à-vis Europe and other geo-political regions. A conversation between the doctor and the colonel highlights issues of knowledge and stereotyping of the other, which García Márquez will address in his Nobel Prize acceptance speech at Oslo in 1987. Mention of the Suez crisis in a newspaper headline that the doctor reads out to the colonel in the third chapter, points to the broader movement of decolonisation that is taking place in areas such as Africa, to the detriment of the Western powers who now find themselves 'losing ground'.[21] For commentators, including Jacques Gilard and the present author, this reference to current affairs signals not merely an interest in global politics but a real identification with peoples and nations of the emerging Third World. Already present in some of the journalism of the late 1940s, that postcolonial sensibility will pervade *One Hundred Years of Solitude* and other texts thereafter.

In Evil Hour

As stated at the start of this chapter, *In Evil Hour* can be viewed as a companion text to *No One Writes to the Colonel,* on account of the shared circumstances of composition and the focus on the same social and political milieu. The geographical setting is a small town next to a river in northern Colombia, whose citizens have to endure a return to a regime of curfews, violence and corruption after a period of relative and short-lived peace. Common narrative details abound and include the character of the diabetic Don Sabas, the circulation of underground news-sheets and the visit of a circus to the town. The temporal setting is again contemporary, as it was in *No One Writes to the Colonel,* with a smattering of references to political events in the wider regional and national spheres.

According to García Márquez, *In Evil Hour* was intended as a corrective to a type of Colombian writing about that country's experience of *la violencia* that, in his view, lacked imagination, ideological complexity and literary merit.[22] Broadening the focus of *No One Writes to the Colonel,* he set out to explore the phenomenon of violence from a perspective that would consider the perpetrators as well as the victims of repression and barbarism. The outstanding example of the first category is the town's mayor, referred to interchangeably in the Spanish original as 'el alcalde' and 'el teniente', who is one of the most finely drawn characters in the book. There is also a wider group of victims and onlookers who share in an atmosphere of tension and suspicion created by a series of lampoons which appear overnight, impugning reputations and precipitating violence from the very start of the narrative. As acknowledged in his memoirs, the device of the whodunnit allows García Márquez to explore the effects of repression and violence on a broad, panoramic scale.

Formally, *In Evil Hour* is modelled on novels such as *Manhattan Transfer* by John Dos Passos and *Mrs Dalloway* by Virginia Woolf. The story covers a period of seventeen days and weaves in and out of the lives and locations of nearly a dozen individuals and their families. It starts on Tuesday, 4 October, the day of St Francis of Assisi, whose daily prayer reads as follows:

> Lord, make me an instrument of your peace.
> Where there is hatred, let me sow love;
> Where there is injury, pardon;

The positive spiritual values and religious promise thus evoked are starkly contradicted by what follows. In the second section of the opening chapter, hunter-cum-landowner César Montero shoots the musician, Pastor, in the first of the narrative's key murders, the second being that of Pepe Amador, caught in possession of subversive propaganda and subsequently tortured, in the final chapter of ten. The intimation, at the close, that the lampoons continue to appear after the detention and death of Pepe Amador conveys a message of pointless suffering and loss which is alleviated, somewhat, by the announcement that opponents of the regime are taking to the hills to join guerrilla factions. The fact that there are some people determined to resist recalls the attitude of the colonel and Agustín in *No One Writes to the Colonel* and introduces a shaft of light into an otherwise dark narrative.

Amongst the principal players in *In Evil Hour,* the narrative emphasises the mayor's venal character and record. Amongst other things, he colludes with the capitalist Don Sabas in a scheme to steal property and livestock from Montiel's widow (also featured in a story of that title in *Big Mama's Funeral*); after César Montero shoots and kills Pastor on a whim, the mayor puts him in a secure gaol cell and sets a price for influencing the official who will investigate the crime; he condones the torture and murder, by González, Rovira and Peralta, of Pepe Amador; and he resorts to bare-faced lies and intimidation when Padre Angel and Dr Octavio Giraldo come to his offices with the intention of viewing Pepe's corpse and conducting an autopsy in compliance with the law. His earlier protestations, that the town is a safer and happier place since he took control some years ago, are made to sound hollow. However, with the benefit of hindsight, coloured, perhaps, by his treatment of the patriarch in *The Autumn of the Patriarch* (*El otoño del patriarca*), García Márquez has stressed the appeal that he felt when developing the character of the mayor, who, he comments, 'became more and more interesting to me as a human being, and I had no cause to kill him off'.[23] This suggests a certain fascination with the complexities of individuals such as the mayor and the judge, Arcadio, who are guilty of dereliction of duty yet possess other dimensions of character, which, in the case of the judge, include trusting and passing information to political opponents of the regime, in Chapter 9, and then subsequently abandoning his wife and position in the town for motives that are left unexplained.

Padre Angel is a less nuanced figure. From a comparative perspective, he is cut from the same cloth as the absent-minded priest of 'One Day after Saturday' and the indolent, sleepy cleric of 'Tuesday Siesta'. His fixation, in the opening section, on the lyrics of the latest song by Pastor blinds him to the coded promise and significance of 4 October within the calendar of the Catholic Church. Some days later, when he pays a visit to the home of a young man who is sick, he encourages the parents to take him to confession, but 'he said it without conviction.'[24] In the final analysis, although Padre Angel attends conscientiously to his duties towards his parishioners, he effectively does little more than go through the motions and certainly provides nothing by way of spiritual leadership for the community.

With the example of *No One Writes to the Colonel* in mind, the reader looks for a figure or two in the populous cast of *In Evil Hour* who might embody the spiritual and political message that was so prominent and tangible a feature of the earlier novella. Of three candidates who suggest themselves for the role, the clarinettist Pastor and Pepe Amador ultimately fail to compel, since their characterisation goes no further than setting them up as the innocent or luckless victims of barbarism. There is pathos, to be sure, in their deaths, but neither of them displays the moral depth and complex motivation of a tragic hero, and they are certainly not invested with the transcendental aura that surrounded Agustín in *No One Writes to the Colonel*.

A third character comes closer to acting as bearer of the novella's moral and political message. This is Carmichael, the long-serving administrator of the Montiel estate who continues to work loyally for the widow after Don Chepe's death. The first time Carmichael is mentioned is in Chapter 3, where he appears as just one of the story's many characters, distinguished, in his case, by the extraordinary number of children that he has (eleven!), and the humorous detail of his corns, which make him sensitive to changes in the weather; in fact, this turns out to be symbolic of his role, later in the narrative, as barometer of moral and political pressures affecting the town. Subsequent chapters (5, 7 and 8) depict Carmichael in a very positive light as a considerate and conscientious employee of the Montiels who handles the finances of their estate with scrupulous honesty.

It is in Chapter 10 that Carmichael's moral stature is most clearly tested and proven, at the hands of the scheming and unscrupulous mayor. Angling to acquire as much of Montiel's property as he can, the mayor sequesters Carmichael (who is dignified throughout the original narrative with the full Spanish title, 'el señor Carmichael') and forces him to remain seated outdoors, exposed to tropical sun and rain, for three days: in this way, he hopes to break Carmichael's will and extract from him information which will allow him to dupe the widow and her children out of their inheritance. However, he has underestimated the character of Carmichael, who puts up stubborn passive resistance, even when the mayor threatens to implicate him in the murder of Pepe Amador. At one of the most sensitive moments in the plot of *In Evil Hour,* Carmichael acts as a champion and barometer of what is morally right. Although he does not make any grand or dramatic gesture that would justify calling him a hero, it is clear that he refuses to be co-opted or frightened by the mayor's intimidation. Ultimately, he comes across as a man of principle, a kind employee and friend, and a loyal family man. The fact that he is black should not be overlooked.

Beyond the panoramic depiction of a community and nation in the grip of lawlessness and moral decay, *In Evil Hour* comprises a meta-literary dimension that complements the political subject matter of the narrative. García Márquez draws on the conventions of the whodunnit and *novela policial,* commenting on them self-referentially and with a modicum of humour directed against the literary-critical establishment. The cultivation of enigma is found elsewhere in the García Márquez corpus, both before and after *In Evil Hour;* the author's inclination towards the *novela policial* will reach its apex in *Chronicle of a Death Foretold,* some twenty years later. More immediately, the narrative of *In Evil Hour* weaves an intertextual patchwork of items from both earlier and contemporary writings by García Márquez, from *Leaf Storm* to the stories of *Big Mama's Funeral.* The result is a kaleidoscope of familiar characters and situations, presented, in some cases, in finer detail than elsewhere: for example, there is a fuller account of the family of Mina and her grandmother, from 'Artificial Roses' ('Rosas artificiales'), in which there is mention of a father conspicuously absent from the earlier story. Other references are in the form not of echoes but prequels, foreshadowing the apocalyptic story of the Buendías and other citizens of Macondo, who will take their places in a fresco constructed on a larger scale in *One Hundred Years of Solitude*.

Concluding this overview, there remains a question about the comparative merits of *In Evil Hour*, especially when set alongside *No One Writes to the Colonel*. Whilst it displays many of the hallmarks of García Márquez's prose, *In Evil Hour* is less compelling than its companion novella and has not achieved the same canonical status; its political message and underlying moral vision are not integrated as masterfully as when they were harnessed to a simpler narrative format in *No One Writes to the Colonel*. Yet, in the context of the author's overall output, *In Evil Hour* lays no less a claim to serious analysis and critical appreciation than *Leaf Storm*: in intrinsic and comparative terms, it occupies a significant place in the evolutionary process that culminates in *One Hundred Years of Solitude*.

NOTES

1. Gabriel García Márquez, *Leaf Storm*, trans. Gregory Rabassa, London: Penguin, 1996, p. 18.
2. Pedro Lastra, 'La tragedia como fundamento estructural en *La hojarasca*', *Anales de la Universidad de Chile*, 140 (1966): 168–86; reprinted in anthologies.
3. Dasso Saldívar, *García Márquez: El viaje a la semilla – La biografía*, Madrid: Alfaguara, 1997, p. 211.
4. See García Márquez, *Vivir para contarla*, Mexico: Diana, 2002, pp. 276–9, along with the author's essay, first published in October 1959, entitled 'Dos o tres cosas sobre "La novela de la violencia"', in *Obra periodística*, Barcelona: Bruguera, 1981–3, vol. IV: *De Europa y América (1955–1960)*, pp. 763–7.
5. García Márquez, *Leaf Storm*, p. 52.
6. García Márquez, *Leaf Storm*, p. 96.
7. García Márquez, *Leaf Storm*, p. 108.
8. García Márquez, *Leaf Storm*, pp. 108–9.
9. García Márquez, *No One Writes to the Colonel*, trans. J. S. Bernstein, London: Penguin, 1996, p. 10.
10. García Márquez, *No One Writes to the Colonel*, p. 1.
11. García Márquez, *No One Writes to the Colonel*, p. 4.
12. García Márquez, *No One Writes to the Colonel*, p. 20.
13. García Márquez, *No One Writes to the Colonel*, pp. 61–2.
14. García Márquez, *No One Writes to the Colonel*, p. 62.
15. René Prieto, 'The Body as Political Instrument: Communication in *No One Writes to the Colonel*', in Bernard McGuirk and Richard Cardwell (eds.), *Gabriel García Márquez: New Readings*, Cambridge: Cambridge University Press, 1987, pp. 33–44.

16. García Márquez, *No One Writes to the Colonel*, p. 1.
17. García Márquez, *No One Writes to the Colonel*, p. 69.
18. García Márquez, *No One Writes to the Colonel*, p. 35.
19. García Márquez, *No One Writes to the Colonel*, p. 69.
20. García Márquez, *No One Writes to the Colonel*, p. 15.
21. García Márquez, *No One Writes to the Colonel*, p. 22.
22. Gabriel García Márquez, *Vivir para contarla*, Bogotá, Norma, 2001, pp. 276–7.
23. García Márquez, *Vivir para contarla*, p. 277; my translation.
24. García Márquez, *In Evil Hour*, trans. Gregory Rabassa, London: Penguin, 1996, p. 50.

4

PHILIP SWANSON

One Hundred Years of Solitude

The publication of *One Hundred Years of Solitude* (*Cien años de soledad*) in Buenos Aires in May 1967 represented, according to the great Latin American writer and critic Mario Vargas Llosa, 'a literary earthquake'.[1] Literariness is a sensitive notion in the criticism of Latin American fiction and is often subordinated to issues of the political impact of texts – be it at the level of authorial stance, interpretation of content or the context of reception and consumption. Yet the literary nature of García Márquez's great work is not a topic that can or should be avoided. Critics who are more consciously politically motivated may feel uncomfortable if we begin with the rather obvious assertion, then, that *One Hundred Years of Solitude* is a work of fiction. The rise of the Latin American New Novel from, roughly, the 1940s and 1950s onwards and its culmination in the so-called Boom of the 1960s was associated in the minds of many observers with a reaction against traditional realism based on an assumption that reality was observable, understandable and translatable into literature.[2] Equally, many would regard 1967 and the appearance of *One Hundred Years of Solitude* as the culmination of that process.

The novel opens with José Arcadio Buendía, the founding father of Macondo (the imaginary town in which much of the narrative is set), inviting his offspring to read with their imaginations rather than in relation to their knowledge of reality: in a room plastered with unrealistic maps and fabulous drawings, he teaches them to read by telling them of 'the wonders of the world' ('las maravillas del mundo') and 'forcing the limits of his or their imagination to extremes'.[3] This prompting to read in a 'marvellous' or magical way is a possible invitation to the reader to approach the work they are about to read as a playful fictional adventure. Moreover, one reading of the ending of the novel is that when the last member of the Buendía family deciphers the seemingly impenetrable manuscripts of the wise old Gypsy Melquíades, he discovers that the manuscripts and the novelistic text are effectively one and the same and that he is therefore no more than a character in Melquíades's narrative who will disappear with the final words of the novel.

This foregrounding of the fictional obviously accounts, at one level, for what is often referred to as the 'magical realist' style of the novel, for, if this is not reality, then the introduction of fantasy is perfectly acceptable. Yet magical realism is also about rethinking rather than negating reality. The Cuban Alejo Carpentier's original notion of *lo real maravilloso* (the 'marvellous real') was based on the idea of rediscovering Latin American reality, and, in an echo of Carpentier, García Márquez has commented that his encounter with the larger-than-life world of Colombia's Caribbean region taught him to perceive reality in a new way, in which the fantastic was part of everyday life.[4] A standard line on Garciamarquian magical realism became that its perspective (in which ice, films, false teeth and phonographs are presented as bizarre, while levitating priests, rains of butterflies and girls ascending into heaven are presented as normal) is striking a blow for authenticity and Latin Americanness by inscribing events from the perspective of a remote rural community. This would allow for a political reading in which a 'developing world' perspective is privileged from within the implicitly 'First World' form of the novel and in which the reader is being invited to exercise his or her imagination in order to invent an alternative and more just reality for the continent.

So far, so good. However, the founding father also introduces his children to the most dazzling and beautiful diamond on earth – actually, it turns out, the previously unknown substance ice. Magical realism in action perhaps – but the reader knows that the beautiful diamond is only ice and must inevitably be engaged in a relationship of ironic complicity with the implied narrator. Thus implied reader and narrator are, if anything, posited as First World. The exoticness of Latin America is assumed as much as it is problematised. Just as the character Gabriel (surname Márquez) leaves Macondo to go to Europe, so too does the magical-realist experiment seem to be departing Latin America at the very moment of projecting its own Latin Americanness. Indeed, the young Gabriel leaves for Paris (like his real-life namesake), on the advice of a 'wise' ('sabio') European bookseller, who has lost his 'marvellous sense of unreality' ('su maravilloso sentido de irrealidad') and who encourages his literary protegés to abandon the fantastic world of Macondo.[5]

The argument can be twisted in another direction, though. Myth and magic are associated with the falsification of reality by an establishment culture that leads ordinary Latin Americans to internalise an essentially unreal version of their own history and identity as dictated by, say, Europe and North America and its clients in Latin America. Critics have often linked the apparent pattern of repetition and the supposedly circular structure of the novel with myth, magic and timelessness. However, while the novel's characters constantly talk about the confusing and circular nature of history and reality, and while the account of Melquíades's manuscripts is willfully complex and obfuscatory, the (complicit?) narrator and reader actually enjoy what is really an essentially clear and largely linear narrative. If anything, *One Hundred Years of Solitude* breaks with the structural impenetrability typical of the New Novel and marks a turn to accessible and, if suggestive, relatively clearly readable narrative. In other words, Latin Americans – like the character Gabriel who is advised by the 'wise' man to leave the marvellously unreal world of Macondo – are being encouraged to see through the myth-making and to take a grip of reality on their own terms. Hence – in two very different but complementary readings of the ending – Edwin Williamson interprets the destruction of Macondo as a punishment for the final Buendía's immersion into the mythical reality of the manuscripts, while Gerald Martin interprets it as a moment of revolutionary change in that the final Buendía not only has proletarian roots but is also the only one to believe in the historical reality of the massacre of striking banana workers, a truth which has been turned into a fanciful myth by official documents that suppress the facts of this massive scandal and replace them with a false history.[6] Fictitious or unreliable 'official' versions of social reality must be questioned, then, and, despite all the talk of 'the marvellous' or 'lo maravilloso', it is vital that truth will out. Even so, a positive political reading of the ending is difficult to reconcile with the last survivor's withdrawal from society, his incestuous romping, which leads to the fulfillment of the long-predicted curse of the birth of a child with a pig's tail, the generally apocalyptic tone of destruction and the final implication of the fundamental fictionality of a text which cannot be taken as a reflection of reality.

Nonetheless, no amount of scepticism can undermine the impression that this novel is very much about Colombian and Latin American history, and the 100-year span of the action effectively corresponds to the story of 'Latin' America from 'discovery' to the modern day. In a sense, what the novel does is to offer an account of Latin American history from the perspective of the privileged and popular classes, so that history becomes a process of facts replaced by myths and myths turned into facts.[7] The founding of Macondo echoes the chronicles of the 'discovery' and colonisation of the 'New World', and the plague of forgetfulness the loss of historical memory regarding the indigenous inheritance, while the rise of the Buendías parallels the emergence of a powerful landowning oligarchy (alluding to the twin myths of the European heritage and of Independence [the latter often seen as merely cementing the interests of a small white creole elite]). The myths of 'civilisation' à la Sarmiento and democracy are explored after the arrival of the corrupting influence of central government, while the myth of progress is played out by the foreign banana company's transformation of the town into a locus of modern economic colonialism.[8] The banana company is modelled on the notorious North American United Fruit Company, an unverified number of whose workers were shot by Colombian troops during a strike in Ciénaga, Magdalena, in 1928 (another true event shrouded in the mists of mystery and disinformation). The key moment in the novel's political narrative is this massacre of striking banana workers by client government troops and the official repression of the facts as truth is turned into a wacky conspiracy theory. This emblematic portrait of suppressed memory and historical truth took on an even greater significance, of course, for readers of the novel in the decades immediately after its publication in the light of the officially denied plight of the disappeared in Latin America's Southern Cone.

Yet, in a notorious passage, this key episode also becomes the fulcrum of the debate concerning tensions between politics, metaphysics, literature and ambiguity. When, years later, the last of the clan, Aureliano Babilonia, the only believer in the truth of the massacre and the possible embodiment of proletarian revolution, asks the town's main source of knowledge and authority, the parish priest, if he believes in the veracity of the massacre, he receives the world-weary reply: 'Oh dear, my son, ... it would be enough for me to be able to believe that you and I exist at this moment.'[9] This is a remarkable introduction of radical doubt at a key moment, and it casts the entire narrative in a state of existential uncertainty. Unsurprisingly, many critics have noticed a pervasive undercurrent of death and hopelessness in the novel, reinforced by a biblical framework that inverts conventional positive belief systems and brackets human experience within the parameters of negative myths such as the Fall, the Great Flood, Plagues and the Apocalypse.[10] The political hero of the novel, for instance, the civil-war legend Colonel Aureliano Buendía, ends up cruel and alienated, spending the rest of his life in the futile circular process of endlessly making little fish from gold, only to melt them down and make the fish again and again.[11] He dies a sad and forlorn figure, pissing against the tree that the mad and disillusioned town founder was once bound to. As he expires, a colourful circus draws into town, but then leaves him behind, the memory gone, an empty and desolate landscape all that remains. No brave new world is imagined here – this is simply the grim reality of emptiness and death or the failure of knowledge and understanding.

One final motif which brings out *One Hundred Years of Solitude*'s seesawing pull between reality and fantasy or optimism and despair is the much-commented-on theme of incest. The Buendía dynasty in Macondo is founded on an Original Sin (echoing another biblical myth) – that of incest. The married couple, José Arcadio and Ursula, are cousins, and their families are terrified that they will engender a cursed child with a pig's tail. Ursula's fear of such a less-than-immaculate conception leads her to deny herself to her husband, and this in turn provokes rumours about his alleged impotence. His public ridicule leads to the violation of Ursula and his murder of his main taunter. However, the subsequent haunting by the victim's ghost compels them to flee their village, and they set off for a new world where they build a town on the spot revealed to José Arcadio in a premonitory dream. Of course, the trek through 'that paradise ... prior to original sin' leads to the inevitable Fall.[12] Not only does José Arcadio's obsession with learning and science lead to madness (he is eventually bound, raving, to a tree, a sort of inverse Tree of Knowledge), but progress, of course, ultimately brings chaos and destruction to Macondo, and the curse of the birth of the child with a pig's tail is fulfilled just as the shattered town is about to be wiped off the face of the earth by a biblical hurricane.

This all sounds rather grim, but the meaning of incest in *One Hundred Years of Solitude* is really very unclear. It has obvious (but contradictory) social and political connotations. The curse of the original sin is repeated from generation to generation in a series of incestuous or pseudo-incestuous relationships, while some family members' deformities of physique or character are said to echo the monstrosity of the pig's tail. The inward-looking nature of incest relates to the notion of a dynastic oligarchy. The much-mentioned 'sino solitario' or 'solitary fate' of the Buendías, then, is the cause and consequence of the selfishness of an entire class or caste: it represents the opposite of social solidarity. Hence, the dynastic reign of 100 years of 'solitude' is wiped out by a revolutionary wind that may usher in a new regime (possibly even a reference to the hope for a new socialist era inspired by the Cuban Revolution).

Incest can also be associated with repression, of course. Martin connects Ursula's paralysing fear of the curse with a mixture of religion and biological determinism reflecting both the inheritance of Catholic Spanish colonialism, on the one hand, and, on the other, European Positivism and the cult of progress after Independence; Williamson meantime links it to the torpor of introspection, dream, myth and subservience to non-historical time.[13] At the same time, though, incest is therefore a form of rebellion (a rejection of the anxiously conservative values embodied in Ursula or the sleepy tie to unquestioned traditional beliefs). The fact is that many of the incestuous relationships in the novel are profoundly healthy ones and often described with an engagingly ribald sense of fun. Moreover, the last-born child, though with a pig's tail, has the appearance of one 'predisposed to begin the race again from the beginning and cleanse it of its pernicious vices and solitary calling, for he was the only one in a century who had been engendered with love'.[14] Is this a triumph of solidarity and hope, after all? The problem is that the child is destroyed as is everyone else. The city of mirrors ('espejos') that José Arcadio Buendía had dreamt of founding in Macondo turns out to be no more than a city of 'mirages' ('espejismos').[15]

In many ways, then, it would seem rather silly to come to any firm conclusions about *One Hundred Years of Solitude.* García Márquez has himself sarcastically commented that 'critics ... who assume the responsibility of deciphering the book's various riddles run the risk of talking a load of old rubbish.'[16] However, the power and appeal of this cornerstone work and of García Márquez's oeuvre as a whole lies precisely in the tantalising mix of possible readings they offer, coexisting in both harmony and tension, and, while exhibiting undeniable literary 'greatness', ultimately and excitingly empowering the reader to engage with and create his or her own narrative – to make the move from passive to active reader that was at the core of the entire New Novel experiment.

NOTES

1. Mario Vargas Llosa, 'García Márquez: From Aracataca to Macondo', *Review,* 70 (1971), p. 129.
2. For a fuller and more nuanced introduction to the rise of the New Novel, see, for example, my *Latin American Fiction,* Oxford: Blackwell, 2005, or Efraín Kristal (ed.), *The Cambridge Companion to the Latin American Novel,* Cambridge: Cambridge University Press, 2005. García Márquez's text contains various mischievous references to individuals who are actually fictional characters from the works of great Latin American novels of the 1960s by the likes of Alejo Carpentier, Julio Cortázar and Carlos Fuentes. In a sense, the novel is wittily setting itself up as a stage in the history of and a commentary on the Latin American New Novel of the 1960s. Incidentally, there is a similar play between fictitious invention and references to García Márquez's family history.
3. Gabriel García Márquez, *One Hundred Years of Solitude,* London: Picador, 1978, p. 20; *Cien años de soledad,* Buenos Aires: Sudamericana, 1967, p. 21. The English translation by Gregory Rabassa has been modified slightly to bring out a potential ambiguity absent in his rendering.
4. Gabriel García Márquez, *El olor de la guayaba,* Barcelona: Bruguera, 1982, p. 71. Probably the best introduction to magical realism is Stephen Hart and Wen-Chin Ouyang (eds.), *A Companion to Magical Realism,* Woodbridge: Tamesis, 2005.
5. García Márquez, *One Hundred Years of Solitude,* p. 325.
6. See Edwin Williamson, 'Magical Realism and the Theme of Incest in *One Hundred Years of Solitude',* and Gerald Martin, 'On "Magical" and Social Realism in García Márquez', both in Bernard McGuirk and Richard Cardwell (eds.), *Gabriel García Márquez: New Readings,* Cambridge: Cambridge University Press, 1987, pp. 45–63 and pp. 95–116.

7. One of the best outlines of this historical pattern can be found in James Higgins, 'Gabriel García Márquez: *Cien años de soledad*', in Philip Swanson (ed.), *Landmarks in Modern Latin American Fiction,* London: Routledge, 1990, pp. 141–60. See also Philip Swanson, *Cómo leer a Gabriel García Márquez,* Madrid: Júcar, 1991, pp. 81–91, which rehearses many of the comments made here in more detail.
8. Domingo Faustino Sarmiento's seminal 1845 work, *Facundo,* introduced the enormously influential topic of *civilización y barbarie* or 'civilisation versus barbarism', in which Latin American modernity was imagined as an overcoming of the threat of innate, interior, rural barbarism by city-based values built around the inheritance of European progressiveness. Many subsequent writers and thinkers located the ills of the continent precisely in the imposition of alien central policies onto otherwise functional traditional communities.
9. García Márquez, *One Hundred Years of Solitude,* p. 330 (my translation).
10. For an excellent survey of these aspects, see James Higgins, '*Cien años de soledad,* historia del hombre occidental', *Cuadernos del Sur,* 2 (1972): 303–14. See also Swanson, *Cómo leer,* pp. 91–101.
11. The long-running civil wars between Liberals and Conservatives, starting in the late nineteenth century, represent an important aspect of the specifically Colombian dimension of history in the novel.
12. García Márquez, *One Hundred Years of Solitude,* p. 17, my translation.
13. See Martin, 'On "Magical" and Social Realism', pp. 105–6, and Williamson, 'Magical Realism and the Theme of Incest'.
14. García Márquez, *One Hundred Years of Solitude,* p. 332.
15. García Márquez, *One Hundred Years of Solitude,* p. 336.
16. García Márquez, *El olor,* pp. 103–4.

5

RAYMOND L. WILLIAMS

An eco-critical reading of *One Hundred Years of Solitude*

The vast majority of critical readings of *One Hundred Years of Solitude* (*Cien años de soledad* [1967]) appeared in the 1970s and 1980s, well before the recent rise of eco-criticism.[1] The pioneer theorist of eco-critical readings, Lawrence Buell, published his seminal book on this subject, *The Environmental Imagination,* in the early 1990s, and since then a growing number of scholars and readers have been increasingly aware of the multiple roles and representations of nature in literature.[2] Inevitably, many discussions of nature in literature lead to parallel considerations of elements that are not considered part of the natural world: culture and technology. In this study, I will begin with a discussion of background canonical literary texts for an understanding of nature and technology in *One Hundred Years of Solitude,* and then move to an eco-critical reading of García Márquez's work, with emphasis on *One Hundred Years of Solitude.* What is eco-criticism? I would bring to the discussion a 1999 definition constructed by the editors of a special issue on ecocriticsm of *New Literary History* that emphasises focus on the non-human.[3]

In this analysis, I will attempt to show how García Márquez constructs an elaborate and complex web of nature of multiple sources, but many of which, in fact, are human rather than non-human parts of nature.[4] Of the human sources, two of the most noteworthy with respect to the representation of nature are, first, other literary texts and, second, oral tradition. I will explore each in this study.

Critical studies on *One Hundred Years of Solitude* with eco-critical underpinnings have been limited to relatively brief commentaries on the presence of varying climatic conditions in García Márquez's work, as well as commentary on the role of nature in the Colombian author's masterpiece. In an introductory study of climate in the fiction of major Spanish American writers, George McMurray notes that the hyperbolic rains in *One Hundred Years of Solitude* remind us of the purifying biblical flood and cause Fernanda's day-long tirade directed at her husband.[5] In his study,

McMurray also refers to climate in García Márquez's other work and concludes that weather change is sometimes a source of humour in his fiction. All in all, McMurray offers a close reading of García Márquez, with an awareness of nature as he carries out his analysis.

In an article on nature and natural sexuality in *One Hundred Years of Solitude,* Patricia Struebig points to the differences between sexuality as it is manifested in the natural world of nature and natural human instinct in Macondo, as well as how sexuality plays itself out within the confines of conventional social mores. She points out how natural behaviour, acts of nature, are portrayed as a threat to the Buendía family and to the town of Macondo and, consequently, metaphorically, to civilisation itself. Struebig emphasises García Márquez's 'approval of the natural or original state of things'.[6] Indeed, nature wars with man to reclaim the space taken by both traditional 'civilisation' and modern technological progress. Struebig concludes that, in the end, García Márquez affirms nature and condemns the incursions of civilisation. Thus, García Márquez, according to this reading, does privilege the non-human.

Indeed, García Márquez is critical of many aspects of the modern progress associated with the rise of the modern capitalistic nation-state. *One Hundred Years of Solitude,* however, is not as unambiguously and consistently supportive of the natural world and unequivocally critical of the modern. To the contrary, this novel is also a celebration of the modern on several levels. For example, *One Hundred Years of Solitude* is a celebration of literary modernism, and all of García Márquez's work represents a triumph of modern innovation over the forces of traditionalism.[7] In a study of broader scope and more closely connected to the current ecological concerns of eco-criticism, Ursula Heise has explored how literary texts, including *One Hundred Years of Solitude,* negotiate issues of ecological globalism and localism and how they link issues of global ecology with those of cultural globalisms ('think globally, act locally'). In this study, she discusses how, in *One Hundred Years of Solitude,* García Márquez translates scenarios of global connectivity and ecological alienation.[8] Heise is interested in how literary texts can reimagine the earth from a perspective that does not privilege human voices over all others. In the end, however, her conclusions deal less with *One Hundred Years of Solitude* than with novels that have drawn upon this novel for ecological wisdom.

Several book-length studies offer commentary on nature and ecology in *One Hundred Years of Solitude* or make allusions to them. Gene H. Bell-Villada's book *García Márquez, The Man and His Work* is typical of many introductory studies that point to the presence of science and technology as the antithesis to the natural environment in *One Hundred Years of*

Solitude.[9] To some degree, nature is a threat, as manifested in the five-year rainstorm that brings ruin to Macondo, and the constant impulse towards incest threatens to create a member of the family with a pig's tail.

García Márquez, of course, is not a pioneer in the imaginative fictionalisation of nature, which, in reality, can be traced back to the original colonial chronicles that he occasionally parodies in *One Hundred Years of Solitude*. The most broadly read and influential of the early writings on nature in Colombia were penned by the German scientist and explorer Alexander von Humboldt. Among his voluminous writings were lengthy descriptions and commentaries on the flora and fauna of Latin America, including those made during a trip to Nueva Granada, the Spanish colony that geographically encompassed the present-day territory of Colombia.[10] Von Humboldt prided himself as a man of the Enlightenment who not only wrote with scientific rigour but who was also at the vanguard of his day on certain social issues. Thus, he was a strident critic of slavery and liked to think of himself as a friend and protector of the North American indigenous peoples in the Americas, North and South. Present-day readers will note, however, that Von Humboldt was actually a racist who sometimes contradicted his own campaign to free the indigenous and African peoples from slavery, a practice he abhorred. Despite the numerous contradictions of his writings, Von Humboldt was a foundational figure for both much of our understanding and some of our misunderstanding of nature in the Americas. A recent book by Aaron Sachs, in fact, argues convincingly that Von Humboldt set forth the foundations for environmentalism in the nineteenth century as a thinker who was well known by American intellectuals such as Thoreau and Emerson.[11]

One Hundred Years of Solitude shows several traces of Von Humboldt's texts, as suggested by the narrator who states in the novel's fourth chapter, in reference to the parchments of Melquíades: 'In reality, the only thing that could be isolated in the rocky paragraphs was the insistent hammering on the word *equinox, equinox, equinox,* and the name of Alexander von Humboldt' ('En realidad, lo único que pudo dislar en las parrafadas pedregosas, fue el insistente martilleo de la palabra equinoccio equinoccio equinoccio, y el nombre de Alexander Von Humboldt').[12] With this sentence, García Márquez not only reveals his awareness of Von Humboldt, but he is also alluding to the title of the Spanish translation (widely available in Colombia) of Von Humboldt's book, *Viaje a las regiones equinocciales del Nuevo Continente*. In his *Personal Narrative,* Von Humboldt vacillates between two general methods of articulating nature. On the one hand, he insists on a highly 'scientific' account of his observations, with abundant lists and categories of flora and fauna in the New World, and often inserting words in Latin, as evoked in the word *equinoccio*. This is the voice of 'Von-Humboldt-the-scientist' which is the predominant voice of the text. On the other hand, however, Von Humboldt occasionally betrays the 'scientific' voice with comments which are more closely allied with the literature of Romanticism. In both his *Personal Narrative* and his later summa of scientific writings, *Cosmos,* for example, Von Humboldt states: 'the view of nature ought to be grand and free'; and, 'Man learns to know the external world through the organs of the senses. Phenomena of light proclaim the existence of matter in remotest space and the eye is thus made the medium through which we may contemplate the universe.'[13] In another passage that reveals the Romantic rather than scientific voice, he states: 'Nature, in the signification of the word ... reveals itself to the single mind and feelings of man as something earthly, and closely allied to himself.'[14] Von Humboldt assumes the voice of both the scientific rationalist and the Romantic writer in his construction of nature.

After the writings of Von Humboldt, then, an important text for the construction of nature in Colombia and for *One Hundred Years of Solitude* is the canonical Romantic novel *María* by Jorge Isaacs (1867). This novel continues the Romantic voice articulated in Von Humboldt's writings and portrays nature as part of an idyllic setting for a love affair. Numerous studies have demonstrated the fact that this idyllic nature was filtered through the lens of European Romantic fiction, the most important of which was Chateaubriand's *Atalá* (1809). Isaacs wrote *María* from 1864 to 1866 while living in the mountains, often isolated. Despite this proximity to nature, *María* is unquestionably the product of the Greater Cauca region's sophisticated and elitist writing culture of the time.[15] Nature serves as a backdrop for the protagonist, Efraín, to overcome his childhood and display his masculinity, after numerous descriptions of him as a child and of childhood as an ideal state. His displays of masculinity involve his hunting in the wilderness: his prizes of ferocious beasts are presented as supposedly impressive proof of what social ideals deem genuine manliness. A brief analysis of these masculine deeds, however, reveals a character who is not convincingly effective in this traditional masculine role in nature. Once in the wilderness, for example, Efraín does not measure up to the hearty Emigdio. When the protagonist picks some flowers, Emigdio warns him: 'Do you want everything to smell of roses? Men should smell like goats.'[16] We note here, in addition, the contrast between a writing-culture value (Efraín's flowers in poetry) and an oral-culture value (Emidgio's human lifeworld of goats). Once involved with the actual hunt, his prize is not the awesome bear that Efraín's father had demanded but an effeminate cat. It is described in the diminutive (*gatico*) and is wounded and weakened before Efraín finally delivers the death blow. This act clearly does not measure up to the aggressive dominance that Efraín desires and believes he needs in order to fulfill his traditional role. He has failed to overcome nature and the natural setting in his desire to demonstrate his masculinity. Isaacs uses nature to communicate the novel's outcome: the protagonist Efraín remains the eternal child, even within the rigid and traditional nineteenth-century societal structures. As such, he remains incomplete – the potential writer who never dictates, the lover who never consummates his desires.

One of the cornerstones of the Latin American novel, as well as one of the most renowned Colombian literary representations of nature to inform *One Hundred Years of Solitude*, was José Eustasio Rivera's *The Vortex* (*La vorágine* [1924]). This text was informed by Spanish American *modernismo*. The turn-of-the century *modernistas* were well known by García Márquez (he parodies them in *The Autumn of the Patriarch* [*El otoño del patriarca*]), and they embraced some aspects of Romanticism. The *modernistas*' renovation of the poetic tradition in the Spanish language was not only a rejection of the major tenets of Romanticism but a rejection of the Romantics' appreciation of nature. More specifically, the *modernistas* embraced art rather than nature as the privileged ideal to be expressed and attained, and ecocritical understandings of nature are difficult to accommodate with the main currents of *modernista* thought and literary production.

A novel often described also as a classic text of Spanish American *criollismo* (early twentieth-century fiction that explored the culture of nationhood via notions of autochthony), Rivera's *La vorágine* promotes the *criollista* agenda of tying national identity with the land, so nature necessarily has some importance in these novels. This specific *criollista* agenda is not as fully developed as in the two other classic *criollista* works *Don Segundo Sombra* (1926) and *Doña Bárbara* (1929), both of which create a more obvious and direct connection between national identity and the land. In *The Vortex*, the protagonist does escape the city and flee to the inland jungle of Colombia, but the jungle never carries the positive connotations attained in *Don Segundo Sombra* (in which the pampa is an aspect of the very essence of authentic Argentine identity) or *Doña Bárbara* (in which the flatlands [the *llano*] serve as an essential backdrop to Gallegos's elaborate discussion of Venezuela's need to resolve the dichotomy between civilisation and barbarism). To the contrary, in *The Vortex*, the natural setting of the jungle serves as the ultimate threat, devouring the protagonist Arturo Cova in the end.

Given the ambiguities concerning this novel's status as a *criollista* text and other questions the reader inevitably faces, the real subject of *The Vortex* has been a matter of considerable debate. Readings have stressed the portrayal of the New World as one of the three classic criollista texts: civilisation versus barbarity, the evil forces of the universe and social injustice. Such forces do indeed operate in the fictional world of *The Vortex*. The costumbrist cockfight scene and the revelation of exploitation of rubber workers are two of several examples of subject matter that supports such readings. The question, however, is whether these are the primary subject matter – the thematic core of this supposedly *criollista* text so tightly tied to nature. The predominant subject of *The Vortex*, I would argue, is not really the fictional representation of the natural world and rural Colombia in 1924 (with its concomitant bedraggled workers) but rather the self in the process of writing. Read in this light, the novel fits squarely in the realm of self-conscious writing culture as a key precedent to *One Hundred Years of Solitude* in its representation of technology and nature.

Several additional problems arise with reading *The Vortex* as a fictionalised replica of Colombia's rural story of the natural world. One basic difficulty with such a reading of this novel as a fictionalised simulacrum of Colombia's rural story is, simply stated, the absence of story. As narrator, Cova constantly vacillates between his role as creator of story and narrator of himself. Many of the novel's narrative segments begin not with the subject matter of the external story (that is, Colombia's rural story) but with intrusions about the self. The reader observes Cova reacting to a world rather than fabricating a story. The novel's first sentence sets the tone and typifies what will take place in the remainder of the work: 'Before falling in love with any woman, I took my chances with my heart, and Violence won' ('Antes que me hubiera apasionado por mujer alguna, jugué mi corazón al azar y me lo ganó la Violencia').[17] In this sentence, five basic elements are in operation with respect to the self and story: three references to the self and two references with the potential of developing the external story, these being 'woman' (love story) and *la violencia* (a Colombian story).

Given the overwhelming presence of the self in this novel, the story is not essentially of a *vorágine*, of natural phenomena in the New World, but of a self in the process of writing, of establishing a writerly identity that interrupts the narration of a story. Interruptions can appear at the most inopportune moments of the narrative's potential as a story. When a group of Indians drowns, Cova's reaction is: 'The spectacle was magnificent'.[18] This passage shows a radical shift of focus from an adventure story to a writer's story. The Indian's death is portrayed as a relatively unimportant event at the end of a narrative segment; Cova's emotional reaction to it turns out to be the subject of the entire first part of the following narrative segment, centred upon this vision of mass death as 'spectacle'. The potential story of an adventure had been subverted by Cova's presence from the beginning of the second part. The narrator does not present the Indians as human beings but as the non-human literary figures about whom Cova-the-writer has read: he characterises them all as being strong, young and with Herculean backs.[19] Indeed, with respect to the orality–writing culture dichotomy, Cova's attitude epitomises a writing culture appropriating an oral culture strictly for literary purposes.

The narrator of *The Vortex* exploits his subject matter of writing in three ways: by the use of metaphor, by means of literary allusions and by dramatising the very act of writing itself. Cova's language is consistently metaphorical: rather than naming the world, he relates what it is 'like' (*como*). Cova's inconsistent story also strives to acquire the status of 'literature' by means of association with classic literary texts or direct allusions to them. Clemente Silva, for example, refers to their trip as 'our Odyssey', and Cova himself characterises his experiences and the book he is writing similarly, referring to them as 'my Odyssey'.[20] In addition to a series of parallels between *The Vortex* and Dante's *Divine Comedy*, references relate the text to Dante's *Inferno* and Virgil's *Aeneid*.

Another way in which *The Vortex* self-consciously seeks the status of high-culture 'literature' is the drama of writing that Cova develops. The figure of 'José Eustasio Rivera' initiates this drama in the prologue, which features as its pre-eminent subject neither Arturo Cova nor the unjust life of rubber tappers but a manuscript. In the final sections of the novel the significant drama is not Cova's struggle with nature, for neither he nor nature has a sufficiently important fictional status. Rather, the tension involves Cova's completion of his writing. Since he has acquired his status as writer, thus assuring his text's status as literature, the only question remaining is the novel's denouement: precisely how and under what circumstances will the text be completed? In the end, the drama of the text culminates in its being left for Clemente Silva; the fact that Cova has been devoured by nature (the jungle) is of little consequence. This is not really a *criollista* text focusing on nature but a novel about writing and literature.

Undoubtedly *María* and *The Vortex* are key predecessors to García Márquez's representation of nature and technology in *One Hundred Years of Solitude*. Nevertheless, between the publication of *The Vortex* in 1924 and the appearance of *One Hundred Years of Solitude* in 1967, numerous other intervening texts of considerable interest in informing *One Hundred Years of Solitude* appeared in print. Among the modernists, three key predecessors with respect to nature and technology were the Argentines Adolfo Bioy Casares, Jorge Luis Borges and Julio Cortázar. Bioy Casares' *Morel's Invention* (*La invención de Morel* [1940]) was a relatively early exploration in Latin America into the possibilities of integrating new technology (at that time, film) into a Latin American novel. Borges's *Fictions* (*Ficciones* [1944]), well known as canonical works for García Márquez himself, were as dramatic a revolution with respect to nature and technology in Latin American literature. In these stories, nature is diminished in value from its privileged role under the guises of the *criollistas* who had dominated the literary scene in Spanish America for over two decades. Even in stories with some natural setting and presence of nature, such as 'The South' ('El Sur'), this natural world is understood as artificial and having literary sources: the South of this story is the southern region of Argentina with an entire literary legacy related to gauchesque literature. In *Hopscotch* (*Rayuela* [1963]), Julio Cortázar sets forth a critique of the very basic tenets of Western Manichean thought, including many Western assumptions about reason. It is a critique of Western assumptions about 'progress' as a value in itself. As such, *Hopscotch* is a noteworthy predecessor to eco-critical thought in that it raises similar questions and critiques the proposition that humans are the centre in opposition to nature, or that the non-human might have a value similar to the human. Cortázar's critique of Western culture's confidence in rational thought is the basis for this fundamental indebtedness of later eco-criticism to the Argentine writer.

In Colombia, the noteworthy predecessor of this period was Álvaro Cepeda Samudio's novel *La casa grande* (*The Big House*, editor's translation [1962]), the author's only novel and one that was situated in the town of Ciénaga, the site of a banana workers' strike in 1928 and massacre by government soldiers. This was the first literary presentation of the strike and massacre which had never been officially recognised by the government and had not appeared in official histories as part of the nation's history. This event reappeared, of course, in *One Hundred Years of Solitude. La casa grande* also places into question the legitimacy of modernisation when it involves the model of foreign capitalist enterprises in Latin America; this region of Colombia, where Cepeda Samudio and García Márquez were born and reared, is the only one dominated by foreign capitalists in the history of the nation. Its questioning of modernisation, the destruction of nature, foreign capitalism and the modern values of patriarchal capitalism make it an important eco-critical predecessor to *One Hundred Years of Solitude*.

In the case of *One Hundred Years of Solitude*, nature, technology and culture are filtered through the texts outlined above, beginning with a nature that associates it with Isaacs's nature in *María*. Not only does the exuberant nature of *One Hundred Years of Solitude* associate with nature in *María*, but a scene in García Márquez's novel directly evokes the classic Romantic novel from Colombia. At the end of the ninth chapter of *One Hundred Years of Solitude*, a window in the home of Remedios la Bella (the Beautiful) is portrayed as the classic scene of romantic love, with the enamoured young man awaiting the beloved below her window embellished with nature. In García Márquez's version, a lovestruck soldier dies of love beneath the window of Remedios la Bella (the original Spanish has him 'dead of love' whereas the published translation loses some of the sense of Romantic melodrama).[21] The passage shows a García Márquez parodying the Romantic tradition, and its nature, in *One Hundred Years of Solitude*. *One Hundred Years of Solitude* evokes *The Vortex* as another self-reflective writerly story. In the end, *One Hundred Years of Solitude* is not only the story of the Buendía family but also a self-reflective book about literature. Numerous critics have pointed to this novel's multiple sources: the Bible, classical Greek literature, Ariosto's *Orlando,* nineteenth-century Russian fiction, the novels of Virginia Woolf, the fiction of Ernest Hemingway and William Faulkner.[22] In addition, *One Hundred Years of Solitude* refers to the act of writing as incessantly as does *The Vortex,* and the latter part of the novel takes the reader to an intensified focus on the text as a piece of literature: the references to characters from other Latin American novels and writers, and the discovery that the entire story of Macondo had already been written on the parchments of Melquíades makes *One Hundred Years of Solitude* a patently literary text that focuses, in the end, on its metafictional qualities and on the text as literature, and not as the representation of the external reality of Colombia or Latin America. With respect to this first point, sustaining an eco-critical reading of *One Hundred Years of Solitude,* it should be noted that many of García Márquez's sources of nature do not point to the natural world itself but rather to other literary texts, from those of Alexander Von Humboldt to those of Isaacs, Rivera and a host of others.

The second source of García Márquez's understanding of nature is the oral tradition of the Caribbean coastal region of Colombia where he was reared listening to the stories that comprised this tradition. My understanding of 'oral tradition' and my explanation of the 'magic realist' elements of the novel are based on the pioneer synthetic work of Walter Ong in his ground-breaking study *Orality and Literacy,* which includes the following key observation concerning oral cultures:

> In the absence of elaborate analytic categories that depend on writing to structure knowledge at a distance from lived experience, oral cultures must conceptualise and verbalise all their knowledge with more or less close reference to the human lifeworld, assimilating the alien, objective world to the more immediate familiar interaction of human beings.[23]

In the case of *One Hundred Years of Solitude,* this 'alien' and 'objective' world is the world of nature and technology. Orlando Fals Borda points to this phenomenon in the Caribbean coastal region of Colombia, for example, the belief in the *hombre-hipoteca,* or 'tortoise-man', is a real-world example of the close reference to the human lifeworld, one in which the human lifeworld and the lifeworld of nature are assimilated.[24] This particular characteristic of oral cultures, closeness to the human lifeworld, seen in the context of ecology, the environment and eco-criticism, should be seen as a positive, eco-critically sound practice. In *One Hundred Years of Solitude,* this noetic process, with characters who are minimally abstract and remain close to the human lifeworld, is often the case – as in that of Ursula. Moreover, this human lifeworld is of nature. Thus, Ursula's reaction to José Aracadio's declaration that 'the world is round, like an orange' is telling. First, it should be noted that even José Arcadio's 'scientific' view is marked by a closeness to nature, with an orange as his metaphor for the world. It is not really the nature of the native natural world of Macondo, Colombia or the Americas, however, for the presence of the orange in the Americas has to do with the history of colonialism and Western technology, having been transported to the Americas by the colonisers in the ships they constructed using the latest marine technology, the cutting-edge technology of the day. Oranges were brought to the Americas by Columbus on his second trip to the New World and first arrived in Haiti in 1493. Ursula, however, reacts negatively to José Arcadio's scientific understanding of the world, as the narrator explains, following José Arcadio's explanation that the world is round like an orange, Ursula lost her patience.

In *One Hundred Years of Solitude,* García Márquez uses situational frames of reference which are minimally abstract in the sense that they remain close to the human lifeworld. The narrator assumes this role as an oral-culture person throughout much of the novel, often using down-to-earth and animal imagery, thus remaining close to the living human lifeworld. In some cases, the narrator, when he takes such positions, is assuming a role similar to the characters. For example, he describes Amaranta at birth using the following animal imagery: 'She was light and water, like a newt, but all her parts were human.'[25]

The narrator assumes other roles typical of an oral mindset. His treatment of Remedios la Bella is that of an oral person both in form and content. The narrator regularly employs the epithet *la bella* for her in Spanish, a form common in oral storytelling. The scene in which Remedios rises heavenward is a typical description of how a person in an oral culture would view such an event. Another characteristic of this narrator's storytelling is his copiousness. Oral performance demands flow: hesitancy is always a vice, and the copious flow of oral performance is effected through repetition and redundancy. The repetition in *One Hundred Years of Solitude* has been well documented.[26] García Márquez has conceived a novel with the copiousness and flow demanded in oral performance, one of the best examples being Fernanda's two-page, single-sentence diatribe.[27]

In addition to the narrator and Ursula, the most prominent examples of oral-culture individuals, other characters in this novel are either oral-culture persons or persons who occasionally react as such. By the twelfth chapter, for example, Macondo's inhabitants seem to be lettered and modern. Nevertheless, the chapter begins with a humorous episode describing an oral-culture person's reaction to modern technology: the people of Macondo become outraged and break the seats of the movie theatre because an actor who died and was buried in one film reappeared later in another alive, now as an Arab.

Oral cultures are also verbally agonistic. The Buendía family history begins as a result of Prudencio Aguilar's verbal challenge to José Arcadio Buendía, questioning the future patriarch's masculinity. The female characters are a special case with respect to orality and literacy. As is common in many traditional cultures, the males of Macondo are the lettered characters, beginning with Melquíades and José Arcadio Buendía, whereas, in contrast, Ursula thinks and expresses herself consistently as an oral-culture person. In the latter parts of the novel, Macondo's women do begin to read, usually finding themselves uncomfortable in the masculine writing culture. The loss of the feminine oral culture (more closely aligned with nature than with the masculine writing culture) affects the novel's denouement: the lettered Amaranta Ursula and Aureliano conceive a baby with a pig's tail not only because he abandoned his studies of the parchments at the point where he would have uncovered their blood relationship but also because neither of them remembers 'Ursula's frightened admonitions'. Their failure also represents the final defeat of a lost oral culture and a parallel loss of nature. In our eco-critical reading of *One Hundred Years of Solitude,* then, the presence and then gradual loss of oral culture has as its parallel the presence and gradual loss of nature, for oral culture and nature are closely linked.

What has often been identified by the now overused and frequently vague term 'magical realism' in this novel is more precisely described as a written expression of the shift from the orality of a culture close to nature to various stages of literacy.[28] The effects of the interplay between oral and writing culture are multiple. García Márquez has fictionalised numerous aspects of his youth in the tri-ethnic and oral culture of the rural Caribbean coastal region of Colombia, one in which the inhabitants lived close to nature when oral culture was still predominant. The unique traditionalism and modernity of this novel are based on various roles the narrator assumes as an oral storyteller in the fashion of the tall tale, as narrator with an oral-culture person's mindset and as the modern narrator of a self-conscious written fiction.

In conclusion, García Márquez portrays an ambiguous relationship between the non-human and the human world, and actually privileges both.[29] Unlike some books identified as 'eco-literature', *One Hundred Years of Solitude* portrays a complex web in which the implied author is attracted to both orality and writing, both technology and nature, both modernity and tradition. He is also critical of them. *One Hundred Years of Solitude* clearly draws from at least two main sources for images of nature: literary texts and the oral tradition. It is perhaps less about nature and technology than about oral and writing culture's images of nature and technology. Clearly, the novel has a multiplicity of filters for the representation of nature. Also, *One Hundred Years of Solitude* is far more complex than more typical books of 'eco-literature' that necessarily privilege nature as centre, as already suggested. Characters such as Ursula live in an oral-culture mindset, close to the human lifeworld and close to nature (using homeopathic herbs such as arnica).[30] Finally, *One Hundred Years of Solitude* does invite the reader to rethink nature as it was and as it is, as well as our relationship with it as it was and as it is. In this sense, *One Hundred Years of Solitude* is a novel that eco-critics can identify as a work of ecological wisdom. Returning to our original definition of eco-criticism, *One Hundred Years of Solitude,* like eco-criticism, claims as its hermeneutic horizon the finite environment the reader occupies thanks not just to culturally coded determinants but also to natural determinants that antedate these, and will outlast them.[31]

NOTES

1. A selection of these early studies of *One Hundred Years of Solitude* includes: Gene H. Bell-Villada, *Gabriel García Márquez: The Man and His Work,* Chapel Hill, NC: University of North Carolina Press, 1990; Josefina Ludmer, Cien años de soledad: *una interpretación,* Buenos Aires: Editorial Tiempo Contemporáneo, 1972; George McMurray, *Gabriel García Márquez,* New York: Frederick Ungar, 1977; George McMurray (ed.), *Critical Essays on Gabriel García Márquez,* Boston, MA: G. K. Hall, 1987; Julio Ortega (ed.), *Gabriel García Márquez and the Powers of Fiction,* Austin, TX: University of Texas Press, 1988; Ricardo Gullón, 'Gabriel García Márquez and the Lost Art of Storytelling', *Diacritics,* 1, (1) (1971): 27–32; Emir Rodríguez Monegal, 'Novedad y anacronismo en *Cien años de soledad', Revista Nacional de Cultura,* 29 (1968): 5; Mario Vargas Llosa, *García Márquez: Historia de un deicidio,* Barcelona and Caracas: Seix Barral and Monte Avila, 1971; Raymond L. Williams, *Gabriel García Márquez,* Boston, MA: Twayne, 1984.
2. The rise of eco-criticism is fundamentally a phenomenon of the 1990s but can be traced back to the 1960s and works such as Rachel Carson's classic *Silent Spring,* Boston, MA and New York: Mariner Books, 1962. Important critical bibliography of key works for eco-critical readings of literature include Leo Marx's early study, *The Machine in the Garden,* New York: Oxford University

Press, 1964; Joseph Meeker, *The Comedy of Survival: Studies in Literary Ecology,* 3rd edn, Tucson, AZ: University of Arizona Press, 1974; Annette Kolodny, *The Lay of the Land: Metaphor as Experience in American Life and Letters,* Chapel Hill, NC: University of North Carolina Press, 1975; Leonard Lutwack, *The Role of Place in Literature,* Syracuse, NY: Syracuse University Press, 1984; Steven Rosedale (ed.), *The Greening of Literary Scholarship,* Iowa City, IA: University of Iowa Press, 2002. See also Laurence Coupe (ed.), *The Green Studies Reader from Romanticism to Ecocriticism,* London and New York: Routledge, 2000; and Andrew Dobson (ed.), *The Green Reader: Essays toward a Sustainable Society,* San Francisco, CA: Mercury House, 1991. The third book by Lawrence Buell on this subject, *The Future of Environmental Criticism,* Oxford: Blackwell Publishing, 2005 (see also his *The Environmental Imagination: Thoreau, Nature Writing and the Formation of American Culture,* Cambridge, MA: Harvard University Press, 1995), and other recent books, such as Glen A. Love, *Practical Ecocriticism,* Charlottesville, VA: University of Virginia Press, 2003, are indicators that eco-criticism is a growing field. The aim of Love's book is to initiate a more biologically informed eco-critical dialogue about literature and its relationship to nature and environmental concerns.

3. Early eco-criticism of the 1980s and early 1990s (now referred to as the 'first wave') placed emphasis on the non-human over the human. The definition of eco-criticism offered by the editors of the special issue on eco-criticism of *New Literary History* is as follows: 'challenges interpretation of its own grounding in the bedrock of natural fact, in the biosphere and indeed planetary conditions without which human life, much less human letters, could not exist. Eco-criticism thus claims as its hermeneutic horizon nothing short of literal horizon itself, the finite environment that a reader or writer occupies thanks not just to culturally coded determinants but also to natural determinants that antedate these, and will outlast them.' Herbert F. Tucker, 'From the Editors', *New Literary History,* 3 (1999): 505.
4. As Buell points out, a second wave of eco-critical thought has allowed for the recovery of the human in ecocriticism.
5. See George McMurray, 'The Role of Climate in Twentieth-Century Spanish American Fiction', in Janet Pérez and Wendell Aycock (eds.), *Climate and Literature: Reflections on the Environment,* Lubbock, TX: Texas Tech University Press, 1995, pp. 55–64.
6. Patricia Struebig, 'Nature and Sexuality in Gabriel García Márquez's *One Hundred Years of Solitude*', *Selecta: Journal of the Pacific Northwest Council on Foreign Languages,* 5 (1984): 60.
7. I have discussed the role of García Márquez and the writers of the Boom as modernists and innovators in 'Modernist Continuities: The Desire to be Modern in Twentieth-Century Spanish-American Fiction', *Bulletin of Spanish Studies,* 79 (2002): 369–93.
8. See Ursula K. Heise, 'Local Rock and Global Plastic: World Ecology and the Experience of Place', *Comparative Literature Studies,* 41 (1) (2004): 126–52.
9. Bell-Villada, *The Man and His Work,* pp. 93–7.
10. The two books discussed here are Alexander Von Humboldt's *Personal Narrative,* New York: Penguin, 1996, and *Cosmos,* New York: Harper & Brothers, 1850. All quotations are from these editions.

11. See Aaron Sachs, *The Humboldt Current*, New York: Viking, 2006.
12. Gabriel García Márquez, *One Hundred Years of Solitude*, trans. Gregory Rabassa, London: Picador, 1970, p. 66.
13. Von Humboldt, *Cosmos*, p. 83; Von Humboldt's *Personal Narrative*.
14. Von Humboldt, *Cosmos*, p. 82.
15. For additional analysis of writing culture in *María*, see my book *The Colombian Novel: 1844–1987*, Austin, TX: University of Texas Press, 1991, pp. 151–60.
16. Jorge Isaacs, *María*, Buenos Aires: Losada, 1966, p. 62. The English translation is mine.
17. José Eustasio Rivera, *La vorágine*, Mexico City: Porrúa, 1976, p. 5.
18. Rivera, *La vorágine*, p. 74.
19. Rivera, *La vorágine*, p. 56.
20. Rivera, *La vorágine*, pp. 82, 128.
21. García Márquez, *One Hundred Years of Solitude*, pp. 158, 173.
22. For more complete discussions of the literary sources of *One Hundred Years of Solitude*, see Suzanne J. Levine, *El espejo hablado: Un estudio de* Cien años de soledad, Caracas: Monte Ávila, 1975, and Edward Waters Hood, *La ficción de Gabriel García Márquez: Repetición e intertextualidad*, New York: Peter Lang, 1993.
23. Walter Ong, *Orality and Literacy*, London and New York: Methuen, 1982, pp. 42–3.
24. Orlando Fals Borda, *Historia doble de la costa*, 4 vols., Bogotá: Carlos Valencia Editores, 1979.
25. García Márquez, *One Hundred Years of Solitude*, p. 37.
26. See Birute Ciplijauskaité, 'Foreshadowing as a Technique and Theme in *One Hundred Years of Solitude*', *Books Abroad*, 47 (3) (1973): 479–84.
27. García Márquez, *One Hundred Years of Solitude*, pp. 298–300.
28. On magical realism, see Seymour Menton, *Magic Realism Rediscovered, 1918–1981*, Philadelphia, PA: Art Alliance Press, 1983; Lois Parkinson Zamora and Wendy B. Farris (eds.), *Magic Realism: Theory, History, Community*, Durham, NC: Duke University Press, 1995.
29. I would add to this first observation concerning the construction of nature in *One Hundred Years of Solitude* by citing Rosedale, *The Greening*. Rosedale argues that now, after eco-criticism has established the importance of the non-human in literature, it favours the following: environmentally useful emphases on the human component of the human–nature relationship. Rosedale's proposition supports my emphasis on the human and humane letters' source of nature when I refer to all the literary texts that have contributed to representation of nature in *One Hundred Years of Solitude*.
30. I owe this observation concerning the mention of arnica in the text to Ruth Cabré, who noticed this herbal remedy in an informal reading and discussion of *One Hundred Years of Solitude*.
31. Tucker, 'From the Editors', p. 505. As a final note, I owe some of the points delineated in this article to a group of graduate students at the University of California, Riverside, who were enrolled in a graduate seminar on the topic of eco-critical readings of the Latin American novel, including *One Hundred Years of Solitude*, in autumn 2006 and winter 2007.

6

STEVEN BOLDY

The Autumn of the Patriarch

The Autumn of the Patriarch (*El otoño del patriarca,* 1975) is a text as robustly resistant to confident evaluation as any other by García Márquez, who described it as 'a poem on the solitude of power', a 'poetic adventure' and a highly personal 'book of confession'.[1] Reminiscing with Plinio Apuleyo Mendoza, he situates his intuition of the mystery of power in a scene he witnesses as a reporter in Caracas in 1958 just after the fall of General Marcos Pérez Jiménez:

> It was nearly four in the morning, when the door opened and we saw an officer, in combat gear, walking backwards, with muddy boots and a sub-machine gun in his hands ... pointing with the machine gun, and dirtying the carpet with the mud from his boots. He went down the stairs, got into a car which took him to the airport, and went into exile. It was at that precise moment, when that soldier was leaving a room where the formation of the new government was being decided, that I had the intuition of power, the mystery of power.[2]

Power is a glass ball in the palm of one's hand, but it may also be a slippery fish 'swimming around without god or law' ('un sábalo vivo que nadaba sin dios ni ley').[3] The initial inspiration for the aesthetic of *The Autumn of the Patriarch* was 'the image of an inconceivably old dictator who ends up alone in a palace full of cows'.[4] Latin American dictators, García Márquez elaborates, are 'feudal-cattle farmer dictators', and indeed the Dominican Republic's Rafael Trujillo was said to be far more fond of cows than people. Cows munch through the tapestries in the palace and look out from the presidential balcony; the Patriarch endlessly squelches through cowshit, burns it to drive away the mosquitoes, recites what he remembers of the 'dense minotaur' (of poet Rubén Darío's 'Marcha triunfal', in the 'tepid cowshit olympus of the milking stables' ('el olimpo tibio de mierda de vaca de los establos de ordeño').[5]

The indifferentiation and liquification associated with the omnipresent excrement are indicated in repeated use of vocabulary such as *chapalear* (squelch), *cenagoso* (boggy), *empantanarse* (to become swamped) as in the phrase 'sloshing through the cow flops in the darkness'.[6] This motif embodies the aesthetic of a novel characterised by paradox, oxymoron, excess, grotesque, carnivalisation and simulacra. The Patriarch has a rebel guard skinned alive to encourage his fellows to confess that they had been coerced into an assassination plot and that they did in fact love him. The lyrical, the erotic, the obscene and the tragic blur, for example, in the scenes of paedophilia with the schoolgirl whom the decrepit dictator seduces, shares asparagus marinated in her own intimate fluids, causes her family to be exiled and leaves her for the rest of her life searching promiscuously for a man who could love her as tenderly as he had. Even this disconcerting cluster of impressions is further affected by unreality: the girls from the school are replaced by whores from the port, dressed up and trained for the job. The same man who has 2,000 children who he had used to rig the national lottery in his favour blown up at sea cares with tender abnegation for his sick mother. The most vulgar and racy celebration of popular Caribbean language sits by the most concentrated and elusive poetic prose, where, for example, the lighthouse is 'the fantastic starlike firefly that fumigated in its orbit of a spinning nightmare the fearsome outpouring of the luminous dust of the marrow of the dead'.[7] The writing of the novel shares most of its characteristics with power itself and the fatherland, forever experienced 'with this feeling of unreality, with this smell of shit'.[8]

Michael Bell sees in this proximity between writing and dictatorship the cause of the adverse reaction of many critics:

> Whereas in *Hundred Years* there was a humorous gap between the Buendías' obsessions and the magical mode of the narrative, in *Autumn* the book itself struggles with the condition it describes. To see the patriarch as a magical realist, albeit in bad faith and *malgré lui,* is a more intrinsic way of explaining the readerly and critical resistance the book has aroused.[9]

Post-structuralists rejoice, while Marxists rage. Patricia Tobin takes the scene when the Patriarch soils himself as he finally deflowers Leticia Nazareno as emblematic of his anti-Manichaean practice: 'It is this vortex, where Señor Signifier shits as he fucks, that is the ultimate focus of the deconstructionists.'[10] His monstrously herniated testicle magically becomes 'deconstructionists' crippled Phallus'.[11] Similarly, González Echevarría sees García Márquez's writing as a deconstruction and demythification of the power of the dictator.[12] Gerald Martin reacted scornfully to the former of these two critics, claiming that 'collage-texts' such as this 'dissolve reality ultimately into myth'.[13] He argues that 'decentering' and 'deconstruction' disguise the real message that 'they were not prepared to confront the powers and authorities they saw only too clearly around them, on behalf of the peasants and workers of the continent.'[14] Other critics seek to resolve the tensions positively. Julio Ortega sees the voice of the people empowered in the popular codes of the text, while Aronne Amestoy sees mythification working to cancel itself out: rationality is finally affirmed by the parodic, self-cancelling excess of mythical narrative.

Powerful men have figured centrally in García Márquez's fiction over many years, from Colonel Aureliano Buendía in *One Hundred Years of Solitude* (*Cien años de soledad* [1967]), through the Patriarch in 1975, to Simón Bolívar in *The General in His Labyrinth* (*El general en su laberinto* [1989]). The move is clearly one into documented history. Aureliano was loosely based on General Uribe and on Márquez's grandfather, while the Patriarch is a compendium of recognisable dictators, but the portrait of the explicitly named Liberator of the final novel depends on a textual dialogue with compendious source documents on Bolívar. Curiously, all three come from the Caribbean or live there, and they (or their family) share with their chronicler a horrified memory of the cold and inhospitable city of Bogotá. Aureliano Buendía, immediately recognisable by his 'stigma of solitude' and his desire to 'sweep away conservative regimes from Alaska to Patagonia once and for all' comes in to *The Autumn of the Patriarch* to ask the Patriarch for support for his cause, only to be dismissed as a hopeless idealist.[15] General Moncada had warned Aureliano that he was on course to become 'the most despotic and bloodthirsty dictator of our history', perhaps something like the Patriarch, which adds curious pathos to the encounter between the young liberal and a likely version of his future.[16]

One Hundred Years of Solitude has two distinct halves: one of growth and plenitude and one of terminal decline and nostalgia. *The Autumn of the Patriarch* does not have this first part but begins with the decline of the Patriarch after the death of his double, Patricio Aragonés. Like *The General in His Labyrinth* it looks back to vitality and promise from physical decrepitude, and one wonders whether the later novel might be seen as a 'pre-sequel' in so far as the failure of the Bolivarian project for America is played out in the stagnant horrors of endless dictatorial regimes, starting with 'the civil wars we were to suffer for the rest of the century', invoked by the sudden appearance of a first-person plural voice.[17] This 'we' refers us back to the distinctly problematic voice at the end of *The Autumn of the Patriarch*, which has been read as a source of non-alienated popular presence by Zamora and Ortega but questioned by others, including Jo Labanyi, who warns: 'The fact that it is anonymous, uninformed and inconsistent means that it cannot be seen as an alternative source of authority.'[18] This voice claims a self-knowledge utterly unforeseen in the novel, and points to a liberated future: 'we knew only too well that it was arduous and ephemeral but there wasn't any other, general, because we knew who we were while he was left never knowing it for ever.'[19] This paradoxical optimism against all odds had been in evidence two years earlier in the Colombian's Nobel Prize speech, where he reversed the damning conclusion of *One Hundred Years:* 'it is not yet too late to undertake the creation of a minor utopia ... where the lineal generations of one hundred years of solitude will have at last and for ever a second chance on earth'.[20] The negative ending of the 1967 novel is of course contradicted internally by the voice of the 'Catalan sage', who leads his young mentees such as Gabriel Márquez out of the crippling nostalgia of Macondo.

Such ambivalence had already been one of the distinguishing marks of the dictatorship novel for more than a century. Domingo Faustino Sarmiento's fascination with the Argentine *caudillo* Facundo Quiroga in his 1845 *Facundo: civilización y barbarie* could be taken as a founding moment. Multi-genre to the extreme, as was magical realism a century later, biography, history, political pamphlet, nationalist romanticism, the work condemns Facundo Quiroga as a paradigm of the barbarism which was to facilitate the tyranny of Juan Manuel de Rosas, while extolling him as the incarnation of the uniqueness of national culture. Sarmiento, states Yahni, 'lucidly admits the coexistence of an aesthetic which admires that which is rejected by his ideas'.[21] Miguel Ángel Asturias's *El Señor Presidente,* which was published in 1946, and deemed by García Márquez an 'awful' novel, is generally considered to be a classic of the genre.[22] It shares with *The Autumn of the Patriarch* a focus on the link between information (more specifically knowing, *saber,* in García Márquez) and power. The all-encompassing web of informants of the President (modelled on Guatemala's Manuel Estrada Cabrera) is echoed by that developed by the Patriarch's torturer-dandy Ignacio Saenz de la Barra. What is also interesting is the parallel between the political power of the dictator and Asturias's extraordinary manipulation of information within the novel, entrapping the reader in its web, and complemented by the strutting display of the new avant-garde literary techniques on parade there. The 1952 short novel, or 'poema satírico', *El Gran Burundún-Burundá ha muerto* (*Big Burundún-Burundá Has Died,* editor's translation) by García Márquez's fellow Colombian Jorge Zalamea offers important stylistic parallels with both *The Autumn of the Patriarch* and 'Big Mama's Funeral' ('Los funerales de la mamá grande').[23] The exuberant and surrealist linguistic virtuosity of the piece interacts intriguingly with the satirical political narrative. The extravagantly named dictator had subjected his republic by the force of his rhetoric until he was suddenly reduced to incoherent mumbling, whereupon he prohibited the use of language by his people. When his coffin is opened at the end of the funeral, it contains not his corpse but a parrot made entirely of printed material, which seems to have the effect of re-empowering the people: 'the mute people were terrified to feel the stubborn root of speech rising in their guts to scream screams of amazement and reproach and refusal and horror.'[24]

The Autumn of the Patriarch was published in the year following the appearance of two dictatorship novels by major writers, *El recurso del método* (*Reasons of State*) by Alejo Carpentier and *Yo el Supremo* (*I the Supreme*) by Augusto Roa Bastos, in 1974, and in the same year as Carlos Fuentes's *Terra Nostra*. The novels of the Cuban and the Colombian feature dictator-figures who are a compendium of various historical leaders, while that of Roa Bastos focuses firmly on the regime of José Gaspar Rodríguez de Francia in Paraguay (1814–40). Carpentier's is an urbane and witty novel, an ironic satire of a Primer Magistrado, who has, surprisingly, many of the features of Carpentier himself. Intertextual right from the Cartesian title through a pastiche of Proust in the first paragraph, it has the Magistrate citing Renan verbatim to the discomfiture of the French Ambassador. While intertextuality in *The Autumn of the Patriarch* is largely restricted to three significant figures, Rubén Darío, Christopher Columbus, and Petrarch on Julius Caesar, Roa Bastos's text engages not only with a wide range of writers from Rousseau to Raymond Roussel but also compiles and dialogues with a vast amount of historiography on the dictator Francia. Seymour Menton treats Roa Bastos's text as a paradigmatic Latin American 'new historical novel' while excluding *The Autumn of the Patriarch* on the grounds that some of the time period it covered was experienced directly by the author.[25] Menton makes the interesting point that whereas the classic nineteenth-century historical novels such as those of Walter Scott favoured by Lukács represented historical movements through decent, average characters rather than 'world-historical individuals', the Latin American new novel has centred on major historical figures such as Bolívar and Perón.

Perhaps the closest he comes to engagement with one major identifiable historical figure is the presence of Christopher Columbus, who was to figure in a series of subsequent novels, stimulated, according to Menton, by the approach of the 1992 quincentennial of Discovery. They include Carpentier's *El arpa y la sombra* (The Shadow and the Harp [1979]), Abel Posse's *Los perros del paraíso* (Dogs of Paradise [1987]), and Roa Bastos's 1992 text *Vigilia del Almirante* (*The Admiral's Vigil*, my translation). There are two major sorts of historical reference in the novel: the carnivalised anecdotes about Latin American dictators and the major currents of Latin American history: principally the emergence of *caudillos* from civil wars, and Spanish, English and North American imperialism. The figure of Columbus is of a different order, more emblematic and deeply symbolical.[26] In many ways he is the polar opposite figure to Rubén Darío, to whom Márquez described his novel as a 'homenaje'.[27] Columbus was the Spaniard who first occupied American lands in the island of Hispaniola, to continue, as Haiti and the Dominican Republic, the victim of constant despoliation by foreign powers, genocide and the tyranny of dictators. Columbus is mentioned regularly throughout *The Autumn of the Patriarch* often in the context of 'the gold spur on his left heel which had been given him by the admiral of the ocean sea so that he would wear it unto death as a sign of the highest authority'.[28] It is Columbus who invests the dictator with his power, and is a sort of maleficent Mequíades figure (the first reportedly dies from 'pellagra in Senegal', and the second from 'fevers in the swamps of Singapore'), who seems to embody a continental historical curse).[29] He is 'condemned to wander from sepulcher to sepulcher until the end of time because of the twisted fate of his expeditions'.[30] The historical reference is to debates about his remains and his burial in Santo Domingo, Havana and Seville, replicated in the three different birthplaces of the Patriarch but also suggests that the 'suerte torcida de sus empresas' is a phantasm not yet exorcised. Though revered by the Patriarch and approached with an apparently playful tone throughout, Márquez has said that Columbus shares with General Santander the role of the historical figures he most despises.[31] In a clever anachronism, the presence together in the sea before the windows of the presidential palace of the three caravels and the battleship of the North American occupying force points towards one aspect of his legacy for García Márquez.

Anachronism and inversion concerning Columbus are put to effective use in at least two other occasions. He is reported in rather magical-realist style as being seen dressed as a Franciscan in the capital (which Columbus did on various occasions), scouring the Caribbean for a cure for hair loss and charting islands while changing 'their old names of military men to the names of kings and saints'.[32] The most obvious reference here would be to the first city of Latin America, originally Santo Domingo, but renamed for a time Ciudad Trujillo. A second, brilliant sequence has received much critical attention. This is a parodic reworking of Columbus's Diary entries for 12 and 13 October 1492 using Columbus's words, but told from the point of view of the savvy natives, who are at once naked and painted and yet able to comment in modern Latin American Spanish on the strangeness of fifteenth-century Castilian. They marvel at the naivety of the Spaniards who do not know their paint to be sunscreen and agree out of mere amused condescension to change their own possessions for red carnival Sunday bonnets, beads and trinkets that they are fully aware cost a mere *maravedí* in Flanders.

Just as Columbus is at once a presence of profound dread and a figure of fun, García Márquez approaches the horrors and idiosyncrasies of the dictators who go to make up the Patriarch. Fuentes describes this well in his chapter on *The Autumn of the Patriarch* in *Valiente mundo Nuevo* (*Brave New World*): 'they are the tragicomic defects that I have evoked here with a grimace of bitter joy' ('un rictus de alegría amarga').[33] What Benedetti and others dismissed as incredible, self-indulgent fantasy or, in Spanish, 'desmesura', becomes, according to the reader's knowledge of Latin American history, a knowing and telling 'grimace of bitter joy' at the reality of very real Latin American republics for much of the twentieth century.[34] The combination of different sorts of temporality in the novel is testing for readers and critics alike. A mythical feeling of timelessness is created around a set of outlandish and hyperbolic episodes: the roasting and serving up for dinner of a plotting general (echoing the fate of the children of Thyestes, served up to their father by his brother Atreus), the dynamiting of 2,000 children, the vanishing of a beauty queen during a solar eclipse, the removal of the sea in numbered lots by a foreign power. Internal chronology is vague and self-referential: the Patriarch is presumed to live between 107 and 232 years, certainly seeing 'the comet' pass twice (Halley's Comet passed in 1834 and 1910), and though precise days and months are usually specified, no years are ever mentioned. Historical periods are the time of the plague, of the comet, of the noise, and so forth. Readers with some historical knowledge will pick out the details of the canny weaving together of strands of documented history.

The Patriarch arrives in his palace in a Caribbean city variously identified as Santo Domingo and Cartagena de Indias as the victor of a bloody civil war but is also seen to have been installed by the English who have deposed the 'illustrious Latinist' President Lautaro Muñoz, the last in a line of fourteen federalist generals. Such generic circumstances could point to the period around 1830 after the great liberators and statesmen such as Bolívar, Sucre, Rivadavia and O'Higgins gave way to a wave of major *caudillos* well adapted to the turbulent times, such as Rosas, Páez, Santa Anna and Francia, or the rapid succession of horrific characters such as Belzú and Melgarejo in Bolivia. Internal details, however, and García Márquez's own testimony suggest that the Patriarch is based on dictators, mainly from Central America and the Caribbean, from the late nineteenth century to around 1960. The Patriarch expelled the Church and confiscated all its properties after the Papal Envoy uncovered the fabrication of evidence behind the bid for the canonisation of his mother Bendición Avarado, only to have the priests and religious orders return with a vengeance at the will of his ex-novice wife Leticia Nazareno. History provides a model for the expulsion in similar action by Antonio Guzmán Blanco in Venezuela (1870–89). Just as the Patriarch swept down to the coast from the *páramo* (a kind of bleak upland), Cipriano Castro (1899–1908) was the first of a series of fierce and rough leaders from the highlands of Táchira to fight their way into Caracas and to tyrannise Venezuela until 1945. The figure and the regime (1908–35) of Juan Vicente Gómez provide some of the main material for the novel. Like the Patriarch, he was thought to have almost supernatural powers of intuition. The eighty children he was said to have sired become 5,000 in the novel. Allegedly he feigned death at one stage to gauge his support and take violent retribution, which is what happens in the novel after the death of Patricio Aragonés, the Patriarch's double. The Patriarch's humiliating incontinence reflects the uremia suffered by Gómez towards the end of his life, and also by Trujillo, otherwise notorious for his obsessive pulchritude. At the end of the regimes of both Gómez and the Patriarch, though both had little active involvement in public affairs, the system continued with its own deathly momentum, and the people, who had almost forgotten how to assert their own opinions, could hardly believe in the reality of their deaths. Another particularly durable dictator, the Guatemalan Manuel Estrada Cabrera (1898–1920), fares less well than the Patriarch in similar circumstances. When the Senate declares him insane, he bombards the capital but is captured and deposed, whereas the Patriarch survives to have the instigator of the plot to have him interned in his own asylum, General Rodrigo de Aguilar, roasted and served for dinner to his fellow conspirators.

Many historical incidents are incorporated to build up an atmosphere of fascinated horror. Haitian Doctor Duvalier, Papa Doc, allegedly had all the black dogs in his country killed to account for an enemy who had turned into a dog to escape his persecution.[35] The Patriarch, conversely, has scruples about killing the dogs which have eaten his wife Leticia and his son. The Patriarch, like the Salvadorean theosophist-dictator Hernández Martínez, had the street lamps clad with red paper to combat an outbreak of measles. Márquez himself complained during the writing that his text has an insatiable appetite for gobbling up enormous amounts of anecdotic material, which helps to account for its rather overwhelming and relentless rhythm. He wrote his novel while living in Spain, and his sheer sense of incredulity at the duration of Franco's regime (1939–75), which he came to fear was 'an experiment in eternity', is expressed in the oxymoronic final line of the novel: 'the uncountable time of eternity had come to an end.'[36]

The history of the Dominican Republic also provides much significant material. The horrors of the regime of Rafael Trujillo (1930–61), born a poor mulatto and trained by the American marines, are present not only in the pages of *The Autumn of the Patriarch* but in numerous other novels, most memorably in Manuel Vázquez Montalbán's *Galíndez* (1990) and Mario Vargas Llosa's *La fiesta del Chivo* (*The Feast of the Goat* [2000]). The Dominican Republic provides probably the most dramatic staging of imperialist intervention in Latin America echoed in the novel: the occupation of the republic by the North American Marines. Officially this was to combat the yellow fever but was in fact designed to shore up Trujillo's regime and to organise his secret services, in the face of the regime's crippling indebtedness, leading to an endless cession of national resources. Such an intervention culminates expressionistically in this novel with the removal of the sea to the Arizona desert, the equivalent to the cataclysmic rains brought on by the Compañía Bananera, the United Fruit Company, in *One Hundred Years of Solitude*. It was Buenaventura Báez, who, around 1870, proposed the annexation of the republic to the USA and also the leasing of the Bay of Samaná.[37] In 1905, Theodore Roosevelt occupied Santo Domingo and took over all its custom houses to settle foreign claims against Dominican debts and governed the country until 1924. General Rafael Leónidas Trujillo took power by a coup in 1930, and many of the aspects of his regime are reproduced in the novel: the 1930 hurricane and his efficacy in rebuilding the country, his brutality in massacring thousands of Haitian settlers, his provision of asylum to many fallen Latin American dictators, such as Pérez Jiménez in 1958. According to John Edwin Fagg, 'improbable "accidents" and "suicides" removed inconvenient persons'.[38] Shortly after the Patriarch took power, his rival generals all fell foul to such accidents. His servants came to give him the 'news' (as if he had no knowledge of the event), 'con la novedad mi general', that General Jesucristo Sánchez had contracted rabies and had been beaten to death with chairs by his staff; that General Narcisco, embarrassed by his incurable pederasty, had 'shoved a dynamite stick up his ass and blown his guts out'; and so on.[39] Trujillo's son, the infamous 'Ramfis', like that of the Patriarch, was made a general from his earliest years. Like the Patriarch, Trujillo attempted to have his mother canonised, a case also reminiscent of Eva Perón after her death in 1952.

The historicity of the events described above, however, is blurred or relativised by their redeployment and combination, and by carnivalisation, parody and hyperbole, which for some readers might muffle their reality. The literary structure of the novel is similarly complex and paradoxical. The major stages of the Patriarch's life are recounted in chronological order, but this order is contested by a pronounced circularity in the framing of chapters and, as in *One Hundred Years of Solitude*, brilliant use of anachronic techniques such as analepsis and prolepsis. All the characters which define the temporal stages in the Patriarch's life are marked by the closure of death or disappearance: Patricio Aragonés, Rodrigo de Aguilar, Manuela Sánchez,

Bendición Alvarado, Leticia Nazareno and Saenz de la Barra. Scenes of condensation, however, suddenly bring the whole temporal span of the novel into focus, as when we see in the presidential garage a series of vehicles that embody important stages in his regime, from the vice-regal carriage to the funereal car with the Positivistic motto 'progress in order', announcing the power of Saenz de la Barra many chapters later.[40]

Prolepsis, as ever in García Márquez, creates a sense of inevitability, formalised here by an internal prediction, as it was in *One Hundred Years of Solitude* by the family curse of the pig-tailed child and the manuscript of Melquíades. Here the prediction is that of the pythoness, the soothsayer who told the Patriarch that he would be found dead in a certain position in his plain cotton uniform. It is interesting to note that the authority of the prediction is almost immediately undermined. Though we read that the Patriarch killed the pythoness straight away so that nobody else would know, many characters clearly do know, which suggests a radical unreliability in the narrative voice even in metatextual or key moments. The framing of the six chapters of the novel initially gives an impression of repetitive circularity, and temporal stagnation. Whereas in *One Hundred Years of Solitude* this circularity was achieved by repetition of character traits and episodes over time, here the effect is narrative repetition of one (or two) episodes: the death and lying in state of the Patriarch (and his double). All the chapters begin with reference to the circumstances of the body, and all but the two middle chapters end similarly. Typically the first and last chapters reflect each other with a nice chiasmus. The first begins with the corpse of the Patriarch in his plain cotton uniform, 'uniforme de lienzo sin insignias', and ends with a description of the state funeral of a corpse (of Patricio) seen as decidedly androgynous, with reference to his 'body of a military stud' and 'hard hands of a dauntless young lady'.[41] The final chapter begins with a similar description of the Patriarch at his funeral, his 'feminine splendour of a dead pope amidst the flowers', and ends with the discovery of his corpse.[42]

The symmetry is of course flawed and highly unstable. The literary artifice is echoed in the fabrication of evidence by not only the Patriarch but also by some of his people, who stage the finding of the corpse to make it coincide with the prediction. The mythical pattern created by the narrative corresponds to a powerful official version of the regime for its political supporters. There is a similar complicity between the character's revision of their memories and narrative patterning in *Chronicle of a Death Foretold*. The Patriarch arranged the corpse of Patricio and 'reproduced the perfection down to the tiniest details that he had seen with his own eyes in the premonitory waters of the basins', while in Chapter 5 one group complains that 'we had not yet managed to make the corpse look like its legendary image'.[43] This, 'we' voice is interesting. At the end of the chapter we read, 'he lied down on his front ... in his coarse cotton uniform ... just as we would find him'.[44] The 'we' either belongs to a different group of people or to the same group of people but who lie on one occasion. The irony is once again stressed when at the end of the novel the Patriarch loses an argument with Death herself about exactly how he would be dressed in his final instants. This whole sequence is a good example of the way in which the text almost simultaneously constructs and dismantles structure and truth.

Some critics have chosen to resolve such movements dialectically, but the resolutions may well be another simulacrum like the television programmes devised solely to conform to the fantasies and desires of the terminally decrepit Patriarch, or the image of the dictator on coins, stamps, lithographs, copies of an original which his people had never seen. The very notion of the simulacrum is unstable, as we see, to take one example, in the relation between the Patriarch and his near-homonym and double Patricio. Patricio Aragonés (already an uncanny echo of Prudencio Aguilar) makes his appearance in the novel when found supplanting the president on a 'false presidential coach'.[45] The carriage is reminiscent of that on which Fernanda del Carpio appears as a rival carnival queen to supplant the already crowned Remedios la Bella, and the web becomes even more bizarre when both Patriarch and Patricio are presented as being in love with a carnival queen. When Patricio confesses his painful love for the queen, his master allows him free run of the presidential concubines, but forgetting the women were just on loan he would 'linger over details' and absentmindedly make even the tightest of women climax.[46] When, later in the novel, the Patriarch falls in love with the adolescent beauty queen Manuela Sánchez, the description of his sex with his concubines is repeated very nearly verbatim.[47] Whereas in *One Hundred Years of Solitude* the confusion between Aureliano Segundo and José Arcadio Segundo is a game resolved with relative ease, here there seems to be real unknowability.

The tensions we see here are deeply embedded in the rhythm of the prose of the novel, indeed between the rhythms of poetry and prose. The careful, knowing structure, such as the framing of chapters, provided by a controlling author, contains a rapid succession of individual voices, often contradicting each other, some of whom, but by no means all, can be identified. Repetition of tropes and syntactical structures gives an impression of homogeneity but harbours chaos. In this it is reminiscent of the Pablo Neruda of *Residencia en la tierra* (*Residence on Earth*): 'Como cenizas, como mares poblándose' ('Like ashes, like seas being populated').[48] The polysyndeton creates syntactic symmetry but contains semantically irreconcilable elements. A melancholy unity of tedium and novelty is generated by the litany of over thirteen variations on the trope 'dragging his great feet of an elephant walking in the snow' or 'arrastrando sus grandes patas de elefante en la nieve'; 'his thick feet of a captive monarch'.[49] Typically, page-long sequences, such as that beginning 'his mother of my heart Bendición Alvarado to whom the school texts attributed', held together by a succession of source of statement-verb of statement-statement and a hypnotic modulation of conjunctions (and, neither, or), will hold together an incredible swirl of anecdotes, speakers, and attitudes.[50]

In a rather wild and risky aesthetic which Canfield describes in terms of Barthesian *jouissance*, Márquez combines conventionally incompatible contents, often focusing on the scatological.[51] The Patriarch's mother watches his generals shitting in the alabaster amphorae more at home in an exotic sonnet by his favorite poet, Rubén Darío, claiming they are portable toilets.[52] Orality and anality are shuffled: 'there comes my ever-loving general giving off crap through his mouth and laws through his poop'.[53] So are anality and genital sexuality, together with tender care and grotesque physicality: Leticia Nazareno 'moved aside the herniated testicle to clean him up from the last lovemaking's dinky-poo.'[54] Senile impotence and 'biblical' sodomitic power alternate as the Patriarch is left cold by the most expensive and beautiful imported whores, but on glimpsing a palace washerwoman, 'he turned her face down on the laundry table and planted her from behind with a biblical drive that the poor woman felt in her soul with the crunch of death.'[55] Within the field of truth and power, power and powerlessness, knowing and not knowing are insistently confused. The Patriarch seems simultaneously to know and not know. Often he explicitly advises his henchmen that he knows nothing of the atrocities he in fact sanctions; sometimes he knows nothing of the manipulations of others, especially Rodrigo de Aguilar; sometimes his secret thoughts or fears seem to be omnipotent orders, as when he thinks that he can no longer stand the tension of wondering whether his wife and child will be murdered, and they are instantly reported devoured by a pack of hounds. It is, however, often impossible to decide. One clear case is the question of the miraculous incorruptibility of the corpse of Bendición Alvarado which leads to his call for her canonisation. The web of historical allusion, genuine popular fervour, commercial interests, political manipulation of the people, and filial devotion is formidable, hence the oxymoronic sequence (which is ironed out a little in the English translation): 'a carnival apparatus that he himself had put together without really thinking about it ... a circus trick which he had fallen into himself without knowing it.'[56]

The persistent association between excrement and the higher faculties in the Patriarch is extended to the archetypal Latin American poet whom he idolises: Rubén Darío.[57] As in César Vallejo's '*Trilce* I', *guano* is transmuted into gold through verbal alchemy, but stubbornly also remains shit. The Patriarch hears Darío declaim the 'Marcha triunfal' and 'Responso a Verlaine', which he later uses as his nightly prayer, and hears 'Sonatina' recited by a beggar. He envies Darío's powerful language: his was a real procession, far grander than any convoked by the Patriarch's puny authority. He muses on the mystery of how 'it is possible for this Indian to write something so beautiful with the same hand that he wipes his ass with'.[58] The language and condition of the dictator and the poet are superimposed. Fuentes instinctively picks up on this: 'Thus language is the common origin of literature and power. The genius of Gabriel García Márquez in *The Autumn of the Patriarch* consists in participating, with pathos, in this greatness and this servitude: what serves to free us also serves to subjugate us.'[59] Darío himself wrote not only the Spanish Americanist 'Salutación del optimista' ('Salutation of the Optimist', editor's translation), but also the pro-Yankee 'Salutación al águila' ('Salutation to the Eagle', editor's translation). Darío and Columbus are the emblematic figures of Latin America in the novel, poet and man of (fractured) power. They do not meet, but one wonders whether, thinking of the 'suerte torcida' (or 'twisted fate', editor's translation) of Columbus's New World enterprise, Márquez did not have in mind Darío's poem 'A Colón' ('To Columbus', editor's translation), the last stanza of which is:

> Duelos, espantos, guerras, fiebre constante
> en nuestra senda ha puesto la suerte triste:
> ¡Cristóforo Colombo, pobre Almirante,
> ruega a Dios por el mundo que descubriste!
>
> (A sad fate has placed in our path
> mourning, horrors, wars, constant fever:
> Cristoforo Colombo, poor old Admiral,
> pray to God for the world you discovered!)[60]

Towards the end of his life, however, in 1915, Darío accepted the hospitality in Guatemala of Manuel Estrada Cabrera. In 1999, Jon Lee Anderson wrote a long report entitled 'The Power of Gabriel García Márquez', portraying the writer as a wielder of international power, an honest broker between heads of states in Latin America and the USA. While they seek out his company, he is fascinated by their power.[61] García Márquez is a friend of Fidel Castro and Bill Clinton. The erstwhile dictator of Panama, General Oscar Torrijos, who rather than losing a sea, regained control of the Panama Canal, said to his friend Gabo forty-eight hours before his death: 'Your best book is *The Autumn of the Patriarch* ... we are all like you say.'[62] Anderson quotes another of his friends: '[Gabo] likes diplomacy, not politics. He says he is *un gran conspirador.*'[63] Fidel Castro, on reviewing his 2002 autobiography *Living to Tell the Tale* (*Vivir para contarla*), wrote: 'I share with him a scandalous theory, which is probably *sacrilegious* for academies and doctors of philosophy, about the relativity of the words of our language.'[64] Power and truth in *The Autumn of the Patriarch* are certainly political, as well as relative, but not the politics readily caught by dialectics or semiotics, by Marxism or deconstruction, but of diplomacy and conspiracy, struggle and strategy. As a Caribbean Nietzsche might have said: 'nada de eso importaba, carajo, ya verán que con el tiempo será verdad'; 'none of that mattered, God damn it, they'll see that with time it will be the truth.'[65]

NOTES

1. Gabriel García Márquez, '*El otoño del patriarca*', in *El olor de la guayaba,* Barcelona: Bruguera, 1982, pp. 122, 123, 127. All translations from the Spanish, except from *The Autumn of the Patriarch,* are my own.
2. García Márquez, *El olor de la guayaba,* pp. 117–18.
3. Gabriel García Márquez, *The Autumn of the Patriarch,* trans. Gregory Rabassa, London: Jonathan Cape, 1977, pp. 44–5.
4. González Bermejo, *Cosas de escritores,* Montevideo: Biblioteca de Marcha, 1971, p. 33.
5. García Márquez, *The Autumn of the Patriarch,* pp. 164, 164, 195.
6. García Márquez, *The Autumn of the Patriarch,* p. 57. The Spanish is 'chapaleando en las tortas de boñiga de la oscuridad', *El otoño del patriarca,* Barcelona: Plaza y Janés, 1975, p. 71.
7. García Márquez, *The Autumn of the Patriarch,* p. 211.
8. García Márquez, *The Autumn of the Patriarch,* p. 132.
9. Michael Bell, 'The Magical and the Banal: *The Autumn of the Patriarch*', in *Gabriel García Márquez: Solitude and Solidarity,* London: Macmillan, 1993.
10. Patricia Tobin, 'The Autumn of the Signifier: The Deconstructionist Moment of García Márquez', *Latin American Literary Review,* 13 (25) (1985): 65–78; p. 72.
11. Tobin, 'The Autumn of the Signifier', p. 73.
12. Roberto González Echevarría, *The Voice of the Masters,* Austin, TX: University of Texas Press, 1985, pp. 64–85.
13. Gerald Martin, 'On Dictatorship and Rhetoric in Latin American Writing: A Counter-Proposal', *Latin American Research Review,* 17 (3) (1982): 207–27; p. 216.
14. Martin, 'On Dictatorship', p. 226.
15. García Márquez, *The Autumn of the Patriarch,* p. 88. Also Gabriel García Márquez, *Cien años de soledad,* Buenos Aires: Sudamericana, 1970, p. 129.
16. García Márquez, *Cien años de soledad,* p. 141.
17. Gabriel García Márquez, *El general en su laberinto*, Madrid: Mondadori, 1989, p. 203.
18. Jo Labanyi, 'Language and Power in *El otoño del patriarca*', in Bernard McGuirk and Richard Cardwell (eds.), *Gabriel García Márquez: New Readings,* Cambridge: Cambridge University Press, 1987, pp. 135–50, p. 147.
19. García Márquez, *El general en su laberinto,* pp. 228.

20. Cited in McGuirk and Cardwell, *Gabriel García Márquez,* p. 211.
21. Roberto Yahni, in his introduction to Domingo Faustino Sarmiento, *Facundo,* Madrid: Cátedra, 1999, p. 16.
22. García Márquez, *El olor de la guayaba,* p. 118.
23. Adriana Sandoval, *Los dictadores y la dictadura en la novela hispanoamericana, 1851–1978,* Mexico City: UNAM, 1989, p. 45.
24. Jorge Zalamea, *El Gran Burundún-Burundá ha muerto,* Bogotá: Carlos Valencia, 1979, pp. 88–9.
25. Seymour Menton, *Latin America's New Historical Novel,* Austin, TX: University of Texas Press, 1993, pp. 198–9.
26. I take most of my information on Columbus in the novel from Michael Palencia-Roth, *Gabriel García Márquez: la línea, el círculo y las metamorfosis del mito,* Madrid: Gredos, 1983, pp. 191–201, and Graciela Palau de Nemes's excellent early study '*El otoño del patriarca:* historicidad de la novela', *Hispamérica,* 4 (11–12) (1975): 173–83.
27. Cited in Palencia-Roth, *Gabriel García Márquez,* p. 201.
28. García Márquez, *Autumn of the Patriarch,* p. 150.
29. García Márquez, *Autumn of the Patriarch,* p. 218; García Márquez, *Cien años de soledad,* p. 22.
30. García Márquez, *Autumn of the Patriarch,* p. 218. In the original, 'la suerte torcida de sus empresas' (*García Márquez, El otoño del patriarca,* p. 258).
31. García Márquez, *Autumn of the Patriarch,* p. 218.
32. García Márquez, *Autumn of the Patriarch,* p. 217.
33. Carlos Fuentes, 'García Márquez: la figura del poder', in *Valiente mundo nuevo,* Mexico City: Fondo de Cultura Económica, 1990, pp. 194–212, p. 204.
34. Mario Benedetti, *El recurso del supremo patriarca,* Mexico City: Nueva Imagen, 1979, p. 19.
35. Cited in Palencia-Roth, *Gabriel García Márquez,* p. 173.
36. Cited in Palencia-Roth, *Gabriel García Márquez,* p. 179.
37. Bolivia also disastrously lost its sea in 1884 as a consequence of ruinous negotiations by Melgarejo and defeat at Chilean hands in the War of the Pacific.
38. John Edwin Fagg, *Latin America: A General History,* London: Macmillan, 1977, p. 594. I have taken much of my information on historical Latin American dictators from this source.
39. García Márquez, *The Autumn of the Patriarch,* p. 59.
40. García Márquez, *The Autumn of the Patriarch,* p. 2; in the original: 'progreso dentro del orden', García Márquez, *El otoño del patriarca,* p. 6.
41. García Márquez, *The Autumn of the Patriarch,* pp. 24.
42. García Márquez, *The Autumn of the Patriarch,* pp. 184.
43. García Márquez, *The Autumn of the Patriarch,* pp. 23, 141. This is my translation. The Rabassa rendition is wrong and misleading: 'we were still unable to tell if' (p. 141).
44. García Márquez, *The Autumn of the Patriarch,* p. 216.
45. García Márquez, *The Autumn of the Patriarch,* p. 8.
46. García Márquez, *The Autumn of the Patriarch,* p. 11.
47. García Márquez, *The Autumn of the Patriarch,* p. 74.
48. Pablo Neruda, 'Galope muerto', in *Residencia en la tierra,* Buenos Aires: Losada, 1969, p. 9.

49. García Márquez, *The Autumn of the Patriarch*, pp. 7, 182.
50. García Márquez, *The Autumn of the Patriarch*, p. 40.
51. See Martha Canfield's outstanding article 'El Patriarca de García Márquez: padre, poeta y tirano', *Revista Iberoamericana*, 50, 128–9 (1984): 1017–56. This is one of the most useful studies of *The Autumn of the Patriarch*.
52. García Márquez, *The Autumn of the Patriarch*, p. 46.
53. García Márquez, *The Autumn of the Patriarch*, p. 66; in the original: 'echando caca por la boca y leyes por la popa', *El otoño del patriarca*, (p. 81).
54. García Márquez, *The Autumn of the Patriarch*, p. 147.
55. García Márquez, *The Autumn of the Patriarch*, p. 224; in the original, 'la sembró al revés con un ímpetu bíblico que' (*El otoño del patriarca*, p. 266).
56. García Márquez, *The Autumn of the Patriarch*, p. 129; in the original, 'un aparato de farándula que él montó sin proponérselo ... un engaño de circo en el cual él mismo había incurrido sin saberlo' (*El otoño del patriarca* p. 155).
57. See Martha Canfield's outstanding article 'El Patriarca de García Márquez: padre, poeta y tirano', *Revista Iberoamericana*, 50 (128–9) (1984): 1017–56, especially pp. 1039–44 and 1053–6. I have found this one of the most useful studies of *The Autumn of the Patriarch*.
58. García Márquez, *The Autumn of the Patriarch*, p. 163.
59. Fuentes, 'García Márquez: la figura del poder', p. 202.
60. Rubén Darío, *El canto errante*, in *Poesías completas*, Madrid: Aguilar, 1968, p. 704.
61. Jon Lee Anderson, 'The Power of Gabriel García Márquez', *New Yorker*, 27 September 1999, available online at www.themodernword.com/gabo/gabo_power.html (accessed 11 February 2010).
62. García Márquez, *El olor de la guayaba*, p. 124.
63. Jon Lee Anderson, 27 September 1999, *New Yorker*, available online at www.themodernword.com/gabo/gabo_power.html (accessed 11 February 2010).
64. Fidel Castro Ruiz, 'La novela de sus recuerdos', in *Granma*, 9 December 2002.
65. García Márquez, *The Autumn of the Patriarch*, pp. 173; in the original Spanish, *El otoño del patriarca*, p. 145.

7

GERALD MARTIN

The General in His Labyrinth

Two central ideas guide this essay. Firstly, *The General in His Labyrinth* (*El general en su laberinto* [1989]), while not perhaps the most important of Gabriel García Márquez's novels, is nevertheless a culmination of his career as a writer, a kind of compact *summa:* not only because it is a literary biography of Latin America's greatest historical icon by a man himself unusually famous and always intrigued by failed heroes, but also because, typologically, it is the book which contains the largest number of different themes and trademark elements which may be identified, in variable degrees, in those other works by García Márquez that preceded and succeeded it. Second, death and burial are perhaps the most compelling and enduring of these central themes that shape García Márquez's writing, just as they shape life itself, and therefore it was particularly appropriate that the Colombian novelist should concentrate on the events leading up to the death of the Great Liberator after so successfully bringing him to life.

García Márquez's road to *The General in His Labyrinth*

Many critics have noticed the way in which an apparently limited set of themes and motifs seem to recur obsessively throughout García Márquez's novels and stories, as if he were constantly harking back to some initial trauma or traumas; or as if, on the contrary, he were constantly trying to write some definitive work of which the actually achieved texts are mere approximations forever doomed, *avant la lettre,* to permanent reiteration. The most obvious and perhaps the most tenacious of these obsessive foundational themes, shorn of their Latin American specificity and of the compensatory emotional and aesthetic satisfactions of the so-called 'magical realism' through which they are filtered, seem to be solitude, power and death.

Needless to say, each of these themes is the nucleus of an entire cluster of related motifs, and each reader and critic would identify and organise them somewhat differently; equally, each of the themes implies a relation of contrast or contradiction to its opposite – solitude against community (or socialism, or love); power against vulnerability (or victimhood, or injustice); and death against life (or creativity, or art). One might also venture to say that, in the works produced during the first half of his career (of which more below), García Márquez tended more to the diagnostic and the condemnatory, whilst in the second half (after the responsibilities of the Nobel Prize settled on his shoulders), he tended more to the exhortatory and the curative. But again these are just emphases.

Both García Márquez's life and his works fall into two chronological halves, with a disjuncture that has often confused his critics and biographers. The first half seems to end with the incomparable *One Hundred Years of Solitude* (*Cien años de soledad* [1967]), a world-historical novel published when the author had just reached forty, and it completes a cycle of works which began with the unpublished 'The House', a book he began in the late 1940s and never managed to finish, though his first published novel *Leaf Storm* (*La hojarasca* [1955]) is the most direct chip off that old – or, rather, youthful – block, and *One Hundred Years of Solitude* itself is the final resolution and consummation of the writer's obsession with his painful yet magical childhood, the small town of Aracataca (Macondo) where he was born and where he spent the first decade of his life, and his memories of his grandfather's house in which he lived as a boy. Curiously, after *One Hundred Years of Solitude,* though most readers have not noticed it, Macondo never appears in García Márquez's oeuvre again. (Neither do colonels.)

Yet in reality, although *One Hundred Years of Solitude* is the book that brought him fame, wealth and even glory unparalleled in the history of Latin American literature, and is coincidentally the novel which, more than any other, is seen as the most important metaphor for the continent's history and identity – hence the frequency with which its author is compared to Cervantes – the end of the first half of García Márquez's own creative cycle can more convincingly be identified with the writing of *The Autumn of the Patriarch* (*El otoño del patriarca* [1975]) between 1967 and 1974. In that work, which he considered a self-portrait, the central themes of solitude, power and death, whilst by no means exhausted as far as García Márquez's later writing and publishing were concerned, reach an early and in some ways definitive climax.

The writer himself may well have seen things this way because after the publication of *The Autumn of the Patriarch* he took a long sabbatical from creative writing and turned to political activism and political journalism between 1974 and 1980, making his notorious vow that he would not write another novel until General Pinochet fell from power in Chile after overthrowing Salvador Allende in 1973. Pinochet did not fall from power, and the political panorama went from bad to worse when viewed from the standpoint of a lifelong socialist such as García Márquez. Thus, in 1981, having frustrated his readers for what seemed to them like an eternity, the writer, by now an international celebrity and a living legend in Latin America, published a new novel, *Chronicle of a Death Foretold* (*Crónica de una muerte anunciada*), with an extraordinary fanfare of publicity all over the continent, unveiling in the process a style still recognisably 'Garciamarquian' but no longer 'magical realist' in any significant way and with none of *The Autumn of the Patriarch*'s 'modernist' impediments to reader accessibility or, indeed, to sales. Given the violence of this new novel's central episode, a brutal murder, it was not at first evident to most critics (though our table of contents shows that it was evident to the perspicacious editor of the present *Cambridge Companion to García Márquez*) that the novel was not only a love story – over the dead body of its hapless protagonist, so to speak – but a love story with an outcome not far removed from a possible happy ending: something which would have been inconceivable in earlier works by this author. Until that time, love had been treated in the same fashion as Colombia itself (Colombia viewed as the microcosmic reflection of Latin America's traumatic experience of history): as a source of continual disillusionment at best and calamitous failure at worst. Hence the theme of solitude: an apparently anthropological curse in the case of human beings and a disturbingly persistent historical curse in the case of Latin America itself.

In 1982, García Márquez was awarded the Nobel Prize for Literature. Even before it he had begun a second novel about love, and this time with that previously proscribed word in the title: *Love in the Time of Cholera* (*El amor en los tiempos del cólera*). This novel, when published in 1985, would repeat the dual achievement of *One Hundred Years of Solitude* by attaining extraordinary success both with literary critics and with the general reading public. Resonance with the critics was the more surprising because this novel set out to meet head-on a challenge scarcely attempted by any previous writer in the twentieth century: to flirt with the 'postmodernist' conventions of radio or television soap operas – which appeared in Latin America as early as the 1930s – by producing a major novel about love which would have, despite everything, an unequivocal happy ending. Love, then, was the grand new topic added to the primordial themes – solitude (its opposite), power and death – of the first half of García Márquez's creative cycle. We therefore have the intriguing phenomenon of a writer who emphasises solitude and death in the first half of his career and love and life in the second;

though, as we shall see, this is merely a question of emphasis, not a significant modification of what is in reality an essentially unchanging poetics.

On beginnings which are endings and on endings which either accept or deny 'the end'

This author's works constantly remind us that in life, as in novels and films, we are unceasingly *waiting for the end*. And the end can arrive when we least expect it: for example, at the start of several of this writer's books. (Of course almost everyone knows that death is an ever-present menace in García Márquez's fiction. What has been much less noticed is the persistence of the related theme of burial.)

'The Third Resignation' ('La tercera resignación'), García Márquez's first published work of prose fiction (1947), is a remarkable beginning. It has been almost entirely ignored by critics and yet it may be the most revealing of all the works written by García Márquez these past sixty years and may indeed constitute the emotional foundation of everything that has followed it. Although its analysis is beyond the scope of the present essay, it may be asserted that the story includes many of the themes explored by Freud in his most seminal essays – particularly those on the uncanny and on melancholy and mourning. Fear of death and postponement of death; fear of burial and postponement of burial; and solitude, abandonment and anxiety as defining features of life itself. Little wonder, then, that García Márquez should have gone furthest of all in dramatising defiance of the certainties of death (and the terrors of burial) in what will almost certainly be his last novel, *Memories of My Melancholy Whores* (*Memorias de mis putas tristes* [2004]).

Although clumsily written in a number of respects, 'The Third Resignation' already sounded something like 'García Márquez' and was strikingly ambitious. This, however, was a García Márquez influenced by Kafka, Dostoyevsky and Poe, a young man from the tropics writing in a cold – and cold-hearted – capital city from which he felt alienated and which, in effect, he would later exile from his work. The story is profoundly subjective, suffused with absurdity, solitude and death, and obsessed with the idea of being buried alive. In fact the narrator has three interconnected primordial terrors: the first of being buried oneself, whether dead or alive; the second of having to bury others; the third the ancestral terror of anyone remaining unburied:

> A dead man can be happy with his irremediable situation. But a living man cannot resign himself to being buried alive. Yet his limbs did not respond to his call. He could not express himself, and that was what inspired the terror in him; the greatest terror of his life and his death. They would bury him alive.[1]

Part of this terror appears to relate to the traditional Hispanic obsession with the soul's imprisonment within the body and the body's imprisonment within a house or a city – all underlined in this case by the fact that the narrator himself is effectively lying in a coma in an open coffin in a house in some undefined urban setting. (Before being born, of course, we are 'buried' inside our mother's womb, as the story reminds us: 'When he feels himself swimming in his own sweat, in a thick, viscous liquid, like he swam before he was born in his mother's womb'.) This first García Márquez is anguished, hyper-sensitive, neurasthenic – far from his later, carefully constructed image as the life-enhancing and heart-warming worker of literary miracles. He would use the stories he wrote between 1947 and 1950 to explore the literary modes of Kafka, Hemingway, Virginia Woolf and Faulkner before settling on the latter pair to begin his first novel in 1950.

That novel, *Leaf Storm* (1955), set in the small town of Macondo, begins, 'I've seen a corpse for the first time', and is narrated so to speak within sniffing distance of death ('The Third Resignation' shows a Freudian obsession with smell), ending half an hour after its start as the aforementioned corpse is carried away for burial. Three central characters reminisce about the dead man: one who knows his story, one who thinks she does but has it wrong, and one, a child, who knows almost nothing at all. The central problematic is that of Sophocles's *Antigone:* the duty the colonel takes upon himself to ensure that the corpse is decently buried in the face of hostility from the community in which he lives. (Of course a mature man of authority, the colonel, is hardly in the same position as Antigone, a helpless young woman.) Shortly before the end of the novel someone refers to 'that final wind ... that will sweep away Macondo, its bedrooms full of lizards and its silent people devastated by memories'.[2] And we realise now what García Márquez himself did not realise then, that he had found the apocalyptic ending to express the death and destruction of his fictional town Macondo, more than a decade in advance, in *One Hundred Years of Solitude.*

No One Writes to the Colonel (*El coronel no tiene quien le escriba* [published 1961]), with García Márquez now in neo-realist mode, begins with a funeral (read, burial), like *Leaf Storm,* and with a man, the colonel of the title, who attends the funeral but spends most of the novel endlessly waiting for one thing or another, above all for the pension the government is clearly never going to pay him:

> It was October. A difficult morning to get through, even for a man like himself, who had survived so many mornings like this one. For nearly sixty years – since the end of the last civil war – the colonel had done nothing else but wait. October was one of the few things which arrived.[3]

But of course, the colonel, at the age of seventy-six, is too old to be waiting for anything but death, though this is not in his conscious mind. We learn that the colonel's son was murdered as just one of the hundreds of thousands of victims of *la violencia* which began to ravage Colombia (not for the first time but this period was the worst) in the 1940s; that the colonel has been caring for his dead son's fighting cock, whose profession is of course killing; and that it has still not had its big fight by the end of the novel. The work ends memorably as his wife asks the stubborn protagonist what, since he refuses to sell the bird – evidently a symbol of resistance and of hope in the future – they can now expect to eat. García Márquez writes: 'It had taken the colonel seventy-five years – the seventy-five years of his life, minute by minute – to reach this moment. He felt pure, explicit, invincible at the moment when he replied: "Shit".'[4] (Which is, among other things, that which must be buried.) Thus is life paradoxically affirmed even in the midst of death and decay.

In general those who should not die – particularly sexually exploited young women – do die in García Márquez's novels, and those very old characters who might reasonably be expected to die do not. Thus the twelve year old protagonist of the later *Of Love and Other Demons* (*Del amor y otros demonios*), Sierva María, would die at the end of that novel, and fourteen-year-old América Vicuña commits suicide in *Love in the Time of Cholera,* while, like the colonel in *No One Writes to the Colonel* and Florentino Ariza in *Love in the Time of Cholera,* the ninety-year-old protagonist of *Memories of My Melancholy Whores* beats all the odds and has not been killed off by his author at the end of what will surely prove to be García Márquez's own last literary gesture of resistance.

The title of the story collection *Big Mama's Funeral* (*Los funerales de la mamá grande* [1962]) speaks for itself – this too is about a funeral – and so does its first sentence: 'This is, for all the world's unbelievers, the true account of Big Mama, absolute sovereign of the kingdom of Macondo, who lived for ninety-two years, and died in the odour of sanctity one Tuesday last September, and whose funeral was attended by the Pope.'[5] Once again, as in our first quotation from *No One Writes to the Colonel,* and as in so many works by Borges, a whole life has been contained and described – begun and ended – in a sentence. The story ends:

> The only thing left then was for someone to lean a stool against the doorway to tell this story, lesson and example for future generations, so that not one of the world's disbelievers would be left who did not know the story of Big Mama, because tomorrow, Wednesday, the garbage men will come and will sweep up the garbage from her funeral, forever and ever.[6]

Another ending, another corpse, another act of burial witnessed by literature (a corpse to be tidied away like shit or garbage) – by a storyteller – on behalf of the Latin American people, still waiting for justice and for some meaning to their existence which might go beyond the merely biological and anthropological.

In 1967, the year in which Miguel Ángel Asturias became the first Latin American novelist to win the Nobel Prize, and the year in which Che Guevara died in the mountains of Bolivia, the 'Boom' of the Latin American novel reached its climax with the showcasing of what was henceforth its most famous exhibit, *One Hundred Years of Solitude*, the emblematic work of so-called 'magical realism'. The novel's protagonist is facing a firing squad in the very first sentence, and the entire world of Macondo is swept away in the final, unforgettable lines. (What does this ending of endings mean? What did it mean to García Márquez in 1965, and what will it mean to future generations? Few literary corpses have been more bitterly fought over for their ideological legacies.)[7] The novel is by now so well known, of course, that its beginning and ending have entered the realm of the archetypal (the comparison with *Don Quixote* is unavoidable).

García Márquez could have written more Macondo novels after 1967 – there appeared to be an insatiable demand – but he, anxious to avoid mummification and exposure in some literary museum, set off in what was, at first sight, a quite different direction. Nonetheless, *The Autumn of the Patriarch* (1975) again begins with an unburied corpse discovered as the people of some unknown Latin American republic enter the presidential palace after the death (again it is merely apparent and illusory) of a dictator they were beginning to think was immortal. They have been waiting for him to die for almost 200 years. And of course the novel, circular as García Márquez's novels so often are, ends where it began: the corpse is found again, only this time it is the real one. The dictator is dead.

By this point in the trajectory, in one's own darker moments, one sometimes wonders whether these beginnings and endings are not merely tricks of the trade, gradually wearing thin, with a tragic poignancy and a dialectic of knowledge and delusion applicable sometimes to the mighty, sometimes to the impotent, and sometimes – as in *One Hundred Years of Solitude* – to both at one and the same time. Or is this, more positively, a writer exploring, exhaustively and obsessively, the world-view and the poetics which he glimpsed, with dramatic and exceptional depth and clarity, when he was little more than an adolescent? (Are we here to praise him or to bury him?)

Whatever the answer, it was a rather more sober García Márquez, who, with *Chronicle of a Death Foretold*, returned to small-town Colombia, to his own past and his own experience, in 1981. It is a work almost universally recognised as a brief literary masterpiece by a narrator who is without doubt the most popular Hispanic writer since the Spanish Golden Age, which the novel inevitably recalls – for this is Lope de Vega's *Fuenteovejuna* in reverse ('none of us is to blame'). *Chronicle of a Death Foretold* begins, 'The day they were going to kill him, Santiago Nasar got up at five-thirty in the morning.' In *One Hundred Years of Solitude* the reader had been at least as certain as here that the executioners of the firing squad would indeed kill the colonel, and the reader had been deceived; here we soon realise that this is a retrospective narration to end all retrospective narrations, and that this protagonist is indeed going to die, and the novel ends with the wretched character trying vainly to tidy away his own drooping intestines and collapsing as he finally reaches the refuge of his mother's kitchen. The horror of the uncovered entrails is an image in miniature of all the unburied corpses we find in García Márquez's other works, which may stand for all the brutally exposed corpses – some with testicles stuffed in their mouths – of the Colombian *la violencia* – or for the unassimilated traumas this incomparable writer was still trying to bury as he wrote this fearful work.

Love in the Time of Cholera (1985), set mainly in Cartagena de Indias, begins with a death, investigated and certified by one of the principal characters, a doctor who himself dies early in the novel (or maybe late in it, because this too is a completely circular book). García Márquez here gets fully into his belated postmodernist mode of soap-opera parody and melodrama, as when, after the doctor falls from a tree, his wife finds her man:

> lying on his back in the mud, dead to this life but still resisting death's final blow for one last minute so that she would have time to come to him. He recognized her despite the uproar, through his tears of unrepeatable sorrow at dying without her, and he looked at her for the last and final time with eyes more luminous, more grief-stricken, more grateful than she had ever seen them in half a century of a shared life, and he managed to say to her with his last breath: 'Only God knows how much I loved you.'[8]

His erstwhile rival for the wife's affections, Florentino Ariza, is present at the doctor's burial. The novel ends with the widow cruising on the river Magdalena with this same suitor who has loved her in vain and in pain for more than half a century:

> The captain looked at Fermina Daza and saw on her eyelashes the first glimmer of wintry frost. Then he looked at Florentino Ariza, his invincible power, his intrepid love, and he was overwhelmed by the belated suspicion that it is life, more than death, that has no limits.
>
> 'And how long do you think we can keep up this goddamn coming and going?', he asked.

> Florentino Ariza had kept his answer ready for fifty-three years, seven months, and eleven days and nights.
> 'Forever, ' he said.[9]

Needless to say, this is very like the conclusion given to *No One Writes to the Colonel* twenty-five years earlier, but sentimentally inverted by a writer now himself on the verge of old age.

The General in His Labyrinth

And so to *The General in His Labyrinth*, published in 1989, a novel written about Latin America's most famous and most glamorous historical figure of all time by perhaps its most celebrated novelist, dealing, perhaps predictably, with the Great Liberator's last journey towards his early death. It might indeed be called the 'Autumn of Another Patriarch', with much the same relation between author and character; or perhaps 'Seven Months of Solitude'. Power, solitude, death – here the great mythological themes of García Márquez's oeuvre unite in a portrait of a real historical personage, a work that no one would have expected yet which somehow seemed the most natural and predictable thing in the world once it was given form by the master narrator.

Although few would consider this work his grandest literary achievement, it is still, in my judgement, a very substantial one judged by the magnitude of the task and the probabilities of failure. What is more, it seems to me, as mentioned, the culmination of García Márquez's entire trajectory as a writer, not only the greatest challenge he ever confronted but the book somehow implicit in all the other great works of his historical trajectory: *No One Writes to the Colonel, One Hundred Years of Solitude* and the *Autumn of the Patriarch*. García Márquez, who admittedly has a tendency always to see his latest novel as his most important, said the same thing in another fashion shortly after the book appeared:

> *The General* has an importance greater than all the rest of my work. It shows that all my work corresponds to a geographical and historical reality. It isn't magical realism and all those things people say. When you read the Bolívar you realise that everything else has, in some way, a documental basis, a historical basis, a geographical basis which this novel demonstrates. It is like *The Colonel* again, but historically based. At bottom I have only written one book, which is the same one going round and round, and continuing.[10]

Though a significant minority of critics have argued that García Márquez's overweening sense of his own glory gets in the way of his presentation of Simón Bolívar – allegedly full of linguistic effects conceived as spectacle, like self-congratulatory fireworks, instead of the appropriate communication of Bolívar's own possible subjectivity, combined with a series of stock phrases and episodic structures whose true function is to draw attention to the García Márquez brand, with the novel as a mausoleum to the writer himself rather than its protagonist – it cannot be ignored that many other distinguished literary critics disagree and that some of the leading Bolivarian historians have expressed admiration for the novel. It would be interesting to know whether any of these have had their perception of the Liberator shifted or even transformed by the magic of the literary imagination.

The territory of the novel and its peculiar atmosphere are immediately familiar, as immediately recognisable as the tropical 'Graham Greene-land' of heat, vultures and hopelessness in which García Márquez's English friend and colleague so frequently immersed his readers. Just as *The Autumn of the Patriarch* begins with a presumption of death which is reminiscent of the real death with which *Love in the Time of Cholera* begins, *The General in His Labyrinth* begins with an image which suggests that Bolívar may have died, immersed – interred – in his bath. And just as *Love in the Time of Cholera* ends with an unmistakable reference, albeit inverted, to the conclusion of *No One Writes to the Colonel, The General in His Labyrinth* concludes with an actual death, that of Bolívar, which fuses the conclusion of *One Hundred Years of Solitude* with that of *The Autumn of the Patriarch*. As the General approaches his 'final objective', he murmurs – as Bolívar himself is said to have done – 'How can I escape from this labyrinth!' And the reader asks himself: what does this mean? If the labyrinth is life and all its woes, the answer seems obvious: death will release him. If the labyrinth is imminent death, then for the materialist pessimist which García Márquez appears to be, there is no escape at all from this final tight corner, except perhaps into the posthumous glory which Bolívar, by now, no longer believes it his destiny to enjoy.

All García Márquez's books after *One Hundred Years of Solitude* received levels of publicity previously unknown in Latin America, but in the mid to late 1980s the news that the Colombian – by now a Nobel Prize-winner – was writing a novel about Simón Bolívar was especially intriguing, not to say provoking. García Márquez, by then one of the best-known personalities in Latin America in any field of achievement, was already acknowledged as perhaps the closest friend of Cuban leader Fidel Castro – surely the best-known Latin American of the twentieth century – and now he had chosen to write a novel about the man who is generally considered the best-known and most influential Latin American in all of history: the Great Liberator. The ambition of the gesture seemed to confirm García Márquez's image among some sectors of Latin American society as arrogant and overbearing, and many critics were hoping that when the book appeared it would be both a critical and an economic failure. Such critics were to be confounded.

Like all Latin Americans, García Márquez had been aware of Bolívar's transcendent historical importance since his own childhood – he was born only 80 kilometres (50 miles) from where Bolívar had died almost a century before – but the idea of writing a book about the Liberator's last journey down the Magdalena river from Bogotá to Cartagena and Santa Marta – and from failure to death – was not his but rather that of his great friend and fellow novelist Álvaro Mutis. Moreover, there had been a novel published quite recently by another Colombian, Fernando Cruz Konfly, entitled *La ceniza del libertador* (*The Ash of the Liberator*, editor's translation [1987]), a somewhat fanciful but skilled and thought-provoking rewrite of Bolívar's story which fully deserved its prompt inclusion in Seymour Menton's well-known typology of Latin America's 'new historical novels'.[11]

When *The General in His Labyrinth* appeared, its acknowledgements, or 'Gratitudes', as García Márquez chose to call them, were to all manner of distinguished academics, diplomats and politicians. Among its very first reviewers were two ex-presidents of Colombia, Alfonso López Michelsen (Liberal) and Belisario Betancur (Conservative), also both friends of García Márquez. Fidel Castro (Communist) did not write a public review of the work, but he had read it even before his two Colombian colleagues. García Márquez had always said that he was intrigued and even obsessed by the theme of power – previously linked in his work to that of solitude – and one wonders if such intimate and yet multiple links between actually existing power and literature have existed anywhere else in the twentieth-century West. One doubts it the more because few other twentieth-century writers have been as famous and as powerful (read, influential) as García Márquez has since 1967.

The book was dedicated to Álvaro Mutis, who was in the process of becoming a major novelist towards the end of a long career as a poet. Mutis had written a story entitled 'El último rostro' ('The Last Face'), which he had subtitled 'Fragment', suggesting that it might have been intended as part of a novel. The story was about Bolívar's stay in Cartagena, in the Pie de la Popa district (where García Márquez's own family had lived when they arrived in the city in the early 1950s), shortly before his death, and was purportedly narrated by a Polish officer recently arrived from Europe. Mutis's classical sobriety makes an interesting contrast with García Márquez's bravura approach to narrative. As García Márquez recalls, Mutis had planned to write the novel García Márquez himself eventually wrote – charting the last months of Bolívar's life from the moment he left Bogotá on the 8 May

1830 until his death at a sugar mill outside Santa Marta on 17 December – but Mutis had put the story to one side and García Márquez asked permission to write it himself.

Bolívar's story spoke directly to García Márquez in many ways, above all to his much-debated identity as a Colombian and a Latin American. Circumstantially, as already mentioned, Bolívar died quite near to where García Márquez was born, and the future writer was taken to San Pedro Alejandrino, where the Great Liberator expired, by his beloved grandfather as a small boy; Bolívar's passage from Bogotá to Cartagena down the great Magdalena river is a journey which García Márquez himself made a number of times in both directions beginning with his trips to and from school in highland Zipaquirá as a teenager; Bolívar's rejection in 1830 by Bogotá, a city García Márquez, as a Caribbean *costeño,* always disliked, produced an inevitable identification (and indeed García Márquez himself was rejected quite aggressively by many *cachaco* – *bogotano* – critics when his novel appeared).

Bolívar's great adversary in Colombia, where Bolívar had been president, was Francisco de Paula Santander, traditionally considered the founder of the Colombian Liberal Party (to which García Márquez's grandfather Nicolás Ricardo Márquez was affiliated and for which he fought in the bloody War of a Thousand Days [1899–1902]), though the novelist suggests that Santander was really a political conservative and that Bolívar's thinking was so advanced that he was the true Liberal (albeit sobered by his reading of the outcome of the French Revolution, not least by Napoleon's self-aggrandisement and eventual authoritarianism) and that his thinking had some elements which were prophetic of socialism. In particular, Bolívar, like García Márquez and his friend Fidel Castro, advocated the unity of Spanish-speaking Latin America whereas Santander stands in García Márquez's mind for petty-minded regionalism, nationalism and, worst of all, the interests of the local post-independence oligarchies of the continent – specifically, in this case, the interests of the allegedly cold-hearted, perfidious, pedantic and legalistic ruling class of Colombia centred on the Andean city of Bogotá. (García Márquez has insisted in his own defence that all the anti-Santander statements in the novel are based upon Bolívar's own utterances and writings.) The novel's epigraph, 'It seems that the devil controls the business of my life', is taken from a letter Bolívar sent to Santander in August 1823. Presumably its inclusion is intended ironically: little did Bolívar know, it implies, that Santander, then his friend, would become his nemesis – the very 'devil'. García Márquez has synthesised all these contradictions quite effectively in one of his most important interviews about this book:

> Our debate about formalism leads irremediably to the eternal difference between two ways of being: Andean and Caribbean. Or, said in Colombian, between *cachacos* and *costeños*. The *cachacos*, irredeemable formalists, say that the *costeños* are not frank but rude. We *costeños*, irremediably loose-tongued, say that the *cachacos* are not well-mannered but hypocritical. A *costeño* insults first and then feels sorry. The *cachacos* overwhelm you with praise before they strike. Bolívar, a *costeño* from Caracas, wanted to make Bogotá the capital of half the world and in the end summed up his failure in a single phrase: 'This is not my theatre'.[12]

This hostility to Bogotá (a word that appears only once in the book – García Márquez has always said he finds it 'too ugly' for literature – the only time it is named he notes that the city is '2,600 metres above the distant sea') and aversion to Santander has led García Márquez on numerous occasions to exalt aspects of Venezuelan history and society against those of his own country and to suggest that he and other Colombian *costeños* might have been happier if history had grouped them in an enlarged tropical Caribbean republic incorporating most of Venezuela, the Colombian Atlantic coast, the Colombian Guajira and Panama. (Only a month before the publication of this novel García Márquez was guest of honour at the inauguration of his friend Carlos Andrés Pérez's second term as president of Venezuela.) Even the bestial dictator of *The Autumn of the Patriarch*, for all his grotesque collection of faults and crimes, seems to be redeemed to some degree by his tropical identity and by the fact that he rules a country, which, like Venezuela, carried out its liberal – and federal – revolution in the nineteenth century whereas Colombia did not even have a Liberal government until 1930, when other countries were exploring new possibilities such as populism and socialism. This is why, in García Márquez's estimation, Venezuela, in terms of race, class and religion, is a much more modern and democratic country, for all its difficulties and in spite of its greater historical tendencies to dictatorship, than Colombia. The latter is a country which has had only a few years in its entire history of overt dictatorial rule but is governed, in the writer's estimation, by a ruthless oligarchy which has never carried out a single important structural reform in the whole of its history; moreover, it secured the assassination in 1948 of the populist Liberal Jorge Eliécer Gaitán, the only leader with mass appeal in the history of the republic, whose death triggered *la violencia* for which Colombia is known, the continuing effects of which are still with the country today.

These points of empathy are carefully inserted into the characterisation of Bolívar in the novel, though arguably without major distortions because there is a genuine coincidence between Bolívar's likes and antipathies and those of the writer. Perhaps the most questionable aspect for many Colombians is not so much the overtly political portrait but the idea of a Bolívar who speaks 'in Caribbean' – not only his accent and diction but his scabrous vocabulary – and whose physical depiction makes it clear that like most inhabitants of the Caribbean regions of Latin America he has black blood flowing in his veins. Curiously enough, García Márquez was quite slow to come to an awareness of his identity as a *mestizo* but in this novel he more than makes up for previous omissions. Nevertheless, in a continent where Bolívar has since been mythologised almost to the point of deification, in several of whose countries his statue appears in almost every town large and small, the idea that Bolívar was already being deformed by myth and exploited by conservative ideology was memorably expressed by Domingo Faustino Sarmiento as early as his *Facundo* in 1845, only a decade and a half after the Liberator's death, when he declared that all the evocations he had read of Bolívar 'take off his poncho and put him in a European dress-coat'. To that extent, some of García Márquez's claims about the novelty and audacity of his own purportedly demystifying portrait may seem exaggerated, though it is certainly true that his challenge to more than a century and a half of mythological accretions did cause uproar in a number of sectors of Latin American – especially Colombian and Venezuelan – society. (On the other hand, several critics have complained that, far from demythologising Bolívar, García Márquez has done exactly the opposite: that Bolívar is here *re*-mythologised according to García Márquez's own allegedly populist-socialist demagogueries.) García Márquez, when accused by Colombians of a lack of patriotism, points out that in 1830 Colombia, Venezuela and Ecuador were one country and thus patriotism is in a sense beside the point: the question was, precisely, whether the different regions should stay together or split into two or three. Santander was for splitting; Bolívar was for unity. Much of what Bolívar has to say about these and other political issues in the novel was said by García Márquez in his speech at the time of the conferment of the Nobel Prize in 1982, a text which should certainly be read by any student of this book.

As we have seen, the word 'Bogotá' is carefully excluded for reasons of euphony and personal allergy. But even the protagonist's name appears only twice, first at the end of the first of the eight chapters and second when the embittered Liberator – known as 'the General' throughout the book – is asked what name to give to an old, ugly, ailing and sorely wounded stray dog. He replies: 'Bolívar'. This is just one more example of one of the central thematic clusters of this and almost every other novel by García Márquez: the motifs of waiting (even the great Bolívar has to wait for permission to leave the country and for his passport to be issued – though of course the powerful also have the power to *delay*), failure, decline, disappointment, disillusionment, decay and eventual death. The Bolívar we see at the beginning of this novel is a hero who has lost almost all his powers – physical and political – and is retreating into exile. Despite his glorious reputation as the man who did more to liberate the entire South American continent than any other individual, he has been rejected by the country he specifically selected as his own 'theatre' and is having to confront his own apparent failure and an illness that may be mortal. As the novel follows him down to the coast the most important events and experiences of the forty-seven years of his previous life are artfully inserted as memories to counterpoint his brilliant rise to glory with the stunning decline and fall of his last months.

As García Márquez has repeatedly pointed out, this last journey down to Cartagena from Bogotá – the first half of this eight-part novel – is the least well documented period of Bolívar's entire public life as a politician-warrior, a fact which has given the author license to invent a significant number of episodes – though always, he insists, within the limitations of historical verisimilitude as decreed by the huge quantities of historical information bequeathed by historians, biographers, archivists and, not least, the thousands of letters which Bolívar himself left to posterity. Georg Lukács famously said that historical novels should not take the most important historical personage as their principal protagonist; but García Márquez wades straight in and depicts one of the most select handful of iconic figures of Latin American history – shall we say Bolívar, Columbus and Castro? – on his own terms and without any apparent self-consciousness. Though there may be many arguments about this book, its essential triumph in the face of its challenges cannot reasonably be denied, as Tariq Ali has declared:

> Carlyle compared Bolívar to Ulysses who required a Homer to do him justice. Márquez is the closest we have got to that injunction. That is why the work of Bolívar's biographers, even taken collectively, has a magnificent rival in Gabriel García Márquez's mesmerising historical novel *The General in His Labyrinth*. This work of fiction contains a wealth of factual details and rare psychological insights that should be the envy of any biographer.[13]

We sense that García Márquez is going to achieve his goals in the very first paragraph where there is a masterly cinematographic presentation of Bolívar who seems to have drowned in his bath in the early morning and is first seen from the viewpoint of his anxious valet José Palacios; then, we emerge from below the waters of the bath with Bolívar and see the troubled steward from the great man's perspective; finally we are shown by the narrator himself that this ailing man, who has lost most of his physical strength (and so much else, as we shall learn), is able to emerge once more with the force of pure willpower and take up his burdens again. It is extremely difficult to paint persuasive portraits of history's great men and women, just as it is extremely difficult to feed large doses of factual information into narrative fiction, but García Márquez rises to the challenge with extraordinary brio and conviction, as Argentinian novelist Osvaldo Soriano has remarked: 'García Márquez has worked the miracle of constructing a literary personage, grandiose and fascinating, but at the same time substantially faithful to the historical figure of Bolívar.'[14] García Márquez uses the techniques of the biographer, the journalist, the travel writer and the historian, as well as the novelist, and manages to produce a relatively seamless narrative. Apart from the depiction of Bolívar as a man of the Caribbean, and the emphasis upon his unifying motivation against Santander's regionalist impetus, the principal departure from most previous views of Bolívar's final months is García Márquez's insistence that, far from planning a journey to exile in Europe, Bolívar was secretly determined to get back to Venezuela and 'start all over again'.

Bolívar was an inspiration to romantic writers all over the Americas and Europe. Quite apart from the dashing image to which his generalship and his sometimes miraculous victories gave rise, the more intimate details of his life provided an aura of solitude which always surrounded him. His father died when he was two and a half, his mother when he was eight; he married when he was almost nineteen and his wife died eight months later. He never married again, and despite his fabled relationship with the Ecuadorean Manuelita Sáenz and an unknown – but undoubtedly considerable – number of affairs (which is why this is also a novel about love), he had no children as far as history is able to determine. García Márquez adds to these facets of his portrait the information that, miraculously, Bolívar was never wounded; that he had spent almost all his considerable fortune on the war effort; and that he wore no special insignia of his rank. Such a combination of solitude and austerity makes Bolívar just one more example of the García Márquez figures condemned to such an existence, most notably the unnamed ex-soldier waiting for his letter and his pension in *No One Writes to the Colonel;* Colonel Aureliano Buendía, mentioned in all the writer's early books and the principal protagonist of *One Hundred Years of Solitude,* whose personality gives that complex novel its most distinctive flavour; and the grotesquely violent dictator of *The Autumn of the Patriarch* wandering the lonely corridors of his vast and sombre government palace.

Thus, García Márquez's Bolívar, the general who did so much in his life, is in some respects related to the colonel of *No One Writes to the Colonel,* a main character who nevertheless does so little, most notably in the obsessive concentration on their ailing constitutions ('The glory had left his body') and their determination to succeed in the face of all the evidence that disaster is just around the corner.[15] Bolívar is also like the protagonist of *The Autumn of the Patriarch* in terms of the minutiae of his relation to power – whether it is early or late, whether he has all of it, much of it or almost none of it. And although no one could reasonably doubt the world-changing impact of Bolívar's achievements, the character himself is at times given to wonder whether there has been any point to his struggles in just the way that Colonel Aureliano Buendía meditates on the futility of all his projects and all his battles in *One Hundred Years of Solitude*. There is even a parallel, technically, with *Chronicle of a Death Foretold*, a novel in which the reader is told from the beginning (and in the title) that the protagonist is doomed to die and yet somehow the writer manages to maintain a high level of suspense; in *The General in His Labyrinth*, Bolívar is trapped in his labyrinth from the outset, and in the very first chapter a British diplomat (one invested with a Garciamarquian turn of phrase and taste for paradox) tells us exactly what is going to happen:

> It was the end. General Simón José Antonio de la Santísima Trinidad Bolívar y Palacios was leaving forever. He had wrested from Spanish domination an empire five times more vast than all of Europe, he had led twenty years of war to keep it free and united, and he had governed it with a firm hand until the week before, but when it was time to leave he did not even take away with him the consolation that anyone believed in his departure. The only man with enough lucidity to know he really was going, and where he was going to, was the English diplomat, who wrote in an official report to his government: 'The time he has left will hardly be enough for him to reach his grave.'[16]

Readers familiar with *One Hundred Years of Solitude* will find echoes here of the encapsulation of the absolute futility of the life and career of Colonel Aureliano Buendía at the beginning of the sixth chapter of that seminal novel. ('Colonel Aureliano Buendía organised thirty-two armed uprisings and he lost them all').[17]

By the end of *The General in His Labyrinth*, readers familiar with García Márquez's artifices wonder which way the ending will go, although they know that in this case, surely, only one conclusion is possible. The moribund Bolívar gazes one last time at his mirror, hears the slaves singing outside his window and sees:

> the diamond of Venus in the sky as it went away for ever, the eternal snows, the creeper whose yellow flowers he would not see bloom the following Saturday in a house closed down by mourning, the last splendour of that life that till the end of time itself would never ever be repeated.[18]

Despite the purple prose we may feel able to see Bolívar for ourselves, as a man who has succeeded in his great task as liberator of a continent but failed in the even greater endeavour of uniting it; and as a man who, mightily fallen, somehow retains his courage and greatness of spirit in even the most desperate and humiliating circumstances, at the end of his 'mad chase between his woes and his dreams'. Clearly García Márquez believes that this is indeed an even more admirable side to the Liberator, whose ultimate greatness (perhaps) lay in his becoming an ordinary Latin American in his last months, the predecessor of all those other magnificent failures who struggle through the pages of Latin American fiction in the arduous kingdom of this world. If this were so, then far from Bolívar becoming a García Márquez adaptation, we could see that it was Bolívar who had, in a sense, created all García Márquez's earlier characters, who had, in short, created the character of the Latin American, with his magnificent dreams, seemingly endless struggles, transient victories and shattering disappointments.[19]

Having read the end of this late novel, it may come as a surprise to go back to the end of that first short story, 'The Third Resignation', published forty-two years before, whose central problematic is that of a young man buried 'alive' in his coffin and kept in the family home until he seems about to 'die' for the third and perhaps final time:

> Resigned, he will hear the last prayers, the last phrases mumbled in Latin and clumsily responded by the altar boys. The cold of the cemetery's earth and bones will penetrate to his own bones and may dissipate somewhat that 'smell'. Perhaps – who knows! – the imminence of that moment will force him out of that lethargy. When he feels himself swimming in his own sweat, in a thick, viscous liquid, like he swam before he was born in his mother's womb. Perhaps at that moment he will be alive.
>
> But by then he will be so resigned to dying that he may die of resignation.[20]

The connection to the last page of *The General in His Labyrinth* is unmistakable.

Yet it was only when, for the purposes of this essay, I recently reread 'The Third Resignation' – a story in which a young man is buried before he even dies and spends his time imagining his definitive demise, which has still not occurred by the end of the story – and when I then returned to *The General in His Labyrinth,* that I realised that, like most other readers, I had fallen prey to an optical illusion. I had always believed that I had witnessed Bolívar's death in *The General in His Labyrinth*. No such thing! In novels at least, unlike history itself, heroes need never die.[21]

NOTES

1. All translated quotations from this story are mine.
2. Gabriel García Márquez, *Leaf Storm,* trans. Gregory Rabassa, London, Picador, 1979, p. 94.

3. Gabriel García Márquez, *No One Writes to the Colonel,* trans. J. S. Bernstein, Harmondsworth: Penguin, 1974, p. 9.
4. García Márquez, *No One Writes to the Colonel,* p. 61.
5. Gabriel García Márquez, 'Big Mama's Funeral', trans. J. S. Bernstein, in *Collected Stories,* New York, Harper, 1991, p. 184.
6. García Márquez, 'Big Mama's Funeral', p. 200.
7. See my 'On "Magical" and Social Realism in García Márquez', in Bernard McGuirk and Richard Cardwell (eds.), *Gabriel García Márquez: New Readings,* Cambridge: Cambridge University Press, 1987, pp. 95–116.
8. Gabriel García Márquez, *Love in the Time of Cholera,* trans. Edith Grossman, London, Jonathan Cape, 1988, pp. 46–7.
9. García Márquez, *Love in the Time of Cholera,* p. 352. See my discussion of this literary moment in 'Translating García Márquez, or, the Impossible Dream', in D. Balderston and M. Schwartz (eds.), *Voice-Overs: Translation and Latin American Literature,* Albany, NY: State University of New York Press, 2002, pp. 156–63.
10. María Elvira Samper, '*El general en su laberinto:* un libro vengativo. Entrevista exclusiva con Gabriel García Márquez', *La Jornada Semanal,* Mexico City, 9 April 1989, pp. 3–9; p. 3.
11. Seymour Menton, *La nueva novela histórica,* Mexico City: Fondo de Cultura Económica, 1993.
12. Susana Cato, 'El Gabo: "Desnudé a Bolívar"', *Proceso,* Mexico City, 3 April 1989, pp. 48–55; p. 54.
13. Tariq Ali, *Pirates of the Caribbean: Axis of Hope (Evo Morales, Fidel Castro, Hugo Chávez),* London: Verso, 2006, p. 128.
14. *Excelsior,* Mexico City, 26 October 1989.
15. García Márquez, *No One Writes to the Colonel,* p. 15.
16. Gabriel García Márquez, *The General in His Labyrinth,* trans. Edith Grossman, London: Penguin, 1991, p. 37.
17. Gabriel García Márquez, *One Hundred Years of Solitude,* London: Picador, 1978, p. 91.
18. My translation.
19. See my *Journeys through the Labyrinth: Latin American Fiction in the Twentieth Century,* London: Verso, 1989, pp. 292–3.
20. My translation.
21. Bolívar was not buried at San Pedro Alejandrino, where he died, but in the cathedral of nearby Santa Marta, the city in which García Márquez's beloved grandfather, Colonel Nicolás Ricardo Márquez, also died and was buried little more than a century later. (His grave has been lost.) Later the body was disinterred and transferred to Caracas. San Pedro now has what is effectively a vast mausoleum without a body.

8

MARK I. MILLINGTON

García Márquez's novels of love

Whatever else one might say about García Márquez's view of love, his treatment of it is remarkably consistent. That view shows love as an irresistible force that overwhelms the rational mind and sweeps those in its grasp to the margins of conventional society. Social practices and institutions are anathema to the kind of passionate obsessions explored in *Chronicle of a Death Foretold* (*Crónica de una muerte anunciada* [1981]), *Love in the Time of Cholera* (*El amor en los tiempos del cólera* [1985]), *Love and Other Demons* (*Del amor y otros demonios* [1994]) and *Memories of My Melancholy Whores* (*Memoria de mis putas tristes* [2004]). Small wonder that love is at times confused with virulent diseases such as cholera and rabies, which cause their victims to be placed in quarantine. Love can seem a distinctly dangerous affliction. And it is an affliction almost always suffered by men – the women's (or usually adolescent girls') stories of love are mere glimpses. Men's suffering seems to bear out the notion that 'nothing in this world is more difficult than love', though fundamentally in García Márquez there is nothing remotely to compare with love's intoxicating wonder.[1]

Chronicle of a Death Foretold focuses on how society impedes the fulfillment of individual lives. In particular, it shows how the most important aspects of human experience are obstructed because social conventions take priority. Unlike the other novels considered here, love does not drive the narrative in *Chronicle of a Death Foretold*. What drives it are the inexorability of social conformism culminating in murder and a collective abdication of responsibility. However, the very neglect of love is a key underlying factor of the novel and part of its social critique. Where love *is* glimpsed, its form anticipates much that is characteristic of it in later novels.

The most significant enigma in *Chronicle of a Death Foretold* is whether Santiago Nasar is the man who took Angela Vicario's virginity. Her naming of him is simply the identification of a man supposedly responsible for one act. But the narrator indicates that nobody believes that Santiago is the man responsible, and he lists all the reasons: that Santiago and Angela belonged to different social worlds, that he was too arrogant to take any notice of her and that he was never known to have a relationship except a conventional one with his fiancée. In addition, many think that she is concealing her real lover by naming Santiago, believing that nobody would dare take revenge against him. Apparently confirming this view, his reaction when told that Angela's brothers are waiting to kill him is utter bewilderment.[2] None of which proves that Santiago was not responsible. Yet, interestingly, Angela herself never claims her loss of virginity as the outcome of love and never suggests that she had a relationship with Santiago. This absence is striking because neither she nor Santiago is immune to strong passions.

Santiago is a conventional man by the standards of the town. The son of a wealthy family, he has the arrogance which goes with the role of sexual predator. For Santiago, visits to the local brothel are routine, and his behaviour towards Divina Flor indicates that he is about to assert his sexual dominance with her. And yet, Santiago also experiences love. When, at fifteen, he first sees the madam of the local brothel, he falls madly in love with her. This passion inverts what becomes the norm in García Márquez, namely that of a mature man for a young girl. However, it does conform with the norm in that it is the male who is struck by the overwhelming emotion rather than the female. His father curtails his passion by insisting on class hierarchy and sending his son away for a year. Thereafter, the relation is one of deep affection but without the disorder that love brings. Santiago can therefore enter into a conventional and loveless engagement with the respectable Flora Miguel.

Angela is also apparently conventional, having been raised in a protective family, which has trained her in the accepted gender role for women, namely that of wife. As the narrator's mother remarks, any man would be happy with Angela and her sisters because they have been brought up to suffer. The connection between marriage and suffering is revealing of the attitude to marriage throughout García Márquez – in short, there is no expectation that marriage will involve love. However, the key expectation of Angela's preparation for marriage is that she should reach the marriage-bed a virgin. Santiago's uncensured sexual exploits are the proof of the double standards here. Where the conventionality of Santiago and Angela breaks down is in the suggestion that they have had sex together. For Angela, the daughter of a modest but respectable family, the lack of virginity is a life-changing problem. For Santiago, a lack of virginity would not be a problem (indeed the opposite would be true for his reputation), but he *is* subject to social norms, which dictate that he have casual sex with prostitutes or women in disadvantaged social positions, and Angela is neither. On that basis, Santiago would have to accept responsibility for what he is alleged to have done with

Angela. The strength of social norms and their capacity to constrain behaviour are manifest here.

When it comes to marriage for Angela, it is her family which decides. Bayardo San Román arrives in the town in search of a wife, a quest which makes no mention of love. He selects Angela as his bride and sets about bewitching her family, who compel her to marry him. When she mentions that she does not love him her objection is swept aside since Bayardo is a significant catch and love is therefore irrelevant. But, although he proves his macho credentials by his aggressive purchase of Xius's house, this acquisition guarantees him nothing, least of all happiness. For, when he discovers that Angela is not a virgin, his macho bravado suffers a decisive blow. His return of his bride to her family underlines his own conformism: he is too conditioned by the honour code and the myth of male dominance to react differently. But it is here that the novel introduces an element of love. For, as her mother punishes her for the loss of virginity and imposes social discipline, Angela falls madly in love with Bayardo. The equation is clear: love is defined in contradistinction to social conformity. Moreover, the more impossible the chances of realising desire, the stronger love becomes. For Angela, love is transforming – it seems to enable her to realise all her potential: 'She became lucid, imperious, mistress of her will and a virgin once more just for him.'[3] The hyperbole here is characteristic of García Márquez's view of love, as are the fact that it is secret, one-sided and that it involves copious letter-writing: Angela sends Bayardo a love letter every week for the next seventeen years. What is unusual in *Chronicle of a Death Foretold* is that the subject of this passion is a woman. These loves beyond the scope of reason are almost everywhere else male experiences. Angela's love and her determination are traits that single her out as an 'unsung heroine' who subverts oppressive gender codes.

Angela demonstrates all the single-mindedness which will later be seen in Florentino in *Love in the Time of Cholera*. And it pays off, for Bayardo returns to her seventeen years later. He brings with him the almost 2,000 letters which she has sent, all neatly ordered and unopened. The couple, of course, are still married, but what is never clear is whether he returns out of love. His meticulous treatment of the letters suggests that they mean something to him even if he does not open them. But his return is enigmatic, and, if based on reciprocated love, it is only the initial step in what might be a mature relationship, something which these novels rarely explore. Indeed, with the exception of Xius, marriage is always seen as a social institution which either has nothing to do with love (for example, Santiago's parents' marriage), or which has an ambivalent relation with it (for example, Fermina and Juvenal's marriage in *Love in the Time of Cholera*). Another institution, the family, as represented by the Vicarios, also stifles love: her mother disciplines Angela, and the narrator indicates that she strove to bring about her daughter's death. There seems to be no place in this family for unconditional love. Instead they seek to imprison Angela in social conformism – a conformism which Angela's indomitable spirit shows to be futile as she finally wins over Bayardo.

Chronicle of a Death Foretold charts both society's capacity to neglect or obstruct love and love's capacity to survive and prosper against all the odds. Where the other novels in this group focus on the experience of love itself and see social obstacles through its lens, *Chronicle of a Death Foretold* focuses on the obstacles and only glimpses love through society's collective failure. By contrast, *Love in the Time of Cholera*'s main preoccupation is the life-long devotion of Florentino Ariza to Fermina Daza. However, it also explores other relationships involving elements of love or sex, which act as contrastive experiences to this main thread. I have implied that *Love in the Time of Cholera* is a novel, though some of its most significant aspects might seem to link it with the genre of romance. All aspects of its plot are driven by the vicissitudes of love, and consequently it provides the reader with something of an emotional rollercoaster. In addition, the characters are not explored psychologically, nor is there any probing of the meaning or causes of desire. Finally, the life-affirming tone and the optimistic ending combine with these other features to create a celebration of love which seems more characteristic of romance than of novelistic realism. And yet there are dark aspects in the book which work against that celebration and reveal emphases which some may find disturbing.

The dominant model of love in *Love in the Time of Cholera* is an all-consuming passion that harbours no doubt and inspires a kind of sublime devotion. The narrative is largely driven by Florentino's emotions: he falls in love at about eighteen and nurtures his passion with total dedication for over fifty years. That starting point and dedication manifest an adolescent obsessiveness that heightens his sensitivity but also attenuates his grasp of reality. So when he returns to the city from his flight up river following Fermina's marriage to Juvenal, its pestilent odour is somehow covered over by her perfume, even though she is nowhere near him. The fascination of the character is his unshakeable commitment: his unquenchable obsession verges on the superhuman, particularly when he reaches his eighth decade. No obstacle, whether Fermina's aloofness, paternal disapproval, class difference or decades of waiting in which he is rarely in her presence, dampens his ardour. Indeed, following the novel's inverse logic, the very number and scale of the obstacles seem merely to increase the intensity of his passion. That intensity is particularly striking because Florentino is such an unremarkable man: his background is modest, his jobs are uninspiring and his looks unprepossessing. And yet the novel conjures up one of its extreme combinations by setting these ordinary traits alongside a quite extraordinary capacity for love. One response to the obstacles to his love is to write impassioned letters – a recurring motif of García Márquez's lovers. Florentino's first, in which he declares his love, reaches sixty double-sided sheets. This sheer excess is a sign of the hyperbolic nature of his emotion, which is always full throttle but also always a closely guarded secret.

The result of his extreme devotion to a woman, who not only rejects him but is also unaware of his feelings for fifty years, is that Florentino has an air of solitude. Almost permanently separated from the object of his love, never fully committing himself to any of the other women in his life and without close male friends, Florentino appears socially marginal. He does have a close friendship with Leona Cassiani, but, even though she is said to be the true woman of his life, neither of them realises it and they are never lovers.[4] But there is no social role for him as an obsessive lover, which is the core of his identity. His marginal condition is clearly perceived by those around him, and rumours circulate about his supposed pederasty, an innuendo which is the best that society can manage in its attempt to understand his solitude. In fact, Florentino epitomises many aspects of heterosexual orthodoxy.

In waiting for a reply to his first letter, Florentino shows signs of illness, which his mother confuses with cholera. Here García Márquez draws on the courtly and romantic traditions which liken love to a sickness. On a literal level, cholera is linked with the city's lack of awareness of public health. But on a poetic level, the fevers of cholera and the sufferings of love intertwine consistently. The most obvious example comes at the end when the desire to perpetuate the idyll of love on the river-boat leads to the declaration of a state of quarantine supposedly caused by a case of cholera on board. The metaphor of cholera poses love as a force of nature with anti-social and life-threatening potential.

An essential feature of this type of love is the asymmetry between the two people involved. Fermina simply does not reciprocate Florentino's love with the same intensity. Her first reaction to his declarations, whether in early adolescence or old age, is caution or rejection, so that she appears prosaic in comparison with the impetuous poetry of his emotions. Whatever the cause of Fermina's cool response (and she is only thirteen at the start), the lack of symmetry between them creates the ideal conditions for narrative: uncertainty and suspense. Once she does commit herself, there is a period of collaboration in the clandestine business of cultivating their love and keeping it secret from her father. And yet, even here, Fermina is reserved about her feelings. When she writes to him it is with 'letters ... designed to keep the coals hot but without putting her hand in the flame, while Florentino Ariza was on fire in every line'.[5] Not that she lacks commitment, and indeed, when her father sends her away, the strength of her feelings is reinforced. And yet, contrarily, when Fermina returns and sees Florentino again, her reaction is immediate and definitive: she is implacable in her rejection of him. Increased proximity and the potential for direct communication work in inverse proportion to her desire to sustain her love.

The asymmetry continues in old age. When, at seventy-two, Fermina is widowed, her reaction to Florentino's declaration of love is anger and then surprise, since she has ceased to see him as a lover and finds the idea of love at their age faintly ridiculous. And yet, she will have no truck with the prejudice that would rule out an intimate relationship at their age, a stance mirroring the novel's challenge to readers' expectations. As a widow, Fermina is moved by Florentino's persuasive powers, though without succumbing to his 'lyrical lies'.[6] In short, she remains cool, practical and realistic, having no illusions about her appearance as a septuagenarian. She even casts doubt on whether their emotions fifty years before amounted to love. Significant though this scepticism is as a counterweight to Florentino's emotional drive, it is doubtful whether Fermina recognises or ever experiences passionate love. However, the narrator does say, after they have finally begun a sexual relationship, that it is as if they had leapt over the arduous calvary of married life and had gone straight to the core of love, a phrase indicative of the sceptical view of love in marriage in *Love in the Time of Cholera*.

In fact, the other type of love in *Love in the Time of Cholera* is the ambivalent one which Juvenal and Fermina experience through their marriage. Florentino's love for Fermina only reaches the beginnings of a relationship at the end, so that we do not know whether his infatuation can be translated into something sustained and shared. Similarly, for all their joy and inventiveness, he never allows his other liaisons to develop beyond a certain level of emotional commitment. Fermina's marriage to Juvenal is therefore the only example of a mature relationship. The question is the extent to which it is based on love and therefore whether the novel really envisages an alternative kind of love to Florentino's.

Fermina shows as much wariness about entering a relationship with Juvenal as with Florentino. When she does accept him it is a pragmatic calculation to safeguard her future. She writes him a terse letter in which she merely agrees that he speak with her father and says nothing about reciprocating his feelings. Indeed, the narrator tells us that: 'In reality, she loved him as little as she did the other.'[7] This beginning sets the tone for their marriage, since it is uncertain whether Fermina and Juvenal truly love each other or whether theirs is a relation of convenience. After their honeymoon, they are very happy, but when living with his mother their relation is put under severe strain. Her mother-in-law severely restricts Fermina, and Juvenal does nothing to help his wife. She blames his spinelessness for her plight, and the love which they had felt is all but destroyed. But once she escapes his mother's influence, Fermina regains control of her destiny and is again convinced that Juvenal is the man whom she would choose above all others. Again it is notable that this commitment is not expressed in terms of undying love. Significantly, after many years of marriage, Juvenal has an affair with another woman. His feelings for his mistress become an all-absorbing passion, and he oscillates between feverish impatience and a desperate wish not to fulfill his sexual desire because he knows he is being unfaithful. In short, Juvenal experiences the kind of intense feelings which Florentino knows and which marriage has not brought him. When Fermina discovers the affair she leaves him, and they spend two years apart, but they are subsequently reconciled and live together contentedly and conventionally until Juvenal's death. The scene of that death does not resolve the ambiguities surrounding their love. His dying declaration that only God knows how much he loved her is counterbalanced by Fermina's plea that she have enough time to tell him how much she loved him whatever doubts they may have had. Doubts resurface even at the moment of death.

On emerging from her initial grief, Fermina thinks that she can now free herself from a servitude in which her identity has been subsumed by Juvenal. She thinks of her marriage as fifty years which have brought happiness but which, because of their social position and Juvenal's public role, have meant that her life was not her own. As her intimate contact with Florentino develops, she discovers that she cannot tell whether what she experienced with Juvenal was love. The implication is that if she has not got an absolute conviction then it is unlikely that this experience was love, at least in the romantic sense. The ambiguity of this 'tamed love' is particularly obvious when set alongside the feelings of Florentino.[8] For that is the decisive contrast in *Love in the Time of Cholera:* a sustained and sometimes fulfilling relationship, with its complex mix of happiness and frustration, is wholly different from the overwhelming emotion which Florentino experiences. For all its difficulties, Florentino's love is never subject to doubt, although the contrast with Juvenal and Fermina also raises the possibility that Florentino's kind of love may be incompatible with a sustained relationship.

Given the frustrations of Florentino's passion for Fermina and the importance of physical love in García Márquez, his innumerable sexual relations with other women come as no surprise. Even though, after Fermina's rejection of him, he vows to remain a virgin until she is available again, he conveniently discovers that sexual relations with other women do no damage to his feelings for Fermina. Despite his obvious shortcomings in terms of sexual attraction – his taciturnity, his scrawniness, his old-fashioned appearance – Florentino is phenomenally successful in his sexual liaisons. In at least two cases, those of Sara Noriega and Olimpia Zuleta, it is said that he falls in love, but at no point is there any question of commitment to a relationship. And this reserve can seem rather selfish: for example, even when her unfaithfulness leads Olimpia's husband to cut her throat, Florentino's only reaction is the fear that Fermina may learn about his 'disloyalty'.

It is in the case of América Vicuña that there are serious repercussions to one of his affairs. She is twelve when she appears and so at almost the same age as Fermina when Florentino's passion for her began, indicating that it is barely adolescent girls with whom he falls madly in love rather than the women in his life. As if that were not problematic enough when he is seventy, there is the added complication that América is a relative and entrusted to his protection by her family while she is at school. From his first sight of her he has an 'awful presentiment' of what they will do together on Sunday afternoons.[9] This hint at the profoundly compromised moral position he gets himself into is not followed up. Indeed, there is a naturalising discourse which glosses over this troubling reality. The narrator admits that América is still a child but claims that Florentino can see the kind of woman she will be, a piece of clairvoyance that conveniently confuses what she is with who she may become. Florentino seduces América by taking her to the circus and buying her ice creams, a process which the narrator chillingly sums up as follows: 'with the gentle cunning of a kindly grandfather he led her by the hand to his clandestine slaughterhouse'.[10] This disturbing image is followed by the apparently mitigating revelation that, after sex with Florentino, 'the gates of heaven opened for her': her life blossoms and her academic work prospers.[11] But it is worth reminding ourselves that Florentino is an old man in his seventies and América a girl of twelve. The novel simply bypasses the full import of what is at stake here and aims to cover over the moral (even criminal) quagmire with deft phrases and witty invention.

This relation lasts for two years, and the narrator stresses the equality of their desires and enthusiasms. The logic seems to be that 'shared emotions' mean that América is not exploited. But the moral distortion of naturalising their relationship is re-emphasised when Fermina is widowed and Florentino decides to focus on winning her for himself. He immediately abandons América, telling her that they will not have sex any more and that he is going to marry. In other words, he is totally self-serving now that another opportunity has appeared. Strangely, he suddenly discovers the difference in their ages, though the readers are left to draw their own conclusions about why this problem did not occur to him before. He struggles to cope with América's deeply wounded response and resists her efforts to seduce him. As a result, she goes to pieces, fails her exams and commits suicide. And yet that tragedy, which is entirely Florentino's responsibility, is neatly brushed aside as he ensures his own survival by eliminating her memory. There is a clear moral cowardice in this manipulation of memory, and yet he does suffer because of the loss of América, locking himself in the bathroom to weep for her, since 'only then was he brave enough to admit to himself how much he had loved her'.[12] This response stresses how *he* suffers because of his love for her with no hint that he feels guilty about her death. Self-centredness enables his survival and also, by implication, the possibility of enjoying the burgeoning relationship with Fermina. The narrator does say that Florentino has no idea how much América suffers because he never realises how much she loves him. But that simply underlines how selfish his emotional world is: he has countless affairs but always maintains a reserve that allows him to cultivate his solitary obsession with a woman who is barely aware of him. There is a strange masculine logic operating here, as if fifty years of solitude were a sufficient end in themselves. Florentino may have a satisfactory sex life and know intense love but he has very little experience of the fulfillment of sharing it: that experience may only be beginning at the novel's end.

The relation with América represents the dark and destabilising underside of the sunny optimism in evidence in Florentino's experience of love. And it brings into focus the element of male egocentricity in these narratives. What drives the different narrative strands is male desire so that what women and female adolescents want is filtered through and potentially distorted by that prism. It seems worth challenging that logic to see what might be missing. For example, it is not clear why, if América can attempt to seduce Florentino just as he initially seduced her, and if she feels such an intense love for him, she is not capable of reacting to his rejection exactly as he does when Fermina rejects *him*. One wonders why América cannot evolve a story of undying commitment and resolution to win Florentino back – and succeed. Such a reaction would not be far removed from what Angela Vicario does in *Chronicle of a Death Foretold* to win over Bayardo. Instead, once rejected, she commits suicide and is rapidly eliminated from the narrative.

As in *Love in the Time of Cholera*, there are different types of love in *Love and Other Demons*, including the unconditional (if belated) love of a father for a daughter, but this discussion will concentrate on the passionate love between Sierva María and Cayetano Delaura. Their relationship bears a certain resemblance to the one between Florentino and Fermina. In the first place, it is initially experienced by the man and only subsequently by Sierva María. The love is overwhelming and leads them to take risks which bring about the destruction of their relationship. But they have moments of great happiness together as the world pales into insignificance. The major difference from Florentino and Fermina is that Sierva María reciprocates Cayetano's love with an intensity that equals his. And that doubly valorises this form of love.

In the course of the narrative, Cayetano moves from insider in the Church to marginalisation, and the driver of this process is his passionate love. He is thirty-six, a priest and the trusted confidant of the bishop. So orthodox is he that he is entrusted with the examination and exorcism of Sierva María when the Church believes that she is possessed by the Devil. Unlike many around him, he is sceptical about her possession and refuses to jump to conclusions. While the nuns in the convent where she is detained have tied her up and subjected her to barbaric indignities, Cayetano talks with her reasonably, and his caring attitude leads her to trust him. He rapidly undergoes a major personal change: he thinks about her constantly, and the nature of his reality begins to shift. His experience of Sierva María is so powerful that it irresistibly propels him out of his obedience to the Church. Given her parents' abandonment of her to their slaves and the horrendous tortures which the doctors inflict on her to 'cure' her of the bite from a rabid dog, it is clear that she has suffered from many things but certainly not 'possession' by the Devil. Cayetano's open-mindedness and feelings for her are therefore projected as balanced and healthy and, crucially, the means to save himself from the colonial church's dogmatism. When he explains rationally to the bishop that Sierva María is terrified rather than possessed, that there is a good reason why she can speak African languages and that the 'evidence' against her is a tissue of superstition and nonsense, the bishop resists. It is clear that the Church lacks the capacity to cope with rational argument. Shortly thereafter, as his heart is fit to explode with his feelings for her, he takes what is the unthinkable step for a Catholic priest of declaring his love. What then happens demonstrates once again that those who principally suffer from love in García Márquez are the male characters, for we are shown Cayetano suffering agonies of doubt and sleeplessness as he prepares for an exorcism which he knows to be unjust. At this point, as with Florentino and Fermina, the love is totally one-sided and male-centred. It also breaks all the rules, a key element of passionate love in García Márquez. In his confusion he turns not to the bishop but to the Enlightenment figure of the doctor, Abrenuncio. Confirming Cayetano's movement into a new intellectual and emotional orbit, he and the free-thinking doctor communicate with ease. When Cayetano next sees Sierva María he tries to undo the ropes with which the Church has tied her up: symbolically, his love liberates her from the tortures inflicted on her. Confused, he resorts to extreme measures to try and return to Catholic orthodoxy: he flagellates himself to extirpate all trace of Sierva María from his mind and body. But, once again, the Church's methods fail, and it then punishes his unpriestly passion by reducing him to washing lepers. Nonetheless, Cayetano's love is such that he breaks the conditions placed upon him and sees Sierva María clandestinely. They spend innocent days and nights together in blissful happiness. And yet, the Church finally triumphs over them by blocking his access to her and then condemning him for heresy – the heresy of falling in love. Unlike Florentino's love, Cayetano's ends in tragedy.

Sierva María is an adolescent like Fermina and América: she is twelve years of age when a mature man falls passionately in love with her. In particular, like Fermina she is somewhat remote, not because she is emotionally aloof but because of her unusual upbringing. Her parents' marriage is loveless, and both reject her because they identify the other spouse in her. She is abandoned by her white parents and brought up by slaves, and in that context learns to speak African languages and acquires a mix of cultures and religions. To the Church, which cannot see beyond its own parochial world-view, this hybridity makes Sierva María dangerous, and the cultural, religious and linguistic richness which she has acquired from the slaves is egregiously misunderstood as deriving from the Devil. The bite she receives from a rabid dog is the trigger for a concatenation of events which delivers her into the violent and intolerant hands of the Church, which eventually kills her.[13] The bishop's sinuous logic even suggests that the bite is the Devil's stratagem for disguising his possession of her. Against this kind of nonsense there is no arguing. Except for the enlightened Abrenuncio, not until Cayetano arrives does anyone dealing with her understand that her refusal to communicate with white people derives from their uncaring or brutal treatment of her, and that other aspects of her behaviour are conditioned by her socialisation within a black culture. But since the reader only sees the character externally and has no access to her thought processes, there is an unaccountability about her which makes her seem remote. Again, the object of male desire is elusive and perplexing. This is the way that García Márquez's discourse of love often creates the female object of love. But, as with América and Angela, there is another story here, a girl's story of neglect and vulnerability. But it is one which is not fully told and which can only be glimpsed through the novel as presented.

And yet Sierva María does fall in love with Cayetano. After his gentle treatment and, significantly, once he too has begun to be punished by the Church and therefore has become an outsider like her, she responds to his declaration of love. And her emotions appear fully engaged by him, for when Cayetano leaves her one day without taking her with him she reacts wildly and destructively, apparently feeling that he is betraying her as so many white people have done before. And indeed, shortly thereafter he is restrained by the Church and disappears entirely from her life, and she is found dead of love in her cell. This tragic ending of unfulfilled love – again, passionate love in García Márquez is not sustained into a relationship – is only partially offset by the fact that Sierva María's spirit remains utterly uncowed by the Church: she stands up to the bishop during her exorcism, outshouting him and kicking him in the groin. Indeed, she continues the rebellion of a free spirit even after death as the hair, which the Church had shaved off her head, grows back in her tomb to the defiant length of 'twenty-two metres and eleven centimetres'.[14] It takes more than fanatical dogmatism to beat the human spirit, and it is that same spirit which renews the narrator's life in *Memories of My Melancholy Whores.*

Memories of My Melancholy Whores tells of an old man's relationship with an adolescent girl, and it resembles the one between Florentino and América, except that the difference in age is even greater here as the man is ninety. A significant contrast between the two novels is that, although very experienced in sex, the nameless narrator-protagonist of *Memories of My Melancholy Whores,* unlike Florentino, never knows love until his ninetieth birthday. Both men are rather ordinary: the narrator describes himself as ugly, shy and anachronistic, traits which Florentino shares. But where Florentino's womanising is conducted on the basis of never paying, the narrator's is conducted on the basis that he always pays. Both of them keep logs of their sexual encounters: at fifty, the narrator's log contains the names of 540 women, a total only slightly lower than Florentino's 622. And neither becomes deeply emotionally involved with these women, though the narrator is particularly remote since, as he says, he always chooses his partners at random and they have sex without love. The aura of solitariness around Florentino is therefore even more pronounced in the narrator, who has lived alone since he was thirty-two.

What changes the narrator's life is the urge on his ninetieth birthday to experience what he euphemistically calls a 'novelty': he wants to have sex with an adolescent virgin.[15] Rosa Chabarcas, the madam who finds a girl for him, alludes to the risk of three years in prison for what they are doing (presumably, procuring and corrupting a minor), but there is no danger of their being arrested because Rosa constantly entertains all the local authorities in her brothel. What they do is evidently a criminal offence but one unlikely to be punished. During their first night together, Rosa gives the girl a sleeping draught because she is so apprehensive, with the result that she is asleep throughout and the narrator limits himself to observing her naked body. What happens in no way reflects any sexual inability on his part, but he is content simply to be with her. That experience is repeated every night that they are together, in so far as one can say that they are together. Indeed, the narrator develops a passionate desire to be with the girl but avoids any possibility that she might be awake and speak with him. Instead, the focus of his attention is on caring for her, drying her perspiring body, and talking and singing to her. There are passages that capture a remarkable sensuousness in his chaste physical contact with her, and the suggestion is that she responds to his touch and his voice via a language of the body, which produces a kind of communication between them. He also talks of their getting to know each other 'as though we were together and awake', although she is unconscious throughout their 'relationship'.[16]

The challenge to the reader in understanding this relationship is to decide on the balance between realistic and poetic truth. The poetic truth is fraught with dangers, and it is evident that the bond which the narrator develops derives from the projection of his desire. He gives the girl the name 'Delgadina' because, being always asleep, she cannot give him her real name, and he prevents Rosa from doing so. In his imagination he transforms her, altering the colour of her eyes, her dress and her age to suit his mood. But he denies that this experience is a hallucination, saying that it is the miracle of first love at ninety. If the suggestion is that these imagined features become real and that love can change reality, then evidently the novel is reaching for a poetic truth beyond ordinary experience. And he is explicit about the unprecedented happiness he feels: in line with the dominant model in García Márquez, he is madly in love. But there is little doubt that this is an emotional truth all about his desire and its projections rather than any reality to do with the girl: this is solipsistic love. 'Delgadina' is his creation: her physical presence stimulates his imagination, but she resembles a blank page on which his desire can write its fantasy. When 'Delgadina' speaks in her sleep she does not respond to his subsequent question, indicating the absence of real communication between them. And he finds a 'plebeian tone' in her voice which he thinks belongs not to her but to someone alien within her.[17] He concludes that he prefers her asleep and therefore, presumably, silent. Here is a rare example of her reality obtruding on their 'relation', and it is one which he prefers to ignore. There is another example of her reality affecting his experience and it is after her disappearance. When she returns he finds her transformed: physically, she is more mature and he approves of that. But she is also made up with false eyelashes and painted nails and is festooned with jewellery. He is incensed by this 'cheapening' of her and calls her a 'whore'. Leaving aside the inconvenient truth that she has been procured for him and that he pays for her to be with him, his reaction reveals the extent to which he wants to maintain control of the 'Delgadina' fashioned by his desire. But he does overcome his revulsion, and it is at least in part due to the advice of women. Casilda Armenta, one of his sexual partners, articulates some clear principles, which could be those of the whole novel. As so often in García Márquez, it is a woman who has an unsentimental grasp of what matters. Casilda tells him not to lose the girl since dying alone is life's greatest misfortune. She also advises him not to indulge in an old man's romanticism and to have a sexual relation with her because he should not die without knowing the joy of having sex with love. This view implies an understanding of the novel's title, the 'putas tristes' being a reference to sex without love. And so, the narrator returns joyfully to 'Delgadina', and Rosa, who does speak with her, assures him that 'Delgadina' is madly in love with him, providing the reassurance of reciprocity. The novel finishes with the narrator committing himself to his lover and finding his true identity at last. Love has opened the way to self-discovery even at the age of ninety: it brings fulfillment and reinvigorates him. And 'Delgadina' remains asleep.

Broadly, *Memories of My Melancholy Whores* fits the pattern of all-consuming love found in *Love in the Time of Cholera:* it takes us through the difficulties of the onset of love and then apparently to the joy of reciprocity. But it also leaves the characters only on the brink of a settled relationship and with unanswered questions about how it can develop when one partner is asleep, about whether the narrator will take Casilda's advice to fulfill his love through sexual intercourse (which presumably would somehow need to avoid waking the girl), and about the moral foundation of a love between a man in his nineties and an adolescent of fourteen. These questions appear literalist and dull when placed alongside the wit and sheer invention of the narrative. The fact that the girl is always asleep, for example, appears to suggest the innocence of the situation, and Rosa's assurance that 'Delgadina' loves him seems to create the kind of 'balance' which was suggested in Florentino's relation with América in *Love in the Time of Cholera*. However, the underlying concern is whether these features can pre-empt questions about the appropriateness of the relationship, about the exploitation for money of a poor girl, about whether it can be called a relationship when she is asleep throughout, and about the apparent absence of any awareness of whatever desire she may have. It is difficult to overlook that 'Delgadina' is largely absent from the meetings with the narrator – she is only there as a body, and, while he may discover his true self through his love for her, her real name is never known. Passionate love in García Márquez is again celebrated but again looks like a strangely solitary and male affair.

In these four novels, the consistent view of love is that of an overwhelming passion. It is constantly shown as challenging social constraints and thriving in the face of the obstacles it encounters. Moreover, there is an inextricable connection between love and the will to live: human vitality finds its most intense expression in love. And matching the intensity of love is the exuberance and inventiveness of love-making. The challenge in the depiction of love in these novels is that it often confronts expectations or takes taboo (though always heterosexual) forms. The assumption that it is inappropriate for the elderly to be involved in passionate love is broken in *Love in the Time of Cholera* and *Memories of My Melancholy Whores*. While that involvement may challenge the reader, an even stronger challenge is that to the taboo against paedophilia, for the passion of middle-aged and elderly men for adolescent girls is precisely that. It is true that adolescents are on the border between childhood and adulthood, and that they seem at times to be like adults and at others to manifest childlike behaviour. But these adolescent girls prove surprisingly amenable to adult male advances and have a troubling willingness to reciprocate the passion directed at them. The novels do not problematise this passion, though they occasionally allude to its illegality or potential for censure. But, in García Márquez's vision, love sweeps through such inconvenient legal and moral constraints and can run perilously close to wish fulfillment. And that underlines a fundamental truth, namely that these are male-centred narratives. Women characters are almost always pragmatic and cool and far less prone than men to powerful emotions. They are often the objects of the whirlwind which is male desire but rarely the subjects of a desire which the narratives explore. For a novelist who delights in stretching expectation and inverting conventional logic, such a view of women and of their capacity for passionate love is unusually tame and conformist. But such perhaps are the defining limits of even the most fertile imagination.

NOTES

1. Gabriel García Márquez *El amor en los tiempos del cólera*, Barcelona: Bruguera, 1985, p. 326.
2. Gabriel García Márquez, *Crónica de una muerte anunciada*, Barcelona: Bruguera, 1981, pp. 182–3.
3. García Márquez, *Crónica de una muerte anunciada*, p. 150.
4. García Márquez, *El amor en los tiempos del cólera*, p. 267.
5. García Márquez, *El amor en los tiempos del cólera*, p. 109.
6. García Márquez, *El amor en los tiempos del cólera*, p. 459.
7. García Márquez, *El amor en los tiempos del cólera*, p. 300.
8. García Márquez, *El amor en los tiempos del cólera*, p. 49.
9. García Márquez, *El amor en los tiempos del cólera*, p. 396.
10. García Márquez, *El amor en los tiempos del cólera*, p. 396.
11. García Márquez, *El amor en los tiempos del cólera*, p. 396.
12. García Márquez, *El amor en los tiempos del cólera*, p. 500.

13. It is notable that, where in *Love in the Time of Cholera* love is confused with cholera, in *Love and Other Demons* the same occurs with rabies.
14. Gabriel García Márquez, *Del amor y otros demonios,* Buenos Aires: Editorial Sudamericana, 1994, p. 11.
15. García Márquez, *Memoria de mis putas tristes,* Mexico: Editorial Diana and Mondadori: 2004, p. 9.
16. García Márquez, *Memoria de mis putas tristes,* p. 75.
17. García Márquez, *Memoria de mis putas tristes,* p. 76.

9

STEPHEN HART

García Márquez's short stories

'Chronicle of a Death Foretold: "Match-Fixing Has to Be Sorted or Someone Will Be Assassinated", Ian Botham, 2001.'[1] The title of the article by Cole Moreton and Arifa Akbar on the mysterious death of Bob Woolmer, the coach of Pakistan's cricket team, is eloquent testimony to the way in which Gabriel García Márquez's fiction, rather like the shining metal cones in Jorge Luis Borges's 'Tlön, Uqbar, Orbis Tertius', has mysteriously infiltrated the empirical world. That is why, perhaps, it is common for readers to measure García Márquez's fiction against the yardstick offered by magical realism, to see it as most authentic when most magical-realist and to view his fiction post *One Hundred Years of Solitude* as less original. But, as I hope to show, there are at least five distinguishing features of the best of his fiction – long and short – and magical realism is but one among five, albeit an important one. In this essay I propose to use the short fiction as a laboratory in which I test a few hypotheses about the distinctiveness of the Colombian's work in more general terms. The first hypothesis is that García Márquez's fiction reached the height of its imaginative powers when it was able simultaneously to combine five features as follows:

1. magical realism, or the deadpan description of uncanny, supernatural or magical events as if they were real;
2. the portrayal of time as a truncated, or dislocated reality rather than an historical continuum, namely, a time in which, for example, the sequence of past, present and future may be reversed, as in prolepsis, or a time which, to use Benjamin's metaphor, has been 'blasted out of the continuum of history';[2]
3. the use of punchy dialogue often characterised by lapidary one-liners whose significance resonates intensely with the world outside the fiction;
4. the use of a humour which is often absurd and sometimes black;

5. the portrayal of events in such a way that they may be interpreted as a political allegory.

The example which could be chosen from the long fiction to illustrate how these five features can operate simultaneously in one text is *One Hundred Years of Solitude* (*Cien años de soledad* [1967]). In that novel we find:

- the deadpan description of magical events such as when Remedios la Bella goes to heaven ('she watched Remedios the Beauty waving goodbye in the midst of the flapping sheets that rose up with her, abandoning with her the environment of beetles and dahlias and passing through the air with her as four o'clock in the afternoon came to an end'[3]);
- the portrayal of time as truncated as in the prolepsis of the first sentence of the novel ('Many years later, as he faced the firing squad, Colonel Aureliano Buendía was to remember that distant afternoon');[4]
- the use of punchy dialogue, as for example when José Arcadio tells Úrsula that 'The earth is round, like an orange', and Úrsula retorts: 'If you have to go crazy, please go crazy all by yourself! ... But don't try to put your gypsy ideas into the heads of the children';[5]
- the use of a humour which is absurd, such as when José Arcadio Buendía says of ice: 'This is the great invention of our time';[6]
- the use of a political allegory, as evident for example in the description of the hurricane ('the second surge of wind') which destroys Macondo in the final chapter of the novel, which may be interpreted (though not all would agree) as an allusion to the man-made disaster of capitalism that wrought such havoc in Latin America when introduced by the West, and particularly by North America.[7] As Stephen Minta suggests, 'it is, of course, the arrival in Macondo of a United States banana company that leads to the eventual disintegration of the town and its inhabitants'.[8] Certainly this is how Colonel Aureliano sees it: '"Look at the mess we've got ourselves into," Colonel Aureliano Buendía used to say at the time, "just for inviting a gringo to eat some bananas".'[9] The equivalent paradigm in the area of short fiction is 'The Incredible and Sad Tale of Innocent Eréndira and her Heartless Grandmother' ('La increíble y triste histories de la cándida Eréndira y de su abuela desalmada'), as I shall be arguing below.

If we use this hypothesis to analyse García Márquez's short fiction, it offers us a helpful measuring stick with which to evaluate its evolution. García Márquez's first published short story was 'The Third Resignation' ('La tercera resignación' [1947]), and it has none of the five features listed above, or if it has any they are so far trapped at a nascent stage. As Philip

Swanson has pointed out, this story does not contain a social or political critique since it is a psychological short story.[10] Above all, it is a story about living death and particularly the thoughts running through the mind of someone who is alive but about to be buried: 'He was in the coffin, ready to be buried, and yet he knew that he wasn't dead'.[11] In this sense its theme allows it to brush shoulders with the first characteristic identified above, that is, the portrayal of the uncanny in a deadpan style, but though the uncanny is present, the matter-of-fact style is not, and the final impression is of a story that does not dramatically go beyond the model of consciousness beyond the grave in one of Émile Zola's stories (i.e. it is realist/naturalist). The dialogue is rather wooden if not even unverisimilar: '"Madam, your child has a grave illness: he is dead. Nevertheless," he went on, "we shall do everything possible to keep him alive beyond death."'[12]

Some of the other techniques of García Márquez's genius were – forgive the pun – still waiting to be born.

A short story he wrote a year later, 'The Other Side of Death' ('La otra costilla de la muerte' [1948]), returns to the same idea – what would it feel like to be dead? – and already we see some of the other techniques of his genius beginning to emerge. The supernatural is here (technique no. 1) but only in a traditional, unimaginative way; there is no dialogue (technique no. 3), but there are the stirrings of a new awareness of the timelessness of time (technique no. 2), as we read in the final paragraph of the story. The narrator is looking at a drop which is forming in the middle of the ceiling above him and he muses: 'Maybe that would fill the room in the space of an hour or in a thousand years and would dissolve that mortal armour, that vain substance, which perhaps – why not? – between brief instants would be nothing but a sticky mixture of albumen and whey'.[13] It is only in García Márquez's novelistic universe that an hour can be separated from a thousand-year period by an 'or'. Finally we might note that there is a hint of technique no. 4 (the use of absurd humour) in the sense of an awareness of the absurd though not the expression of that awareness via humour: 'Resigned, he listened to the drop, thick, heavy, exact, as it dripped in the other world, in the mistaken and absurd world of rational creatures.'[14]

'Eva Is Inside Her Cat' ('Eva está dentro de su gato'), published in the same year (1948), reveals García Márquez experimenting – like an improvising jazz musician – with a repertoire of techniques.[15] A rewriting of Kafka's *Metamorphosis,* it explores, like the previous two stories, the realm of non-rational consciousness (before expressed as the unconscious or dream or life after death) but now does it in terms of the consciousness of a cat. Like the other stories, techniques such as expression of the uncanny or the absurd are present, but they are inchoate, unarticulated. However, it is important to note that this story shows the emergence of one new technique (technique no. 4), the lapidary one-liner, which would come to dominate his best fiction in later years, and it occurs at the end of the story: 'Only then did she understand that three thousand years had passed since the day she had had a desire to eat the first orange' – but it does not work.[16]

The story 'Dialogue with the Mirror' ('Diálogo del espejo' [1949]), published a year later, shows a definitive improvement on the previous stories in terms of a more concrete sense of the passing of time ('eight-twelve'; 'eight-seventeen'; 'eight-eighteen').[17] Despite its title, the dialogue is not innovative or punchy in the style of García Márquez's mature fiction, but there is nevertheless a concerted attempt to introduce a punchy one-liner at the conclusion of the story: 'And he felt satisfaction – positive satisfaction – that a large dog had begun to wag its tail inside its soul.'[18] A similar dialogue occurs in 'Bitterness for Three Sleepwalkers' ('Amargura para tres sonámbulos' [1949]), except that now the dialogue is with a woman who sleepwalks rather than a mirror. It is also important to note that 1949, the year when these two stories were published, is often seen as the *annus mirabilis* of magical realism, since it was the year in which Alejo Carpentier's *The Kingdom of This World* (*El reino de este mundo*) was published, along with the important prologue defining 'lo real maravilloso'. It is fair to say, however, that at this point in time, García Márquez is still only halfway along the journey towards his style.

Yet he does solve one aspect of technique the following year, and this is technique no. 3, the use of punchy dialogue along with lapidary one-liners. 'Eyes of a Blue Dog' ('Ojos de perro azul' [1950]) shows how it works.[19] The story opens with what looks like an ordinary enough domestic setting:

> Then she looked at me. I thought that she was looking at me for the first time. But then, when she turned around behind the lamp and I kept feeling her slippery and oily look behind me, over my shoulder, I understood that it was I who was looking at her for the first time. I lit a cigarette. I took a drag on the harsh, strong smoke, before spinning in the chair, balancing on one of the rear legs.[20]

Yet, by the end of the first paragraph of this story, we already see García Márquez's genius emerging, in the form of the lapidary one-liners in a dialogue we are intrigued by since we are one step removed from its referential meaning: 'It was then that I remembered the usual thing, when I said to her: "Eyes of a blue dog." Without taking her hand off the lamp she said to me: "That. We'll never forget that." She left the orbit, singing: "Eyes of a blue dog. I've written it everywhere."'[21]

We come across more and more intriguing one-liners in the rest of the story: '"I think I'm going to catch cold," she said. "This must be a city of ice."'[22] This is continued throughout the story until we reach the final section, which is lapidary but also has a twist: '"You're the only man who doesn't remember anything of what he's dreamed after he wakes up".'[23] It throws the reader's expectations into disarray since the site of consciousness, the perceptor of the narrative, has been told that he is actually the site of non-knowledge, thereby reversing or upsetting the dichotomy knowledge/ignorance established up until that point in the short story. It was an important step towards the creation of a new literary idiom which would impact hugely on the literary world.

In the period 1950–2, García Márquez achieved – though in two different stories – the successful expression of four of the five techniques which would one day make him one of the greatest writers of the twentieth century. 'The Woman Who Came at Six O'Clock' ('La mujer que llegaba a las seis' [1950]) employs three techniques in an arresting manner which is recognisably Garciamarquian.[24] It excels in the use of technique no. 3, punchy dialogue, along with memorable one-liners:

> José went over to where she was. He put his great puffy face up to the woman while he tugged one of his eyelids with his index finger.
>
> 'Blow on me here,' he said.
>
> The woman threw her head back. She was serious, annoyed, softened, beautified by a cloud of sadness and fatigue.
>
> 'Stop your foolishness, José. You know I haven't had a drink for six months.'[25]

The story also demonstrates an innovative awareness of time as truncated and discontinuous. The prostitute comes into José's restaurant every day at six o'clock and yet, though in Jose's eyes, it is six o'clock ('every day the clock says six, then you come in and say you're hungry as a dog'), and although the clock says three minutes after six, the prostitute believes that she has been there for a quarter of an hour: '"It just struck six, queen," José said. "When you came in it was just finishing." "I've got a quarter of an hour that says I've been here," the woman said.'[26]

The anomaly between the ways in which both individuals perceive time is never satisfactorily resolved. It is left as a mystery hovering over the text. One possibility – certainly sustainable from a reading of the text – is that Reina (or Queen) has just killed one of her customers and therefore needs an alibi covering her for the time (5.45–6.00 p.m.) when she killed the client. This, however, remains as a potential reading of the text since it is only based on the fact that Queen begins to talk obsessively about killing a man: 'Would you defend me if I killed him?' she asks José.[27] At the end of the story she suddenly states that she wants 'another quarter of an hour', and the story ends: '"I really don't understand, queen", he said. "Don't be foolish, José," the woman said. "Just remember that I've been here since five-thirty."'[28] This can certainly be interpreted as a case of the woman making sure that her alibi is watertight, but because the story ends with Reina asking for a further fifteen minutes, another reading suggests itself – that Reina is, as it were, going back in time, and the final impression is of a world similar to that in Beckett's *Waiting for Godot* in which the passing of time is undercut by absurdity, and the suggestion that life may be timeless but that human beings parcel it up arbitrarily into hours or, as in García Márquez's story, into quarters of an hour. Time, indeed, is presented in 'The Woman Who Came at Six O'Clock' as a dislocated reality; an awareness of its fundamental absurdity undercuts the apparent comfort zone of the time ticking in a detective novel (this story indeed contains in essence one of the overriding features of the portrayal of time in *Chronicle of a Death Foretold* [*Crónica de una muerte anunciada*] published thirty-one years later). Not only does this story contain techniques no. 2 and no. 3, it also contains technique no. 4, the use of absurd or black humour, as when José says: 'I'll cut off my arm if that clock is one minute slow.'[29]

It was two years later when García Márquez perfected the technique of magical realism by, in 'Someone Has Been Disarranging These Roses' ('Alguien desordena estas rosas' [1952]), letting us hear a ghost speak to us in a deadpan, natural way.[30] The ghost, as he explains, is attempting to take some roses to his child's grave (or is it his own grave?), and the roses he tries to take are those the woman he visits every Sunday puts on her altar. The story is obscure – deliberately so – but it appears that the ghost is that of a young boy who died when the stairs in the stable collapsed underneath him, and who was like a brother to her.[31] This supposition, however, does not square with the other possibility, i.e. that the ghost is that of an older individual (for how else could he have had a child at whose grave he wants to lay flowers, as indicated at the beginning of the story?).[32] Clearly the story is built around an aporia, since the different components cannot all add up:

> That's the way she's been for twenty years, in the rocker, darning her things, looking at the chair as if now she weren't taking care of the boy with whom she had shared her childhood afternoons but the invalid grandson who has been sitting here in the corner ever since the time his grandmother was five years old.[33]

If we presume the invalid grandson to be the child whose body now 'rests, mingled now, dispersed among snails and roots', then we are clearly faced with a non sequitur, not only because it is difficult to know how the individual addressed as 'Boy! Boy!' could have had a child, but also because it is difficult to imagine how a grandson can have been sitting in a corner ever since 'his grandmother was five years old', which would mean that his consciousness of his grandmother preceded his birth.[34] García Márquez has clearly telescoped individuals from different generations into a single person, undoing the Gordian knot of sequentiality, cause and effect. In this sense we can speak of 'Someone Has Been Disarranging These Roses' as exploring, even perfecting, techniques no. 1 and no. 2, that is, magical realism (the presentation of the uncanny as an everyday event) and the presentation of time as a truncated reality. As suggested above, these two short stories, 'The Woman Who Came at Six O'Clock' and 'Someone Has Been Disarranging These Roses', between them combined the four techniques underlying García Márquez's mastery. The only technique which remained to be explored and then perfected was the political allegory, and it is to this technique that I now turn my attention.

Even while García Márquez was perfecting his storytelling abilities, another window was opening in his soul: politics. As Stephen Minta has pointed out, García Márquez 'was closely involved with the Colombian Communist Party in the early 1950s', and from 1954 to 1957 he 'continued to pay monthly contributions to Party funds, and to collect contributions from fellow journalists'.[35] He was present in Caracas in January 1958 when the Venezuelan President Marcos Pérez Jiménez was ousted from power and shared in the popular and public jubilation that accompanied this event. When Batista was defeated in Cuba in January 1959, García Márquez commented that 'it seemed as if time had gone into reverse and Marcos Pérez Jiménez had been overthrown for a second time.'[36] The Colombian's metaphor is redolent of Benjamin's alluded to above: 'The awareness that they are about to make the continuum of history explode is characteristic of the revolutionary classes at the moment of their action. The great revolution introduced a new calendar.'[37] Reading the Latin American writer's metaphor via Benjamin's historical materialism allows us to see García Márquez's sense of time going 'into reverse' as predicated on a sense of popular revolution being explosive and regenerative rather than cyclical and vicious. The Colombian writer was invited to Cuba, along with his stalwart friend and fellow writer, Plinio Apuleyo Mendoza, as a friend of the Revolution, and commented: 'For those of us who had lived in Caracas throughout the previous year, the feverish atmosphere and the creative disorder of Havana at the beginning of 1959 were no surprise.'[38] He was subsequently invited to open the Bogotá office of the recently founded Cuban press agency, Prensa Latina, and he also worked for a period in Prensa Latina's New York office. As Minta suggests (though written in 1987 this is arguably still true): 'García Márquez's enthusiasm for the Cuban Revolution has remained undiminished to the present day, and, if he has had some private reservations about the direction which the revolution has taken, he has never doubted that its achievements have been of far greater significance than its limitations.'[39]

Despite all of the above, the political allegory is one of the most difficult techniques to identify within García Márquez's fiction since an allegory is by definition hidden from immediate view. Indeed, symbolism is never obvious or overdetermined in the Colombian writer's fiction. Finding a political symbolism in García Márquez's work can be like looking for a needle in the proverbial haystack, but we find the first hint of its existence in a story, 'The Night of the Curlews' ('La noche de los alcaravanes') which may be read as an allegory of political blindness within the Colombian nation.[40] Thus the phrase 'We can't get out of here. The curlews have pecked out our eyes' would be interpreted in a political and contemporary sense rather than a universal and eternal sense.[41] The scepticism towards the official story of state discourse would also be seen to hover around the following sentence: 'she said that's what the newspapers had said, but nobody had believed them'.[42] The gap between what the people think and what the newspapers say introduces a motif which resonates with those readers familiar with García Márquez's later fiction, such as *One Hundred Years of Solitude,* where the state is revealed to make things up to suit its political purposes. The fiction of this period – the mid to late 1950s – is characterised by the portrayal of a latent political anger within a country, which, in Ángel Rama's words, 'lives in a permanent state of violence, which is either open, or underground and threatening'.[43] But it was in a collection of short stories published in 1962, *Big Mama's Funeral* (*Los funerales de la mamá grande*), that García Márquez would perfect his use of the fifth technique of political allegory.

'One of These Days' ('Un día de éstos') was written before March 1958 and is one of the clearest examples of the emergence of a political allegory in García Márquez's work. Barely four pages long, it uses the rather comical rivalry between a dentist, Aureliano Escovar, and the local mayor (unnamed) to draw a broader canvas. The dentist forces the mayor to accept a tooth extraction without anaesthetic and comments after the tooth has been pulled out: 'With this, lieutenant, you are paying us back for the twenty dead', the idea being the local mayor has been repressing the local community and has with impunity killed twenty of his political opponents (on whose side the 'liberal' dentist finds himself).[44] The novelistic *coup de grâce* occurs in the hyperbolic conclusion of the short story:

> – Send me the bill – he said.
> – To you or the town hall?
> The mayor did not even look at him. He closed the door, and said, through the metal grid.
> – It doesn't make any difference.[45]

This hieroglyphic which traces the equals sign between impunity, corruption and state power tore the veil from the rhetoric of state discourse which had remained in power since the days of the Conquest. With these thirty-five words, the political allegory was born in Latin America.

It is, however, in the short story 'Big Mama's Funeral' that García Márquez inaugurates rather than simply hints at the short story as an allegory of contemporary Latin American history, when he uses the funeral of a woman conveniently named Big Mama (I say convenient since it cannot be anything other than allegorical as it is so little tied to a specific historical reality) to allegorise the grotesque nature of post-colonial political reality in Latin America. 'Big Mama's Funeral' was written in May–June 1959, which means that the short story can almost be seen as a direct response to the ideology underlying the Cuban Revolution.[46] At first flush, there is nothing in this story which specifically defines it as a political allegory, but the list of powers over which Big Mama specifically has control are such as to persuade me that this short story is an allegory of the folly and misuse of power initiated by the Spanish conquistadors and continued to the present day – and the reaction to this short story in the 1960s when it came to greater public attention can only have been a revolutionary one. All of the details, particularly with regard to the various material and abstract entities to which Big Mama lays claim, gradually turn the *récit* into a *reductio ad absurdum*. How can Big Mama, for example, really be the owner of

> the richness of the subsoil, territorial waters, the colours of the national flag, national sovereignty, traditional parties, the rights of man, citizens' rights, citizens' freedoms, the first magistrate, the second official request, the third debate, letters of recommendation, historical proof, free elections, beauty queens, traditional speeches, grandiose demonstrations, distinguished young ladies, upright gentlemen, military honour, his illustrious lordship, the supreme court of justice, import-banned articles, liberal ladies, the problem of the flesh, linguistic purity, examples for the world, legal order, a free but responsible press, the Athens of South America, public opinion, democratic elections, Christian morals, lack of hard currency, the right to asylum, the communist threat, the ship of the state, the high cost of living, Republican traditions, the disadvantaged classes, messages of support.[47]

Has there ever be any more grotesque or ironic description of the rights and privileges that the *caciques* of Latin America have arrogated to themselves because of the lack of any dissenting voice? Has any Latin American writer ever stated in such denuded terms the vacuity underlying the amalgamation of rights, privileges and taboos decreed by the Latin American oligarchy?[48] For, since there is no 'loyal dissent' of the other house, nor even the voice of the subaltern to be listened to, then the *latifundistas* can simply arrogate to themselves privileges, and rights, and things as if they were godlike. Surely it is the case that – given that the story was written in 1959 – García Márquez was attacking the grotesque arbitrariness of colonial rule in Latin America, and therefore, by implication, though not stating so as such, expressing an allegiance by one step removed to the anti-colonialist ideology of the Cuban Revolution. Indeed, 'Big Mama's Funeral' might well be read as a warm letter of self-introduction to Fidel Castro and all that he stood for in those heady years of the 1960s, for it is a satire about the grotesque nature of the rights and privileges claimed by the conquerors of Latin America – and indeed by their successors in post-Independence Latin America. It certainly contains within it the seeds of a radical, anti-colonial reading of the history of Latin America, but this is nowhere an over-obvious paradigm and, indeed, may be dismissed as an overdetermined interpretation by the historicist critic; but, notwithstanding this, it is a potential reading and as such hovers around the text. It can, for example, be read as a portrayal of the lethargy of the tropics. García Márquez himself has stated that it offers 'a rather static and exclusive (*excluyente*) vision of reality', and Robin Fiddian has noted the depiction of 'the texture of tedium' in this and other stories written from the mid to late 1950s.[49] Certainly there are some circles – perhaps in Cuba in the early 1960s, or the left-wing intelligentsia in France or the USA, or the hierarchy in the Soviet Union – whose members would chuckle self-knowingly over the obviousness of such a paradigm, but let us for the time being read it as a short story with a number of intended meanings, political and otherwise, none of which is necessarily encoded or predetermined.

'The Incredible and Sad Tale of Innocent Eréndira and Her Heartless Grandmother' ('La increíble y triste historia de la Cándida Eréndira y de su abuela desalmada'), published in 1972, can be considered the zenith of the style of the short-story genre in García Márquez's hands. But before turning to, I want to make a quick detour in order to discuss a short story which shows how García Márquez was feeling his way towards the creation of the political allegory, for first he needed to perfect the form before he could add the message. 'The Sea of Lost Time' ('El mar del tiempo perdido' [1961]) is an example of a fiction that explores the creative depths of allegory but one in which the expressiveness of allegory has not reached its expressive zenith. For here allegory appears in the form of the smell of roses which stands for the secret of death. Yet this meaning of the allegory is only released to the reader little by little. The opening of this story is careful to underline that the flowers of death associated with the sea have a significance which the inhabitants of the town recognise but cannot decipher: 'something very strange happened last year.'[50] Gradually, however, the transcendent significance of the mysterious smell of roses is revealed. As Clothilde says: 'A smell of roses can only be a message from God.'[51] That the smell of roses is a reference to the secret significance of death is only revealed when, in a rather surrealist if not magical-realist turn of events, Mr Herbert invites Tobías down to the depths of the sea where they both witness the dead swimming around.[52] Going to an empirically impossible place to witness the life of the dead is not, of course, a new idea (we find extraordinary examples in the Old Testament, in Book VI of Virgil's *Aeneid,* and in Dante's *Divine Comedy*), but the way in which García Márquez presents it is striking for he uses an allegorical instrument to do so, with the physical (the smell of roses wafting up from the sea) used to allude to the spiritual (life after death). It was, however, only later on – in 1972, to be precise – that García Márquez was able to use the instrument of allegory in order to make a barbed though not over-obvious political point about the distress of capitalism.

It is in 'The Incredible and Sad Tale of Innocent Eréndira and Her Heartless Grandmother' that I argue can be found simultaneously present the five characteristics of García Márquez's style which are identified as the magic mix needed to create García Márquez's personal brand of narration.[53] Julio Ortega has pointed to the parodic and ironic function of this tale of a woman's woe, one in which the story of Cinderella is carnivalised and reversed in order now to tell the story of a prostitute.[54] 'The Incredible and Sad Tale of Innocent Eréndira and Her Heartless Grandmother' uses magical realism, in the sense of the deadpan description of a fantastic event, namely, the banishment of a granddaughter to sexual slavery for having accidentally burnt the family home down, a slavery which would furthermore last 200 years if the debt were to be paid off fully. Though this is first presented as a fantastically exaggerated event, its fantastic logarithm is allowed to produce a formula. ('At this rate she'll need two hundred years to pay me back.'[55]) Likewise, there are numerous examples of how this brilliantly developed short story portrays time as a truncated or, more accurately, timeless reality: '"Take advantage of tomorrow to wash the living-room too," she told Eréndira. "It hasn't seen the sun since the days of all the noise."'[56] 'The Incredible and Sad Tale of Innocent Eréndira and Her Heartless Grandmother' is also full of one of the most engaging aspects of García Márquez's fiction: his use of punchy dialogue: '"I never saw the sea," she said. "It's like the desert but with water, " said Ulises.'[57] There are also examples of absurd humour in this short story: '"Then why do they have you here as mayor?" the grandmother asked. "To make it rain, " was the mayor's answer.'[58] Finally 'The Incredible and Sad Tale of Innocent Eréndira and Her Heartless Grandmother' can be read as a political allegory in that the debt slavery which Eréndira suffers – but which she, it ought to be underlined, does not complain about – may be interpreted as the impossible situation in which Latin America finds itself with regard to its creditors as a result of its overwhelming debt. Intriguingly, this man-made disaster is – and here we can draw a line of similarity between 'The Incredible and Sad Tale of Innocent Eréndira and Her Heartless Grandmother' and *One Hundred Years of Solitude* – presented not as the result of a disastrous human or social decision but rather in terms of a natural disaster or human error, that is, something which cannot be helped. Eréndira's mistake, like the 'second surge of wind' in *One Hundred Years of Solitude,* is also created by the wind:[59]

> Overcome by the barbarous chores of the day, Eréndira didn't have the strength to get undressed and she put the candlestick on the night table and fell on to the bed. A short while later the wind of her misfortune came into the bedroom like a pack of hounds and knocked the candle over against the curtain.[60]

At this point Eréndira's fate is sealed. The mansion burns down. The Indians of the village try to rescue the remains of smoking ashes of the mansion: 'the charred corpse of the ostrich, the frame of a gilded piano, the torso of a statue.'[61] The grandmother is implacable: '"My poor child," she sighed. "Life won't be long enough for you to pay me back for this mishap".'[62] And thus Eréndira's nightmare begins, as she attempts to pay back her debt: 'she began to pay it back that very day, beneath the noise of the rain, when she was taken to the village storekeeper, a skinny and premature widower who was quite well known in the desert for the good price he paid for virginity.'[63] Eréndira's debt is paid back through prostitution, a common topos in García Márquez's work – here it is a transaction that defiles her as much as her clients and masters.[64] García Márquez thereby explodes the syntax of Cinderella, both in the sense of its timelessness (set in the achronos of 'Once upon a time') and its rhetoric of social cohesiveness (the prince who marries the poor girl). Like Benjamin's historical materialist, the Colombian novelist 'leaves it to others to be drained by the whore called "Once upon a time" in historicism's bordello. He remains in control of his powers, man enough to blast open the continuum of history.'[65] It is only in the last two paragraphs of 'The Incredible and Sad Tale of Innocent Eréndira and Her Heartless Grandmother' that we suddenly realise the tide is beginning to turn on the story; Eréndira refuses her knight in shining white armour (Ulises) who comes to save her, and instead she starts to 'run along the shore away from the city'.[66] Her flight begins to 'blast open the continuum of history' since she runs somehow forwards and backwards at the same time:

> She was running into the wind, swifter than a deer, and no voice of this world could stop her. Without turning her head she ran past the saltpetre pits, the

> talcum craters, the torpor of the shacks, until the natural science of the sea ended and the desert began, and she still kept on running with the gold vest beyond the arid winds and the never-ending sunsets and she was never heard of again nor was the slightest trace of her misfortune ever found.[67]

The liminal zone between where the sea ended and where the desert began operates simultaneously in this paragraph as a magical-realist space combining reality and fantasy, and as a revolutionary space where the 'misfortune' of her slavery is cancelled out. Not only does Eréndira manage to escape the sacrificial syntax of the West with its indebtedness and slavery but she also manages to cut the sinews of that redemptionism which is complicit with the Cinderella complex. Eréndira is running towards the Revolution.

NOTES

1. Cole Moreton and Arifa Akbar, 'Chronicle of a Death Foretold: "Match-Fixing Has to Be Sorted or Someone Will Be Assassinated", Ian Botham, 2001', *The Independent on Sunday* (25 March 2007), pp. 16–17.
2. Walter Benjamin, 'Theses on the Philosophy of History', in *Illuminations,* ed. Hannah Arendt, trans. Harry Zohn, London: Fontana Press, 1992, pp. 245–58; p. 253.
3. Gabriel García Márquez, *One Hundred Years of Solitude,* trans. Gregory Rabassa, London: Picador, 1970, p. 195.
4. García Márquez, *One Hundred Years of Solitude,* p. 5.
5. García Márquez, *One Hundred Years of Solitude,* p. 12.
6. García Márquez, *One Hundred Years of Solitude,* p. 22.
7. García Márquez, *One Hundred Years of Solitude,* p. 335.
8. Stephen Minta, *Gabriel García Márquez: Writer of Colombia,* London: Jonathan Cape, 1987, p. 163.
9. García Márquez, *One Hundred Years of Solitude,* p. 189.
10. Philip Swanson, *Cómo leer a Gabriel García Márquez,* Madrid: Júcar, 1991, p. 14.
11. Gabriel García Márquez, 'The Third Resignation', in *Innocent Eréndira and Other Stories,* trans. Gregory Rabassa, London: Picador, 1981, pp. 68–75; p. 69.
12. García Márquez, 'The Third Resignation', p. 69.
13. Gabriel García Márquez, 'The Other Side of Death', in *Innocent Eréndira and Other Stories,* pp. 76–82; p. 82.
14. García Márquez, 'The Other Side of Death', p. 82.
15. Gabriel García Márquez, 'Eva Is Inside Her Cat', in *Innocent Eréndira and Other Stories,* pp. 83–91.
16. García Márquez, 'Eva Is Inside Her Cat', p. 91.
17. Gabriel García Márquez, 'Dialogue with the Mirror', in *Innocent Eréndira and Other Stories,* pp. 92–7; pp. 92, 94, 95.
18. García Márquez, 'Dialogue with the Mirror', p. 97.
19. Gabriel García Márquez, 'Eyes of a Blue Dog', in *Innocent Eréndira and Other Stories,* pp. 102–7.
20. García Márquez, 'Eyes of a Blue Dog', p. 102.

21. García Márquez, 'Eyes of a Blue Dog', p. 102.
22. García Márquez, 'Eyes of a Blue Dog', p. 103.
23. García Márquez, 'Eyes of a Blue Dog', p. 107.
24. Gabriel García Márquez, 'The Woman Who Came at Six O'Clock', in *Innocent Eréndira and Other Stories,* pp. 108–17.
25. García Márquez, 'The Woman Who Came at Six O'Clock', p. 109.
26. García Márquez, 'The Woman Who Came at Six O'Clock', p. 109.
27. García Márquez, 'The Woman Who Came at Six O'Clock', p. 113.
28. García Márquez, 'The Woman Who Came at Six O'Clock', p. 117.
29. García Márquez, 'The Woman Who Came at Six O'Clock', p. 109.
30. Gabriel García Márquez, 'Someone Has Been Disarranging These Roses', in *Innocent Eréndira and Other Stories,* pp. 118–21.
31. García Márquez, 'Someone Has Been Disarranging These Roses', pp. 119, 120.
32. García Márquez, 'Someone Has Been Disarranging These Roses', p. 118.
33. García Márquez, 'Someone Has Been Disarranging These Roses', p. 120.
34. García Márquez, 'Someone Has Been Disarranging These Roses', pp. 118, 120.
35. Minta, *Gabriel García Márquez,* p. 55.
36. Minta, *Gabriel García Márquez,* p. 59.
37. Benjamin, 'Theses', p. 253.
38. Quoted in Minta, *Gabriel García Márquez,* pp. 59–60.
39. Minta, *Gabriel García Márquez,* p. 59.
40. Gabriel García Márquez, 'The Night of the Curlews', in *Innocent Eréndira and Other Stories,* pp. 122–6.
41. García Márquez, 'The Night of the Curlews', p. 122.
42. García Márquez, 'The Night of the Curlews', p. 123.
43. Ángel Rama, 'Un novelista de la violencia americana', in Mario Benedetti, *Nueve asedios a García Márquez,* Santiago de Chile: Editora Universitaria, 1969, pp. 106–25; p. 113 (my translation).
44. Gabriel García Márquez, 'Un día de éstos', in *Los funerales de la Mamá Grande,* Buenos Aires: Editorial Sudamericana, 1977, pp. 21–6; p. 25 (my translation).
45. García Márquez, 'Un día de éstos', p. 26 (my translation).
46. Dasso Saldívar, *García Márquez: El viaje a la semilla – La biografía,* Madrid: Alfaguara, 1997, p. 356.
47. Gabriel García Márquez, 'Los funerales de la Mamá Grande', in *Los funerales de la Mamá Grande,* Buenos Aires: Editorial Sudamericana, 1977; p. 137 (my translation).
48. Philip Swanson argues that 'Big Mama's Funeral' satirises 'la influencia de las oligarquías rurales en América Latina' ('the influence of rural oligarchies in Latin America'); *Cómo leer,* p. 26.
49. Quoted in Swanson, *Cómo leer,* p. 22.
50. Gabriel García Márquez, 'The Sea of Lost Time', in *Innocent Eréndira and Other Stories,* pp. 46–60; p. 47.
51. García Márquez, 'The Sea of Lost Time', p. 47.
52. García Márquez, 'The Sea of Lost Time', p. 58.
53. Gabriel García Márquez, 'The Incredible and Sad Tale of Innocent Eréndira and Her Heartless Grandmother', in *Innocent Eréndira and Other Stories,* pp. 7–45.
54. Julio Ortega, 'García Márquez posmoderno: el relativismo de la verdad', *Ínsula,* 723 (March 2007): 12–15; p. 12. Special number entitled 'Ciento cuarenta años de soledad y ochenta de vida'.

55. García Márquez, 'Eréndira', p. 11.
56. García Márquez, 'Eréndira', p. 9.
57. García Márquez, 'Eréndira', p. 20.
58. García Márquez, 'Eréndira', p. 22.
59. García Márquez, *One Hundred Years of Solitude,* p. 335.
60. García Márquez, 'Eréndira', p. 10.
61. García Márquez, 'Eréndira', p. 10.
62. García Márquez, 'Eréndira', p. 11.
63. García Márquez, 'Eréndira', p. 11.
64. Prostitution is a constant theme of his memoirs, *Living to Tell the Tale,* for example, and reappears in his most recent work *Memories of my Melancholy Whores,* called by Adam Feinstein, 'an imperfectly formed little jewel': Adam Feinstein, 'Sleeping Seamstresses', *TLS,* 10 December 2004, p. 23. For further discussion, see Lorena E. Roses, 'Las putas alegres, tristes, pero sagradas de García Márquez: *Cien años* a cuarenta años de distancia', *Ínsula,* 723 (March 2007): 3–5.
65. Benjamin, 'Theses', p. 254.
66. García Márquez, 'Eréndira', p. 45.
67. García Márquez, 'Eréndira', p. 45.

10

ROBERT L. SIMS

García Márquez's non-fiction works

Gabriel García Márquez has been a journalist and fiction writer all his life, and the two genres have intertwined throughout his career. Raymond L. Williams pointedly explains that

> journalism has been a constant presence in García Márquez's literary career and personal biography. García Márquez the novelist has gained far more from journalism than just 'contact with reality'. A reading of his journalistic writings during this period, in fact, shows a writer experimenting with a variety of styles, techniques, and genres. Both the enormous volume of García Márquez's journalism and its intimate relationship to his fiction make his journalistic writings essential to a complete study of this work.[1]

The connection between García Márquez's fiction and his non-fiction is represented by the *refrito*, or follow-up story, which provides information discovered or events happening after the publication of the original story. The fact that the follow-up story builds upon an already published story often gives it a pejorative connotation and lowly status among journalists. The intersection of his fiction and non-fiction starts during the investigative reporting phase of his work for *El Espectador* in Bogotá, Colombia in 1954–5. García Márquez wrote three series of follow-up stories in which his writing and narrative technique start to develop.

Before examining three major *refritos* that García Márquez wrote during his time at *El Espectador,* we have to backtrack to the beginnings of his journalistic and literary careers. Chronologically, his first journalistic piece appeared eight months after the publication of his first short story. It is important that his first short stories were published in the limited space of the newspaper which is governed by strict formal criteria. García Márquez's journalistic debut deviated from the norm in several significant ways:

> It is not easy to detect the different basic structures of a newspaper column which, like 'Another Story' in Cartagena and 'La Jirafa' in Barranquilla,

> allowed the inclusion of absolutely everything that the journalist wanted to write in it, from a formal point of view, without, it seems, a chief editor calling his attention to any style book. The fact that the journalist in question lacked any formal training and that, presumably, he only knew that the column had to be well written, do not help explain the situation.[2]

García Márquez's atypical debut in journalism requires framing the context in which he started to write.

He never seems to have suffered from the 'blank page' syndrome or, in this case, the 'blank space of the newspaper column', when his only criterion was that he had to 'write well'. This situation was quite prevalent in the Colombian press because there existed a general practice of 'assigning those spaces in the newspaper to people who "write well" and who, except in rare cases, do not oppose the newspaper's philosophy. Consequently, in these authentic fiefdoms, the reader can find almost any topic.'[3] Beyond García Márquez's more stimulating work as a columnist, his labours also included writing headlines, correcting teletype copy and working with the layout staff. Thus, García Márquez's training in journalism not only afforded him the opportunity to experiment within the elastic formal and thematic constraints of the column but also involved him in the more anonymous aspects of the newspaper which undoubtedly helped him develop his writing style and narrative.

During the first phase of García Márquez's career as a journalist, which extends from May 1948 to December 1949, his signed output consists of thirty-eight pieces published in the column 'Another Story' ('Punto y aparte') of the Cartagena daily *El Universal*. From January 1950 to December 1952, he wrote nearly 400 pieces in the column 'La Jirafa' ('The Giraffe') for *El Heraldo* of Barranquilla. After these two phases, García Márquez's journalistic peregrinations turned inland from the luminous land of the Caribbean towards Bogotá, the domain of the *cachacos,* a name which the coastal inhabitants of Colombia apply to the inhabitants of these landlocked, sombre cities. From February 1954 to July 1955, García Márquez worked in Bogotá as a member of the staff of the Liberal newspaper, *El Espectador.* The distinguishing features of this brief but significant stage in his career are the new journalistic environment and the diversity of activities to which he would dedicate his time and energy. García Márquez's move from the coast to Bogotá also produced a spatial change in his journalism. The longer articles, published in several parts, afforded him the opportunity to develop his writing and narrative techniques in a more coherent way. These longer articles proved especially important because the unity of vision of his previous journalistic pieces still lacked a narrative framework which could enable him to communicate his totalising vision in a sustained manner:

> In his newspaper reporting García Márquez found exactly what he needed, since what is a newspaper article but a narration, and even more, a narration based on a story. That is exactly what the Colombian writer's narrative style is. Like many writers before him – such as Hemingway, one of his masters – García Márquez discovered in newspaper articles not only an increased contact with the 'street', – and in many cases his articles were based on documentation and interviews – but also an area for narrative experimentation, honed by the requirements of mass communications, which would also serve him well in his stories and novels.[4]

García Márquez's journalistic work for *El Espectador* branched out in three directions: film criticism, short articles written for 'Day to Day' and feature articles, usually appearing in instalments, on topics ranging from a long series on a noted Colombian cyclist to the return of the Colombian soldiers from the Korean war and their subsequent neglect by the government. Of the three areas in which he worked for *El Espectador,* investigative reporting is the most crucial to his writing: while investigative reporting enabled García Márquez to develop a continuous space for his writing, this same space still imposed strict limits in which he had to write.

These longer articles resemble the hybrid genre variously labelled 'the literature of fact' or 'literary non-fiction writing' and which is often identified with the style of writing christened New Journalism. García Márquez's investigative reporting combines factual reporting and literary techniques, and he focuses primarily on the human context in which the events took place. He also seeks meaning within the limits of the facts. These spatial and factual limitations provide him with a well-delineated framework in which he can develop his writing techniques, themes and a vision of reality that simultaneously respects the facts and transcends them. His articles show that he moves interpretatively, not imaginatively, beyond the facts in order to find patterns of human meaning embedded in the events. Human involvement in the events fills in and completes the factual, skeletal framework, and this constitutes the overall pattern in most of these articles.

García Márquez's first long article investigates the human dimensions of a tragic event in 'Evaluation and Reconstruction of the Catastrophe in Antioquia', which appeared in three parts on 2–4 August 1954. This first venture in investigative reporting established a pattern that the author would follow in much of his subsequent journalism and fiction: the *refrito* in which he investigates an event which has already occurred and has been 'interpreted' by the press and official sources. Frequently, he has to confront the official version, which he inevitably opposes and subverts in his own articles. Pedro Sorela describes this decisive moment in García Márquez's writing career:

> The paper sent García Márquez on his first assignment to undertake the thankless task of reporting on something that, in principle, had already been fully covered. Upon arriving in Medellín, the journalist was just about ready to return and forget his assignment. His story would have been different. He did not do it and quite the contrary he returned with his article whose principal characteristics were already announced in the title – *evaluation and reconstruction* – and which would capture the attention of the newspaper's editors.[5]

The first assignment not only played a key role in the development of García Márquez's approach to reality but it also allowed him to perfect his writing techniques. The space of the news stories expands rapidly, especially in the *refritos,* because the young reporter does not have to limit himself to the narrated story, which could fit into a still more restricted space. The spatial expansion occurs above all in the narrating where he can develop a variety of narrative possibilities embedded in the voices which have been temporarily silenced by the official version.

Two other crucial *refritos* appeared during his stint with *El Espectador:* a series on the Chocó entitled 'The Chocó Ignored by Colombia' and another entitled 'From Korea to Reality' demonstrate his intense interest in politics and culture. In these three articles García Márquez has directly challenged the official discourse of the Colombian government. The subversiveness of García Márquez always aims directly at *how an event occurred* and never at *what happened.* Behind the veneer of *what happened* in these three articles lies a whole human context that produced the event, and this is what he searches for in his news stories. The facts and events cannot be detached from their human context without losing their meaning. The *refrito* affords him the opportunity to restore the human context. In this struggle to liberate the human context, *The Story of a Shipwrecked Sailor* (*Relato de un náufrago* [1970]) represents the most perilous encounter with power and the official world.

From the inception of the hyphenated writing career of García Márquez in 1947, we encounter a series of confrontations with the official world and its versions of historical events. Three separate articles on the naval accident appeared in *El Espectador,* and they trace a direct path to his spectacular story on the accident of the Colombian naval destroyer *Caldas* in which eight sailors were washed overboard and disappeared. The only survivor, Luis Alejandro Velasco, spent ten days adrift in a life raft before reaching the Atlantic coast of Colombia. García Márquez interviewed Velasco for many hours, and his story was published in a fourteen-part series in *El Espectador* in 1955 and then as a book in 1970.

Throughout his career, García Márquez has endeavoured to penetrate the inner circles of power, and this quest is accompanied by a continuous fascination and obsession with the phenomenon of power and the concomitant effort to undermine it through narrative discourse. One of the forms that power assumes is the archival power of official history which offers itself as the only authentic version of the facts. García Márquez fully realises the futility of producing another historical variant because it will only end up reconfirming the official version.

His confrontation with the official world in *The Story of a Shipwrecked Sailor,* unlike the oblique encounters in the preceding journalistic series, drew an immediate response from the High Command of the Navy upon the republication of the story as a special supplement which included a number of compromising photographs. After the publication of the special supplement, the military's account of the accident and the newspaper's version showed striking differences.

In the first chapter of *The Story of a Shipwrecked Sailor,* Velasco alludes to the contraband cargo when he describes his friend, Miguel Ortega, who used all his money to buy an automatic washer, radio and a stove for his wife. A little further on, Velasco refers to the false sense of security that the illicit cargo offers: 'Amid the refrigerators, washing machines, and stoves that were tightly secured on the stern deck, Ramón Herrera and I lay down, carefully positioning ourselves to avoid being swept away by a wave.'[6] García Márquez continues to contextualise the discourse until it appears for a third time in the most suspenseful and emotional moment of the story. He deliberately chooses this moment because it crystallises the confrontation between his strong desire to approach the centre of power and to undermine it through narrative discourse.

García Márquez restores the human dimension of the event so that the reader can witness the unfolding drama of Velasco as if it were taking place for the first time. The author merges the *seen* and the *lived* experience to create what is called in electronic journalism 'live coverage' in which the words of the reporter are broadcast without being scripted. Moreover, the narrative follows the action so closely that they can almost be considered simultaneous. The double narrator enables the author to achieve the same effect. The creation of a gestalt image through the clash of discourses and languages surrounding the contraband cargo materialises the historical event in the reader's mind, and he proceeds to furnish the missing details.

García Márquez succeeds in transforming the accusatory photos into narrative discourse by constantly stressing the presence of the objects. He also reactivates the different discourses that the official world tried in vain to silence. Beyond the visual impact of the photographs, their reassilimilation into the narrative reveals the subversive strategy of the author. He not only spectacularises the story's most dramatic moment on the textual level by employing action and visual verbs, but he also skilfully synchronises the two moments to create live coverage which is *seen* and *lived*.

The Story of a Shipwrecked Sailor confirms the corrosive power of narrative and reveals the dualist position of García Márquez before the phenomenon of power: an attraction–repulsion movement that impels the author to find the power centre and to subvert it without losing its specular value. Specularisation constitutes a fundamental aspect in the bigeneric writing of García Márquez. Drawing close to power does not signify being absorbed, nor much less corrupted by this phenomenon, but it does signal a profound desire to observe it from the absolute centre. The subversion of power through narrative discourse cannot bring about a final defeat because, in the dialogic world in which the author is writing and living, no one has the final word. The discourse of power, whether dictatorial, revolutionary or military, constitutes one of the numerous discourses populating the dialogical world. García Márquez combats it most effectively by activating and setting in motion other discourses that oppose it. *The Story of a Shipwrecked Sailor*, the culmination of the *refrito* in García Márquez's journalistic writing, establishes the paradigm for much of his later non-fiction and fiction writing.

In 1986, García Márquez published *Clandestine in Chile: The Adventure of Miguel Littín* (*La aventura de Miguel Littín clandestino en Chile* [1987]). Littín, a Chilean film-maker who had been permanently exiled by the Pinochet dictatorship, assembled an expert team whose secret mission was to enter Chile in order to provide a visual record of his beloved country governed by the iron fist of Augusto Pinochet. Littín disguised himself as a Uruguayan businessman. So complete was his transformation that Littín's new identity became much more than a disguise and clashed with the deep nostalgia and attachment he felt for Chile in his true identity. The constant danger of exposure and capture, the clash between his dual identities and the nostalgia and memories of his former Chile and the new reality imposed by Pinochet's dictatorship, the profound sense of loss and separation and the sudden reencounter with his beloved country, all contribute to a story in which García Márquez foregrounds the human drama of Miguel Littín who must confront a constant series of incongruities.

García Márquez offers us another work whose structure and form derive from the *refrito*. Again, García Márquez, through a series of interviews with Miguel Littín, recaptures the voice of the Chilean film director and creates another double narrator:

> Early in 1986 in Madrid, when Miguel Littín told me what he had done and how he had done it, I realised that behind his film there was another film that

would probably never be made. And so he agreed to a grueling interrogation, the tape of which ran some eighteen hours. It encompassed the full human adventure in all its professional and political implications, which I have condensed into ten chapters.[7]

The often maligned *refrito* in journalism undergoes a creative epiphany in the hands of García Márquez because it frees him from the necessity of repeating the story so that he can recreate it through the construction of a double narrator who also possesses a dual identity:

I preferred to keep Littín's story in the first person, to preserve its personal – and sometimes confidential – tone, without any dramatic additions or historical pretentiousness on my part. The manner of the final text is, of course, my own, since a writer's voice is not interchangeable, particularly when he had to condense almost 600 pages into less than 200.[8]

He specifically identifies the work as a *refrito:*

In its nature and its method of disclosure, this is a piece of reporting. Yet it is something more: the emotional reconstruction of an adventure the finality of which was unquestionably much more visceral and moving than the original – and effectively realized – intention of making a film that made fun of the dangers of military power.[9]

From the beginning, the tension between two narrative voices and identities of Miguel Littín creates a dramatic situation which sustains itself to the end of the story. The multiple dualisms and conflicts present in Littín coincide with the dualistic attraction–repulsion of García Márquez in relation to the phenomenon of power, a constant foregrounding and backgrounding of this highest and lowest expression of the human spirit. Both men share the dual quest of filming and entering the centre of power, the very office of Augusto Pinochet.

Littín's transformation unleashes multiples layers of dualisms and contradictory forces in this story:

Becoming another person was the hardest part, more difficult than I could have imagined. Changing personality is a daily battle in which, wishing to continue being ourselves, we keep rebelling against our own determination to change. I had to resign myself to giving up being the man I had always been and transform myself into another, different one, above the suspicion of the same repressive police who had forced me out of my country. I had to become unrecognizable even to my friends.[10]

As is normal with his double, past-present narrators, García Márquez restricts or eliminates the prerogatives of the first-person narrator who has already undergone an experience and who can judge, explain, justify and speculate about his personal experience. Instead, he creates a dual narrator who relives his experience in a vulnerable manner so that the reader can identify with him and accompany him on his journey:

> Later on, after all had turned out well, I would recognize that I had done her an injustice because I had, in a subconscious way, judged her according to the disguise we had both adopted. Recalling that strange experience now, I wonder if ours wasn't the perfect parody of a contemporary marriage: we could hardly stand being under the same roof together.[11]

As Littín travelled around Chile, and the sights, sounds and feelings of his former life there constantly threatened to overwhelm him and to expose his real identity, he came to realise that he was a dual exile, exiled from and within his own country.

The most dramatic moment of the story takes place when Littín (and García Márquez) enter the centre of power. The film crew, after repeated attempts to film inside the Moneda Palace where Pinochet exercised his rule, suddenly was granted permission to film. Littín observes: 'The general impression after a complete tour of the palace was that everything had been completely changed for the sole purpose of expunging the memory of the assassinated president [Salvador Allende].'[12] Unexpectedly, during the second day of filming, Littín captured a momentary but crucial glimpse of General Augusto Pinochet:

> We had no idea what this was all about until we saw General Augusto Pinochet himself, his face puffy and greenish, on the way to his office, accompanied by one military and two civilian aides. It was a momentary glimpse, but he passed so close that we clearly heard him say as he went by, 'You can't believe a woman even when she's telling the truth.'[13]

Even Pinochet seems disguised, and, indeed, the succession of narrative and human disguises continues uninterrupted to the end of the story. García Márquez's dualistic narrative strategy enables him to move surreptitiously between the centre of power and the outside world and maintain the authorial position advocated by Gustave Flaubert according to which the author resembles God, invisible but omnipresent.

In 1993, García Márquez's Colombian friends, Maruja Pachón and Alberto Villamizar, asked him to write a book about Maruja's kidnapping ordeal. During his work on the first draft, García Márquez realised that he could not separate Maruja's kidnapping from those of nine others which occurred during the same period. This decision required three more years of work until 1996 when *News of a Kidnapping* (*Noticia de un secuestro* [1997]) appeared. García Márquez again resorts to the *refrito* and surreptitiously moves from the centre of power, the hermetic and secretive domain of the drug cartels, to the outside world of the affected families' reactions to events, their hopes and fears, their interminable waiting for 'news of a kidnapping', the efforts to free the hostages and the many twists and turns produced by such events.

In the preface, entitled 'Acknowledgements', after García Márquez realised that the kidnapping of the ten people constituted 'a single collective abduction of ten carefully chosen individuals, which had been carried out by the same group and for only one purpose', he and his friends were obligated 'to begin again with a different structure and spirit so that all the protagonists would have their well-defined identities, their own realities'.[14] This realisation required him to adopt a more standard reporting perspective in the third person. García Márquez again resorted to interviewing to compile much of his information. If *News of a Kidnapping* is not a book by the author but rather by those who experienced the horrors of kidnapping, then it is not only a book that chronicles the events but a *felt* history of this horrible tragedy suffered by the victims: 'To all the protagonists and all my collaborators, I offer eternal gratitude for not allowing this gruesome drama to sink into oblivion. Sadly, it is only one episode in the biblical holocaust that has been consuming Colombia for more than twenty years.'[15]

Although García Márquez does not 'appear' in the first person in this book, his presence can be detected at the structural level in the alternating movement from the inside and secretive world of the kidnapping to the outside world of secret negotiations, collective suffering, criss-crossing communications and frenetic activity. The first chapter marks the passage from the exterior world to the claustrophobic space of kidnapping. The other ten chapters oscillate between these two worlds: outside world: Chapters 2, 4, 6, 8 and 10; inside world: Chapters 3, 5, 7 and 9. Chapter 11 combines the two worlds as the moment of Maruja Pachón's liberation approaches. The epilogue reunites the two principal characters identified in the preface, Maruja Pachón and Alberto Villamizar. If they form the central axis of the book, then kidnapping constitutes the link between the inside and outside worlds. In effect, everyone in the book is kidnapped to one degree or another: the ten protagonists, their guards, the members of the Medellín drug cartel, then President Gaviria, the government, the country and, perhaps as well, the narrative, the narrator and even the author.

From a journalistic standpoint, *News of a Kidnapping* constitutes yet another *refrito* in the sense that this story had already received extensive coverage in the different news media. García Márquez reconstructs the event, imbuing it with a more literary narrative form. Like many of his fictional works, *News of a Kidnapping* opens *in medias res*, or at an indeterminate moment:

> She looked over her shoulder before getting into the car to be sure no one was following her. It was 7:05 in the evening in Bogotá. It had been dark for an

> hour, the Parque Nacional was not well lit, and the silhouettes of leafless trees against a sad, overcast sky seemed ghostly, but nothing appeared to be threatening. Despite her position, Maruja sat behind the driver because she always thought it was the most comfortable seat.[16]

The narrator opens two lines of narrative in this first sentence, one literary and the other cinematographic. When Maruja 'looked over her shoulder before getting into the car', it is not only her perspective but that of the omniscient narrator. The camera eye of the narrator scans the surrounding area with or without Maruja's participation, and sometimes he zooms in on other scenes: 'From a small corner café half a block away, the eighth man, the one responsible for the operation, observed the first real performance of an action whose intensive, meticulous rehearsals had begun twenty-one days earlier.'[17] The cinematic structure of the books is another indicator of the author's presence: 'What Maruja and Beatriz could not see were the three men getting out of the Mercedes that had pulled in behind them.'[18]

Once the women are abducted, the reader enters the enclosed world of the drug cartels where the omniscient narrator must intervene to see what Maruja and Beatriz cannot see or hear: that is, a world in which invisibility is the dividing line between life and death. *News of a Kidnapping* is a work in which García Márquez writes and materialises the visible and the invisible worlds. The alternating scenic structure of the work not only reveals its filmic structure but also the author's desire to see, penetrate, witness and participate in the dark world of the drug cartels from near and afar. Kidnapping constitutes a chronotope, a fusion of time and space, and it affords the narrator a bifocal perspective from which he can examine this phenomenon in its immediate effect on the ten victims and from a more distant, global one that focuses on its negative consequences for Colombia.

News coverage and the flow of information keep everyone informed, but this information does nothing to help resolve the problem of kidnapping which has reached industrial proportions in Colombia. Francisco (Pacho) Santos, one of the kidnapped victims, sees a parodic image of himself on the television: 'When it was over, he saw himself on the nine-thirty news on file footage, wearing a dinner jacket, and surrounded by beauty queens. That was when he learned his driver was dead.'[19] Pacho Santos witnesses his own kidnapping as a spectator, a victim, in a sense, of the incessant production of images that penetrate even the recondite and private spaces. García Márquez reveals the problematic of truth claims when he refers to public opinion:

> Not knowing what to expect, the presidency alerted the public to a proliferation of false communiqués and asked the people not to put more faith in them than in announcements from the government. But the grave and bitter truth was that the public had implicit trust in the Extraditables' communiqués.[20]

What is true one day is false the next until truth is transformed into a series of truth claims. The truth is relativised to such a degree that one can only find it by eliminating the falsities.

In a sense, then, *News of a Kidnapping* narrates its own kidnapping because García Márquez cannot rein in the reach and extension of kidnapping within the textual borders of his work. It is possible that 'the truth of kidnapping' in Colombia can never be completely known nor narrated, so there is no final word on the subject. What García Márquez achieves in *News of a Kidnapping* is to surpass the simple recording of the historical events and to portray the *felt history* of the kidnap victims. The feelings, words and emotions of the victims provide a transhistorical record of this horrible experience to which all of us can relate to one degree or another.

García Márquez's latest non-fictional work, *Living to Tell the Tale* (*Vivir para contrala* [2003]), the first volume of his projected three-volume autobiography, spans the writer's life from his birth in 1927 to the start of his career as a writer and journalist on the Caribbean coast of Colombia and then in Bogotá in the 1950s and concludes with his proposal to the woman who would become his wife.

The precise generic label for this work proves difficult because in part, like writers such as Albert Camus and Jean-Paul Sartre, who would work on a literary work to express certain ideas with which they were grappling in their more philosophical works, García Márquez published his own 'literary (auto)biography' in 2004, *Memoria de mis putas tristes* (*Memories of My Melancholy Whores*). Since he was most likely working on both books at the same time, the relationship between fiction and (auto)biography is less clearly defined. One critic defines autobiography as 'the retrospective narrative in prose that someone makes of his own existence when he puts the principal accent upon his life, especially upon the story of his own personality'.[21] *Living to Tell the Tale* really constitutes a hybrid work that combines literary, journalistic and non-fictional genres, so the best term to apply to it is *life writing*: 'An overarching term used for a variety of non-fictional modes of writing that claim to engage the shaping of one's life. The writing of one's own life is autobiographical, the writing of another's biographical; but that boundary is sometimes permeable.'[22]

Generic boundaries are almost always porous in García Márquez, and he has constantly and continuously crossed and violated these artifical boundaries from the inception of his writing career. The title of his book and the epigraph contain and embody this foundational element of his writing. One must 'live' to 'tell the tale' or as the epigraph says: 'Life is not what one lived, but what one remembers and how one remembers it in order to recount it.'[23] *Living to Tell the Tale* is a book of memories, arranged not in chronological order but rather according to the principle of *felt history,* or the human context of historical events.

This work begins *in medias res:*

> My mother asked me to go with her to sell the house. She had come that morning from the distant town where the family lived, and she had no idea how to find me. She asked around among acquaintances and was told to look for me at the Librería Mundial, or in the nearby cafés, where I went twice a day to talk with my writer friends.[24]

A few pages later he again emphasises the human essence of every historical event:

> Neither my mother nor I, of course, could have imagined that this simple two-day trip would be so decisive that the longest and most diligent of lives would not be enough for me to finish recounting it. Now, with more than seventy-five years behind me, I know it was the most important of all the decisions I had to make in my career as a writer. That is to say: in my entire life.[25]

This work constitutes the most extensive and eloquent expression of the *refrito*. The 'original article' is his lived life, memory the raw materials of his life and the 'follow-up story' is his 'telling the tale'. Once again, García Márquez's work demonstrates to what extent the *refrito* constitutes one of the fundamental components of his writing and the crucial role that journalism has played in his development as a writer.

Living to Tell the Tale contains important revelations and surprises concerning the relationship between his life and his work. One of the most dramatic moments is the confrontation in *One Hundred Years of Solitude* between official history and human, felt history concerning the 1928 banana massacre of the striking banana workers:

> Later, I spoke with survivors and witnesses and searched through newspaper archives and official documents, and I realized that the truth did not lie anywhere. Conformists said, in effect, that there had been no deaths. Those at the other extreme affirmed with a quaver in their voices that there had been more than a hundred, that they had been seen bleeding to death on the square, and that they were carried away in a freight train to be tossed into the ocean like rejected bananas. And so my version was lost forever at some improbable point between the two extremes. But it was so persistent that in one of my novels I referred to the massacre with all the precision and horror that I had brought for years to its incubation in my imagination. This is why I kept the number of dead at three thousand, in order to preserve the epic proportions of the drama.[26]

Travelling with his mother on the train back to his birthplace, Aracataca,

> the train stopped at a station that had no town, and a short while later it passed the only banana plantation along the route that had its name written

> over the gate: *Macondo*. This word had attracted my attention ever since the first trips I had made with my grandfather, but I discovered only as an adult that I liked its poetic resonance. I never heard anyone say it and did not even ask myself what it meant.[27]

The magical word *Macondo* remains embedded in his memory, and when he arrives in Aracataca, fiction and reality merge in his memory:

> The first thing that struck me was the silence. A material silence I could have identified blindfolded among all the silences in the world. The reverberation of the heat was so intense that you seemed to be looking at everything through undulating glass. As far as the eye could see there was no recollection of human life, nothing that was not covered by a faint sprinkling of burning dust.[28]

He experiences a convergence of his past, present and memory:

> Everything was identical to my memories, but smaller and poorer, and leveled by a windstorm of fatality: the decaying houses themselves, the tin roofs perforated by rust, the levee with its crumbling granite benches and melancholy almond trees, and all of it transfigured by the invisible burning dust that deceived the eye and calcinated the skin.[29]

García Márquez's memories always manifest themselves in relation to concrete objects or events:

> Memory, apparently so immaterial and personal and elusive, is always implicated in materiality, whether it be the materiality of sound, stone, text, garment, integrated circuits or circuit boards, or the materiality of our very bodies – the synapses and electrons of our brains and our nervous systems. Memory is evoked by the senses – smell, taste, touch, sound – and encoded in objects and events with particular meaning for the narrator.[30]

In other words, *Living to Tell the Tale* evokes memories which belong to the realm of *felt history*, and they cannot be confined within chronological, official history. His childhood and early memories played a decisive role in García Márquez's personal and literary development.

Names had a magical resonance for the young child:

> On the other hand, the names in the family attracted my notice because they seemed unique. First those on my mother's side: Tranquilina, Wenefrida, Francisca Simondosea. Then that of my paternal grandmother: Argemira, and those of her parents: Lozana and Aminadab. Perhaps this is the origin of my firm belief that that characters in my novels cannot walk on their own feet until they have a name that can be identified with their natures.[31]

In his fiction, names such as Ursula Iguarán, José Arcadio Buendía and Pilar Ternera in *One Hundred Years of Solitude* and Angela Vicario, the twins Pedro and Pablo Vicario and Santaigo Nasar in *Chronicle of a Death*

Foretold offer just a few examples of the onomastic power of the names in his fiction.

García Márquez's youthful fascination with words is captured in an episode in which his grandfather, the Colonel, took him to see animals in the circus. When the Colonel identified an animal as a camel and was corrected by a bystander that it was a dromedary, the Colonel seemed mortified and decided to correct the situation immediately:

> That afternoon he returned dejected to his office and consulted a dictionary with childish attention. Then he and I learned for the rest of our lives the difference between a dromedary and a camel. In the end he placed the glorious tome in my lap and said: 'This book not only knows everything, but it's also the only one that's never wrong.'[32]

García Márquez's reaction to the dictionary is magical: 'In church I had been surprised by the size of the missal, but the dictionary was thicker. It was like looking out at the entire world for the first time.'[33]

It is worth noting that in this episode, as in much of the rest of his memoir, that the two basic questions concerning point of view, 'who perceives?' and 'who speaks?', receive different answers most of the time. García Márquez often perceives like a child and speaks like an adult. In the above example, the use of words such as 'glorious tome', 'illustrated book' and 'holding the vault of the universe' contrasts with the child's reactions. Although this division persists, it also confirms the importance that García Márquez attributes to memories and to their abiding transtemporal significance in his personal development and evolution as a writer. García Márquez believes that history is composed of a continuous and seamless web of stories and voices, and each one contributes to his life and writing.

García Márquez helped to reinvent the lost art of storytelling, and it is no surprise that *The Thousand and One Nights* made such an impact on him as a child since it involves the figure of Scheherazade who must keep telling stories to King Shahryar to stay alive. When García Márquez found the book in the storeroom of his house, 'it was tattered and incomplete, but it involved me in so intense a way that Sara's fiancé had a terrifying premonition as he walked by: "Damn! This kid's going to be a writer." Said by someone who earned his living as a writer, it made a huge impression on me. Several years went by before I know that the book was *The Thousand and One Nights*'.[34]

One of the most important facets of his youth is the role of women:

> I believe that the essence of my nature and way of thinking I owe in reality to the women in the family and to the many in our service who ministered to my childhood. They had strong characters and tender hearts, and they treated me with the naturalness of the Earthly Paradise.[35]

This is confirmed by the opening of his memoir with the trip to Aracataca with his mother, an event to which he returns throughout his memoir:

> The trip with my mother to sell the house in Aracataca rescued me from the abyss, and the certainty of the new novel indicated to me the horizon of a different future. It was decisive among the many I have taken in my life because it showed me in my own flesh that the book I had tried to write was pure rhetorical invention with no foundation at all in poetic truth. The project, of course, shattered when it confronted the reality on that revelatory journey.[36]

What he realises is that while he cannot go home again because time has passed and changed him, he must mine the well of his personal experience to create his fictional universe.

In *Living to Tell the Tale,* García Márquez comes full circle in his non-fiction writing by exploring the most personal of his *refritos,* his own personal life. His memories are deeply rooted in the sights, sounds, senses and history of Colombia, and he realises that the countless human events of his life make up the essence of who he is as a person and a writer. While García Márquez establishes many parallels between his life and his writing, he maintains the distinction between the man who lives and the man who writes. His work cannot be explained by his life because the raw material of his fiction always undergoes a transformation in the creative process of writing. His journalism taught him that another story always existed behind the obfuscatory veil of official history. García Márquez has said that a writer really writes only one work with many different titles, and his non-fiction works not only form an integral part of that totality but also represent the primary source from which his creative energies spring.

NOTES

1. Raymond. L. Williams, *Gabriel García Márquez,* Boston, MA: Twayne, 1984, p. 134.
2. Pedro Sorela, *El otro García Márquez: los años difíciles,* Madrid: Mondadori, 1981, p. 51. All translations of Sorela are mine.
3. Sorela, *El otro García* Márquez, p. 51.
4. Sorela, *El otro García Márquez,* p. 78.
5. Sorela, *El otro García Márquez.*
6. Gabriel García Márquez, *The Story of a Shipwrecked Sailor,* trans. Randolph Hogan, New York: Knopf, 1986, p. 14.
7. Gabriel García Márquez, *Clandestine in Chile: The Adventures of Miguel Littín,* trans. Asa Zatz, New York: Henry Holt, 1987.
8. García Márquez, *Clandestine in Chile,* p. 4.
9. García Márquez, *Clandestine in Chile,* p. 4.
10. García Márquez, *Clandestine in Chile,* p. 4.
11. García Márquez, *Clandestine in Chile,* pp. 6–7.

12. García Márquez, *Clandestine in Chile,* p. 104.
13. García Márquez, *Clandestine in Chile,* pp. 104–5.
14. Gabriel García Márquez, *News of a Kidnapping,* trans. Edith Grossman, New York: Penguin, 1997, p. 1.
15. García Márquez, *News of a Kidnapping,* p. 2.
16. García Márquez, *News of a Kidnapping,* p. 3.
17. García Márquez, *News of a Kidnapping,* p. 4.
18. García Márquez, *News of a Kidnapping,* p. 5.
19. García Márquez, *News of a Kidnapping,* p. 34.
20. García Márquez, *News of a Kidnapping,* p. 38.
21. Sidonie Smith and Julia Watson, *Reading Autobiography: A Guide for Interpreting Life Narratives,* Minneapolis, MN: University of Minnesota Press, 2001, p. 1.
22. Smith and Watson, *Reading Autobiography,* p. 197.
23. Gabriel García Márquez, *Living to Tell the Tale,* trans. Edith Grossman, New York: Vintage, 2004, p. 1.
24. García Márquez, *Living to Tell the Tale,* p. 3.
25. García Márquez, *Living to Tell the Tale,* p. 4.
26. García Márquez, *Living to Tell the Tale,* p. 69.
27. García Márquez, *Living to Tell the Tale,* p. 21.
28. García Márquez, *Living to Tell the Tale,* p. 23.
29. García Márquez, *Living to Tell the Tale,* pp. 23–4.
30. Smith and Watson, *Reading Autobiography,* p. 21.
31. García Márquez, *Living to Tell the Tale,* p. 56.
32. García Márquez, *Living to Tell the Tale,* p. 99.
33. García Márquez, *Living to Tell the Tale,* p. 99.
34. García Márquez, *Living to Tell the Tale,* p. 105.
35. García Márquez, *Living to Tell the Tale,* p. 75.
36. García Márquez, *Living to Tell the Tale,* pp. 401–2.

11

CLAIRE TAYLOR

García Márquez and film

> [My relationship with cinema] is like that of a poorly-matched married couple. That is to say, I can't live with cinema, and I can't live without it. And, to judge by the number of offers that I get from producers, cinema feels the same way about me.[1]

García Márquez's provocative statement regarding his relationship to cinema provides a sound starting point for the consideration of this Colombian writer and his filmic endeavours. Certainly, the number of Garciamarquian film projects is large and still growing, as attested to by British director Mike Newell's filming of *El amor en los tiempos del cólera* (*Love in the Time of Cholera*) (released in the Americas in 2007), Mexican director Carlos Carrera's filming of *Noticia de un secuestro* (*News of a Kidnapping*) and Costa Rican Hilda Hidalgo's 2009 film of *Del amor y otros demonios* (*Of Love and Other Demons*). The frequency of García Márquez's film-related projects, and those of others to bring his work to the big screen, is thus clear, but these, for a variety of reasons as will be discussed below, have not always lived up to their potential.

Whilst García Márquez is undoubtedly best known as the Nobel Prize-winning novelist, his contribution to, and adaptations within, the cinematic realm cannot be underestimated. His relationship with cinema has been prolonged and complex, and he has played a variety of roles, ranging from film critic, scriptwriter, director, member of a variety of film-related organisations and, of course, inspiration for the large number of cinematic adaptations based on his narrative output. We can thus consider his contribution to cinema in terms of three broad areas: García Márquez *on* cinema, García Márquez *as* cinema and García Márquez *in* cinema.

García Márquez *on* cinema

García Márquez's first forays into the realm of film came during his early years as a journalist, writing first for *El Universal* of Cartagena and *El Heraldo* of Barranquilla, and subsequently for the Bogotá-based national newspaper, *El Espectador.* Whilst writing for the *costeño* press, García Márquez contributed a general-interest column, which included some early examples of his interest in cinema, from high-society gossip and comical musings to more serious – albeit sketchy – film reviews, such as those on Vittorio de Sica's *Bicycle Thieves,* or on William Dieterle's *Portrait of Jennie.*[2] From early 1954, when García Márquez joined *El Espectador,* he began writing on film in earnest, in the form of a weekly film column entitled 'El cine en Bogotá: estrenos de la semana' ('Cinema in Bogotá: This Week's New Releases'), essentially a series of brief reviews of films currently being shown in the capital. These tend to be fairly routine reviews of movies, covering mostly US, European and Mexican productions, with mention in places of the nascent Colombian film industry. Indeed, critics have noted issues such as García Márquez's lack of training and expertise in film criticism and have argued that, since he did not set out to be a 'conscientious film critic', his reviews 'fulfill a purely quick, informative role'.[3]

Nevertheless, during this year and a half that García Márquez worked as film critic for *El Espectador,* his writings were to a certain extent pioneering: as Montoya notes, 'he was the first in Colombia, because prior to him, others had written reviews, commentaries, and high society gossip, but never criticism.'[4] Moreover, whilst it is true that an overarching film theory may be difficult to deduct from his film reviews, certain trends can be distinguished. It is notable, for instance, the frequency with which García Márquez praises the close-up; what he calls a 'human cinema'; realism, in particular Italian neo-realism; and films that are critical of *status quo.*[5] That said, what is more noticeable from these film reviews are the criticisms García Márquez directs *against* certain ways of making cinema. Amongst these, he reserves particular venom for what he terms 'impersonal directing'; melodrama; poor scripts, characterised by rhetoric or pomposity; and the loosely defined 'commercial cinema', which can range from standard Hollywood fare to Mexican *comedias rancheras.*[6] Whilst these disparate, and at times patchy, writings on film do not of themselves provide a coherent cinematic theory, they nevertheless do serve to indicate García Márquez's preference for a human cinema, concerned with emotions and motivations of characters, with social elements.

In addition to these shorter, self-contained pieces on cinema of the earlier period of his career, one of García Márquez's most notable writings on cinema of later years is the extended journalistic essay published in book format as *La aventura de Miguel Littín clandestino en Chile* (*Clandestine in Chile: The Adventures of Miguel Littín* [1986]). García Márquez's engaging prose provides the reader with an insight into Chile's most prominent film-maker, Littín, with a particular focus on the conditions under Pinochet's dictatorship. Again, although this work is by no means a work of film *theory* – the book is more dedicated to narrating the fascinating story of Littín's daring escapades working in Chile in disguise than to analysing his films as such – García Márquez's admiration for a director working against the odds, and for a socially committed cinema, is clear.

Moreover, García Márquez's passion for cinema did not purely remain on the level of written criticism. When, fortuitously, he was sent by *El Espectador* to Italy in 1954 as correspondent for that newspaper, he was able to study a course in film direction at the Rome-based Centro Sperimentale in 1955, then the leading centre in cinematic experimentation, and hotbed of the much-vaunted Italian neo-realism. However, despite the promise that the Centro offered, and the opportunity to meet up with film-makers such as Cuba's Tomás Gutiérrez Alea with whom García Márquez was to collaborate in the future, he remained there for only a year, complaining that he felt it too restrictive, commenting that it was 'like I was in a straight jacket'.[7] Then, after brief periods in Paris, Caracas and New York, García Márquez moved to Mexico, motivated by the desire to make a living by writing film scripts. Nevertheless, whilst this period in Mexico proved fruitful economically for García Márquez, he later expressed his frustration with the entire cinematic process:

> The problem with cinema is that ... it's a mass creative process. I wrote a film that I'd worked on for more than a year, I read it about ten times around the production table, and I had to make changes to it many more times; in the end, the only thing that remained of my original story was a two-minute scene in which a gunman knitted a pair of socks. Fortunately, the film is good, but its resemblance to my story is minimal ... These experiences showed me that the writer is merely one cog in the huge machinery.[8]

In terms resonant with one of the central debates on film theory in recent years – that of the (re)definition of cinema as a popular, commercial, collaborative exercise in contrast to the overly idealistic claims of *auteur* theory – García Márquez's comments highlight the tensions between literary and cinematic practice. It is interesting to note that García Márquez is opposed to the collaborative nature of cinema – we might surmise, coming as he does from literature, the realm of the *auteur,* that he would be predisposed to adopting such a critical stance. Whatever the validity of García Márquez's comments on the status of cinema, what is clear from his statement are the inevitable tensions involved in the relationship between the lone writer and the collaborative, commercial project of film-making.

This is not to say, however, that García Márquez has become entirely disillusioned with cinema, and indeed his more recent ventures into cinema are evidence of his continuing commitment to the medium, such as the co-founding in 1986 of the Escuela Internacional de Cine y Televisión in San Antonio de los Baños, Cuba, an NGO with the aim of promoting and training Third World film-makers. Similarly, his recent work in running workshops on scriptwriting, which led, amongst other things, to the publication of *Cómo se cuenta un cuento: taller de guión de Gabriel García Márquez* (*How to Tell a Story: Gabriel García Márquez's Scriptwriting Workshop* [2003, originally published 1995]) indicates he has not rejected outright the importance of scriptwriting. Rather, what we can detect is that there is no easy relationship between the two media, and that it is never simply the case of a direct and unproblematic transferral of a Garciamarquian story to the big screen.

García Márquez's writing *as* cinema?

Whilst these early journalistic works provided examples of García Márquez's writing *on* cinema, several critics have noted the 'cinematic' qualities of his fiction in itself and have suggested how his training in cinema has directly influenced his writing. Some, such as Donald M. Morales, have gone so far as to say that 'before *Solitude,* everything he wrote was thinly disguised cinema ... there is a certain static quality in the fiction that would arguably fare better as film'.[9] Kathleen McNerney, meanwhile, has argued that 'all García Márquez's works usually considered minor are characterized by their very visual imagery', and that we can therefore 'appreciate the influence film has had on his fiction'.[10] Similarly, García Aguilar notes what he terms 'that almost cinematographic attention to detail' which can be found, in his view, in *El coronel no tiene quien le escriba* (*No One Writes to the Colonel* [published 1961]), the collection *Los funerales de la mamá grande* (*Big Mama's Funeral* [1962]) and the story 'La increíble y triste historia de la cándida Eréndira y de su abuela desalmada' ('The Incredible and Sad Tale of Innocent Eréndira and her Heartless Grandmother' [1972]).[11] Similarly, Montoya describes *No One Writes to the Colonel* as 'a novel written with a camera in his hand', and García Márquez himself has said of it that it 'has a completely cinematic structure, and its style is similar to cinematographic editing; the characters barely speak, and words are used very sparsely'.[12] Meanwhile, the later work, *Crónica de una muerte anunciada* (*Chronicle of a Death Foretold* [1981]), has been the subject of a comparative analysis with Alfred Hitchcock's concept of suspense, in which Matías Montes-Huidobro argues that Hitchcock's concept is the basis for the narrative principles that lie behind the novel.[13]

Instances of this 'cinematic' style of writing can be easily seen in *No One Writes to the Colonel.* The very opening lines to the novella reveal an attention to visual detail which has a cinematic quality:

> The colonel took the top off the coffee can and saw that there was only one little spoonful left. He removed the pot from the fire, poured half the water onto the earthen floor, and scraped the inside of the can with a knife.[14]

These precise descriptions of character movements and the objects used read as an exposition of cinematic *mise en scène,* as much as a literary scene-setting. The focus here on the character in terms of actions and movements – reminiscent of the cinematic conception of 'behaviour of figures' as a feature of *mise en scène* – rather than interior psychology, has clear parallels with cinematic techniques.[15] The preponderance of verbs of action and concrete nouns, with even the exactitude of specified measurements – 'la mitad del agua' – produce the effect of a very close attention to detail and the description of the physical.

Indeed, this technique of opening a chapter with precise details occurs throughout the novella: other chapters begin with lines such as: 'He brought over to the little table in the living room a block of lined paper' (Chapter 4); '"Wait a minute, my friend, and I'll lend you an umbrella." Don Sabas opened a cupboard built in to the wall of the office' (Chapter 5); 'Through the window, the whining of the castrated animals penetrated the interior of the office' (Chapter 6). These opening lines, with their precise use of language chosen for visual description rather than metaphorical meaning, as if describing a film set, often recall stage directions in a screen play.

These and other cinematic strategies can be noted in several of García Márquez's works. These strategies can be summarised as including an emphasis on visual imagery; a use of brief, concise descriptions; a relatively sparse use of metaphors; and a tendency towards a more linear temporal succession. However, while these works betray a cinematic style that is undeniable, it has frequently been noted that García Márquez became disillusioned with cinema by the mid to late 1960s and turned his back on this medium. Indeed, regarding his masterpiece *One Hundred Years of Solitude,* several critics, and García Márquez himself, have declared it 'anti-cinematic'. The author has described the genesis of this novel as being a reaction *against* cinema, declaring that: 'In 1966 I said to myself "Damn it! I'm going to write against cinema!" ... I wrote a novel with entirely literary solutions, a novel which is, if you like, the antithesis of cinema: *One Hundred Years of Solitude.*'[16] Indeed, García Márquez has described all his works prior to *One Hundred Years of Solitude* as being 'hindered' by his cinematic preocupations, which he has defined as 'an excessive eagerness to visualise characters and scenes, a very precise relationship between the time that dialogue and action take place, and even an obsession with signalling points of view and framing'.[17] Moreover, as is famously known, García

Márquez has frequently declared that he will never allow *One Hundred Years of Solitude* to be made into a film.

García Márquez's writing *in* cinema

Whilst García Márquez's contribution to writing on film has thus waned over the decades, and the relative 'cinematic' qualities of his fiction may be contested, an abiding force remains the contribution that his writings have made to films themselves; that is, the number of adaptations which have been made of his works. Standing in 2007 at some forty works, films that cite García Márquez in the writing credits, either as scriptwriter or as source of the original novel or short story upon which the film is based, range across some fifteen countries, from the more expected Colombia, Mexico, Cuba and Brazil to the more unusual Estonia, Russia, Georgia and China.

That said, critics – and García Márquez himself – have not always been positive about cinematic adaptations of his works. Discussing his doubts about the success of adaptations of his works to date, García Márquez has related them to the issue of the visual in his fiction. Arguing that the apparently 'visual' nature of his prose is deceptive, he states that in fact this effect is created through 'magic of the words'. Thus, the task of adapting his works is not as easy as it first appears, since directors 'find that the words crumble and they have to turn everything into images'.[18] Whilst such a declaration could perhaps be seen as typical of an author who wishes to maintain control of his work and dislikes seeing it interpreted by others, García Márquez's concerns are not without foundation. Critics have frequently coincided with his view, although they have given more concrete reasons for the problematic transferral of his prose to the silver screen. Ramírez Ospina, for instance, highlights the relative freedom of prose in contrast to the fixity of the cinematic medium, commenting that, whereas in a written narrative 'everything seems free and possible', cinema tends to reproduce 'very concrete people and things in swift, precise shots'.[19] Linking this general concern with García Márquez's writing in particular, Ramírez Ospina goes on to note that he frequently mixes a 'journalistic style using detailed documentation' with 'images that go from the highly unusual to the impossible', and that this proves problematic for the transferral to the screen.[20] Ramírez Ospina therefore concludes that the majority of the scriptwriters of Garciamarquian fiction (including García Márquez himself) 'do not succeed in resolving the paradoxes of his works which easily skillfully alternate between concrete fact and the resonance of that fact in the collective imagination'.[21] For this reason, Ramírez Ospina states that in his view there are only three Garciamarquian films of worth at the date of his writing (1996): *En este pueblo no hay ladrones* (*There Are No Thieves in This Village,* dir. Alberto Isaac [1965]), *Tiempo de morir* (*Time to Die,* dir. Jorge Alí Triana [1985]) and *Milagro en Roma* (*Miracle in Rome,* dir. Lisandro Duque Naranjo [1988]), thus dismissing the majority of adaptations to date.

Julián David Correa, meanwhile, writing in a compilation article which in many cases summarises some of Ramírez Ospina's arguments, has enumerated six principal reasons for the failure of cinematic adaptations of the Colombian writer:

> There are six stumbling blocks which are due precisely to the excessive nature of his works: the first is the suggestive power of Garciamarquian prose, and linked with this, the difficulty of finding actors capable of portraying this excess; the third is García Márquez's talent for incorporating the fantastic into the most everyday contexts, to which we can add the use he makes of fluctuating timeframes, marked by nostalgia; the fifth difficulty lies in the evident fear of filmmakers – including Gabo himself – of betraying the original written work, and the sixth is that there has yet to be found a cinematic style capable of conveying what his works propose.[22]

The various reasons identified by Correa indicate a series of problems that arise in Garciamarquian adaptations, some with more frequency than others, and some which depend on the style of the source text. In the light of these various problems and tensions, this section will now consider some of the most salient of Garciamarquian adaptations.

García Márquez's contribution to cinema has ranged from screenplays written by him which are adaptations of other's works (such as *El gallo de oro* [*The Golden Cockerel*] or *El año de la peste* [*The Year of the Plague*]), original screenplays entirely written and conceived for the cinema (such as *Time to Die*) and, by far the most numerous group, screenplays written by García Márquez or by a third party which are adaptations of his own stories or novels. His first recorded contribution to film is in 1954, when he was cited in the writing credits of a medium-length film of some twenty-nine minutes entitled *La langosta azul* (*The Blue Lobster*). However, the actual contribution of García Márquez to this film is disputed, and he later stated that his friend Álvaro Cepeda Samudio listed him in the credits as a favour. His first contribution to film which has been definitively corroborated is the 1964 movie *The Golden Cockerel,* for which he was the scriptwriter. Directed by Roberto Gavaldón, this film is based on a short story by the acclaimed Mexican author Juan Rulfo, and García Márquez was joined by Carlos Fuentes, a Mexican contemporary of his, in the writing of the dialogue. As García Márquez notes, 'I'd written the dialogues in Colombian rather than Mexican', hence Fuentes was brought in to help Mexicanise the script.[23] Although the film is of interest in that it provides an example of an abiding theme in Garciamarquian works, the cockfight and its relationship to machismo, for critic Collazos, 'its director, Ricardo Gabaldón [sic], "did things in his own way," and the result was a mediocre film.'[24] Whilst the notion of a director 'doing things his own way' is not necessarily a failing (indeed, the best adaptations are ones in which the directors make the film their own), certainly the film owes much to the stock types of the Golden Age of Mexican melodramas and is replete with mariachis, a seductive singing temptress and numerous scenes of Mexican *ferias*.

Whilst *The Golden Cockerel* was a case of García Márquez adapting the work of another writer, a year later the first adaptation of one of his short stories came out: *There Are No Thieves in This Village,* directed by Alberto Isaac, which won second place in the Experimental Cinema Competition in Mexico. The film also included García Márquez playing a minor role – as ticket-seller in the cinema – along with a variety of other literary and cultural figures, including Mexican painter José Luis Cuevas as a billiard player, Mexican author Carlos Monsiváis and Mexican political cartoonist Abel Quezada as domino players and Spanish film-maker Luis Buñuel as the priest. José de la Colina has praised the 'magnificent literary realism' of García Márquez's writing which is successfully brought to the screen by Isaac.[25] Mora, meanwhile, commenting on the original story, indicates that, since this is a 'more realist García Márquez', it therefore makes for a more 'manageable' adaptation to the cinematic medium.[26]

Conversely, *Time to Die* of 1966 was the first Garciamarquian film that started out life as a truly cinematic endeavour; that is, it was not based on a pre-existing literary source, whether by García Márquez or another writer. It was the first film of Mexican director, Arturo Ripstein, with whom García Márquez was to collaborate in future. The main narrative thrust of the film – the story of Juan Sáyago who returns to his home town after eighteen years, having been imprisoned for killing another man, and who finds himself caught up in the honour code and machismo, ultimately unable to escape the role he is assigned – is one which has often fascinated García Márquez, in both his written and filmic works. Nevertheless, whilst the film may focus on a quintessentially Garciamarquian theme, it has not met with great critical acclaim. Although, according to García Aguilar, the screenplay is one of García Márquez's most accomplished, the critic does not accord the same value to the film in itself.[27] García Aguilar highlights the 'interference of commercial structures' in this and other early Garciamarquian films, lamenting in particular that *Time to Die* 'had to turn itself into a Western'.[28] This sentiment has been echoed by other critics, such as Ramírez Ospina who notes 'a parodic feel of a Western' about this film, or Eligio García Márquez who comments that it was 'dolled up with an impersonal feel of a Western as demanded by the producers'.[29] This indicates one of the central problems with Garciamarquian works on the big screen: the need to negotiate between generic or commercial concerns inherent to cinema and the specificities of García Márquez's prose.

Moving somewhat later, in 1974 the film *Presagio* (*Portent*) was released, based on a short story by García Márquez, and for which he also wrote the screenplay in conjunction with Luis Alcoriza. Telling a tale about a town beset by rumours, this film has again been subject to scrutiny as to the success of the adaptation. For critic García Aguilar, the 'beautiful poetic story' is not successfully transferred to the screen.[30] Four years later, 1978 brought the release of the film *The Year of the Plague,* for which García Márquez himself suggested the idea to the great Mexican director, Felipe Cazals, who was already famous for directing such classics as *Las poquianchis* of 1976. Based on Daniel Defoe's *A Journal of the Plague Year* (1722), which was originally set in London, the film transfers the action to Mexico, with several sections filmed in Teotihuacán. Although ostensibly concerned with a plague, as the director notes, García Márquez saw this as a prextext for examining bureaucracy and power.[31]

In the following year, García Márquez was involved in the screenplay for *María de mi corazón* (*Mary My Dearest*), directed by Mexican Jaime Humberto Hermosillo. Based on a short story by García Márquez, 'Sólo vine a hablar por teléfono' ('I Only Came to Use the Phone') of 1978, the film tells the harrowing, although at times absurd, tale of a woman locked up by mistake in a madhouse. Although the screenplay was officially co-written by both Hermosillo and García Márquez, Hermosillo has clarified that in fact García Márquez came up with the ideas, whilst he, Hermosillo, wrote them down. According to Hermosillo, García Márquez refused to do the writing himself since he argued that 'he would spend all his time polishing his literary style, which, at the end of the day, couldn't be seen on screen' – an indication of García Márquez's growing frustration with the scriptwriting process.[32]

In the same year, *La viuda de Montiel* (*Montiel's Widow*) came out, directed by the Chilean director Miguel Littín, with whom García Márquez was to work again some years later in his famous journalistic piece. Based on García Márquez's short story of the same title (included in the collection *Big Mama's Funeral* of 1962), this film tells the tale of a wealthy family living in the country, in which the wife becomes widowed and whose fortune diminishes. According to Aguilar, the story upon which this film is based is one of the most 'cinematographic' of García Márquez but also one of the least interesting, and he concludes that the 'message' is 'too obvious'.[33] Similarly, Ramírez Ospina believes that, despite the collaboration of García Márquez on the screenplay, the film is a disappointment.[34]

Moving on to the 1980s, one of the most well known of Garciamarquian adaptations was to come in 1983: *Eréndira,* directed by the Brazilian Ruy Guerra. The genesis of this film is somewhat convoluted; García Márquez had written the story originally in the form of a screenplay which he had given to Margot Benacerraf but did not keep a copy for himself. The screenplay then became lost, and, in the meantime, García Márquez wrote the novella or story 'The Incredible and Sad Tale of Innocent Eréndira and Her Heartless Grandmother.' Then, for Ruy Guerra's film, García Márquez had to rewrite the screenplay, basing it on the novella, which was in turn merged with another short story, 'Muerte constante más allá del amor' ('Death Constant Beyond Love') to give the film we now have.

Whilst revealing beautiful cinematography in places, *Eréndira* has split critics – even the director himself – as to its success. Whilst Kathleen McNerney finds that it is 'brilliantly directed' by Ruy Guerra and argues that it 'captures visually some of the images García Márquez makes us conjure up in our minds', and García Aguilar considers it 'the most successful in García Márquez's long cinematic trajectory', being the film which 'perhaps is the closest to his universe', others have found fault with it.[35] Reflecting back on *Eréndira,* even Ruy Guerra himself admits that it is 'somewhat rigid' and thinks that 'perhaps, with *Eréndira,* I was too faithful to the screenplay', rather than trying to create a film in its own right.[36] Critic Ramírez Ospina, meanwhile, in his comparison of the opening paragraph of the screenplay with the film, comments that whilst it is a 'beautiful way' to begin a screenplay, it is nevertheless 'full of problems', given the difficulties of attempting to convey visually the majesty of the grandmother whilst seated on a donkey.[37]

Indeed, we may consider this film as illustrating more broadly the problems of attempting to convey García Márquez's more magical-realist works on the big screen, problems which are less a failing of Ruy Guerra than of the cinematic medium in itself. That is, the visual nature of cinema renders the doubly encoded writings of García Márquez (where the real and the magical coexist in an indeterminate space) all too *real,* all too evident in the screen space. For, if magical realism in its literary form inhabits precisely an intermediate zone between the real and the fantastic, where the narrative oscillates between deadpan expression and fantastical occurrences, then in cinema, a predominantly *visual* medium, the ambiguities of magical realism are ironed out. So, for instance, we may read in the novella *Eréndira* the following: 'As soon as he [Ulises] touched them, the glass and the bottle changed color. Then, out of pure play, he touched a glass pitcher that was on the table beside some tumblers and the pitcher also turned blue ... "Those things happen because of love," his mother said.'[38] On screen, however, we actually see Ulises's hand turning the glass blue. Whereas, to quote theorist Wendy B. Faris, literary magical realism 'merges different realms' and produces 'doubts in the effort to reconcile the two contradictory understandings of events', the film leaves us in no doubt, as the event is clearly conveyed for us on screen.[39]

Moving on to a much more realist, rather than magically real narrative, two years later, in 1985, a remake of Ripstein's 1966 original, *Time to Die* appeared, this time directed by the Colombian Jorge Alí Triana. This new version is generally acknowleged to be the superior version. That said, it remains a somewhat slow-moving film, whose one central conceit (the overriding codes of machismo which end up destroying the principal characters) is perhaps not enough to sustain a feature-length film. Female characters in the film function as mere foils to the men, and the psychology of the male protagonists is also at times shaky; it is unclear why the younger brother, who has been the reconciliatory figure for most of the film, makes an about-face and enters into the duel. Nonetheless, the cinematography is of a high quality, and the closing sequence in the cockfighting ring is particularly well done, inviting clear parallels between the macho posturing of the men and the strutting cocks, who blindly fight to the death. A further pleasing touch is the use of the coastal folk-song form, the *vallenato,* over the closing credits, which roots the film firmly in a Colombian setting and perhaps suggests the film could be read as one long *vallenato* – a folk tale of the exploits of the male protagonists.

Following hard on the heels of *Time to Die* came *Chronicle of a Death Foretold,* directed by veteran Italian film-maker Francesco Rosi and filmed between May and September 1986. Rosi and García Márquez had met personally many years prior to the making of the film, shortly after the success of the latter's *One Hundred Years of Solitude,* and indeed had discussed the possibility of collaborating on a cinematic project, although this did not come to fruition. When the opportunity of working together on *Chronicle of a Death Foretold* arose, García Márquez approved wholeheartedly of Rosi as director (indeed, this was one of his conditions of allowing the novella to be filmed), although he refused to be directly involved himself in the process, instead giving Rosi a free reign with the script.

At first sight, this film would appear to have all the necessary ingredients for a successful adaptation: first, it was directed by Rosi, one of García Márquez's favoured directors and one whom he highly respected; second, it is an adaptation of a work which has been has been frequently identified as 'cinematic' by Garciamarquian literary critics; and third, it had a substantial budget in comparison to other Garciamarquian adaptations to date, totalling some $8.5 million. Yet these factors have not guaranteed its success, and indeed it has been described by Ramírez Ospina as 'the most spectacularly disappointing' of all adaptations of García Márquez's work.[40]

The screenplay for the film follows very closely the original novel, although there are inevitably some minor changes, which are common to most cinematic adaptations.[41] Yet this excessive striving for fidelity does not necessarily result in a better film. Amongst the drawbacks to the film is the issue of casting: Rupert Everett, whilst no doubt a major star, seems miscast as the hero here and does not have the immediate physical presence such a role would demand. Moreover, the fact that Everett was filmed originally speaking English throughout and later dubbed into Spanish leads to a less satisfactory effect overall. One further problem is that, despite its large budget, it tends towards what we might term a '*telenovela* aesthetic', with frequently exaggerated gestures and movements on the part of the actors. Rosi himself has commented on the lack of dialogue in the film and highlighted the use instead of 'looks and gestures' to convey the story; one of the problems with the excessive reliance of this film on the gestural, however, is that this is frequently at the expense of the subtlety of the acting.[42]

Moving on from *Chronicle of a Death Foretold,* in the late 1980s there then followed a series of films which were especially commissioned and financed by the Spanish television company TVE and released under the collective title *Amores difíciles* (*Difficult Loves* [usually rendered, literally, as *Dangerous Loves*]). Shot by six different directors, including Spain's Jaime Chávarri along with five Latin Americans, all films were made in 1988 and premiered at the Valladolid Film Festival, subsequently being aired on Spanish television in October, November and December of that same year.

Three of the six – *Yo soy el que tú buscas* (*I'm the One You're Looking For*), *Fábula de la bella palomera* (*Fable of the Beautiful Pigeon Fancier*), and *Cartas del parque* (*Letters from the Park*) – are based loosely around small segments of García Márquez's novel *El amor en los tiempos del cólera* (*Love in the Time of Cholera* [1985]). The first of these, *Yo soy el que tú buscas,* directed by Chávarri, has little of a Garciamarquian feel to it. Highly derivative of Spain's Pedro Almodóvar, it includes several of his trademark features such as the excessive array of wacky characters, the Almodovarian use of garish colour, farcical scenes and even the use of one of Almodóvar's favoured actresses, Chus Lampreave, in one of the lead roles. Whilst it is hard to assess as a Garciamarquian film, since it is based on only a short three-line section from *Love in the Time of Cholera* and is transposed to a clearly Spanish setting, as a film in its own right it is somewhat disappointing, and it is apparent that Chávarri has not apparently found his feet here. Moreover, the subject matter of the film – the story of a young woman who is raped and subsequently becomes obsessed with her rapist, to the extent of falling in love with him – has provoked controversy. Chávarri comments that what García Márquez wanted to do in choosing this topic for a film was 'to stick his finger in an open wound which at that time was the main hobbyhorse for feminists'.[43] Whether Chávarri's film deals in a sufficiently subtle manner with such delicate subject matter is another question.

Fábula de la bella palomera, meanwhile, signalled a return to collaboration between García Márquez and Ruy Guerra, who some years previously had directed *Eréndira.* Based on a five-page section of the novel focusing on the affair between Olimpia Zuleta and Florentino Ariza (now called Fulvia and Orestes in the film version), the film stars Claudia Ohana in the lead role – the same actress who played the female lead in Guerra's *Eréndira* some years previously. This film has a similar feel to Guerra's earlier work, and there are some striking images, with pleasing shots, in particular of Fulvia dressed in white, flowing attire which mimics the movements of the pigeons. Nevertheless, the psychology of the characters is somewhat unclear; it is hard to comprehend why the beautiful Fulvia would fall for the stuffy and frankly unattractive Orestes, and her lengthy monologue detailing how she cannot live without him serves to confirm Garciamarquian women as constantly needing men to affirm their existence. Moreoever, the film's ending – when, after her one night of passion with Orestes, Fulvia is murdered by her husband upon his discovering her infidelity – produces the rather gloomy conclusion of women as the target of male possession and violence.

Cartas del parque, based on a short section from *Love in the Time of Cholera* that narrates Florentino Ariza's wait for Fermina Daza, was directed by veteran Cuban director, Tomás Gutiérrez Alea. Much less political than most of Gutiérrez Alea's work, this film follows a Cyrano de Bergerac-style plot in which two young people in love communicate through letters written by a penman and the woman discovers she is really in love with the letter-writer. However, this film has again been the subject of critcism due to its portrayal of gender relations: critic Susan Conde, for instance, in her in-depth analysis of the film, has argued that it is pervaded by a traditional overdetermination of gender roles, in which the women in the film fall into *machista* perceptions.[44] Indeed, regarding these three *Love in the Time of Cholera* films as a whole, Donald M. Morales has concluded that 'the license Márquez takes with these films confirms stereotypes of women ... The lives of María, Fulvia, and Natalia rest upon their slavish need for men.'[45] For Morales, García Márquez's image of women in these films is therefore 'troubling' as they represent 'the misconstrued patriarchal imagination'.[46]

The remaining three of the *Difficult Loves* come from other sources. *El verano de la señora Forbes* (*The Summer of Miss Forbes*), directed by the Mexican Jaime Humberto Hermosillo, is based on a short story that later appeared in the collection *Doce cuentos peregrinos* (*Strange Pilgrims*). Set on the Sicilian island of Pantelaria, the film tells of the life of an austere German nanny and the children in her care who feel tormented by her strict routine. As Claudia Cabezón Doty notes, whereas the short story gives the perspective of the children, the film encourages identification with Señora Forbes; now the focus is on the tragic tale of a mature woman and her unfulfilled sexual passion.[47] *Un domingo feliz* (*Happy Sunday*), meanwhile, directed by Venezuelan Olegario Barrera, was based on a short story, which in itself was based on a newspaper article that García Márquez had written some time earlier in Rome. The film version is set in Caracas and tells the story of a child who runs away from home and fakes his own kidnapping. The 'happiness' of the film's title refers to the child's experiences as he discovers the excitement of Caracas's nightlife, but this happiness is soon cut short.

It is *Milagro en Roma* (*Miracle in Rome*), however, directed by Colombian Lisandro Duque Naranjo, which is perhaps the most accomplished of the *Difficult Loves* films. It is also the one in which the director was given the freest rein; according to Duque Naranjo, García Márquez gave him a choice of six different topics, some from *Love in the Time of Cholera* and some from his newspaper articles, and allowed him to select which he felt most appropriate. Duque Naranjo chose one of the newspaper articles as the source for his film, based upon which García Márquez went on to write the short story 'La santa' ('The Saint'), which later appeared in the collection *Strange Pilgrims*. Starring veteran Colombian actor Frank Ramírez, the film captures well the Colombian setting of the early part of the story and has found a convincing formula for the portrayal of the magical-realist elements.[48] The sequence in which Evelia dies at the beginning of the film, for instance, having run home into the arms of her father, is filmed entirely 'straight' and could indeed be taken on one level as a realist account of what actually happened. Yet at the same time subtle indicators throughout the sequence incline us to believe she was really run over as she ran across the road and never made it home at all; the narrative remains suspended within this ambiguity which is never resolved. Moreover, as much as being a film about the 'miracle' (the preservation of Evelia's body some twelve years after her death and her eventual resuscitation), the film has much to say about stifling bureaucracy, both European and Colombian, and the persistence of *palancas* (political connections), in deciding the fate of everyday citizens.

After this burst of activity in the late 1980s, there followed some lean years in the early 1990s in which there were few noteworthy Garciamarquian adaptations. From the mid-1990s onwards, however, interest began to grow again in adapting García Márquez for the cinema, with films that stand out including *Edipo alcalde* (*Oedipus Mayor,* [1996]), directed by Jorge Alí Triana. A modern version of Sophocles' classic tale of incest, the film is set in Colombia and stars the prominent Cuban actor Jorge Perugorria in the lead role. However, critic Hugo Chaparro Valderrama does not find it a successful adaptation and points to problems with the script, which he declares is full of 'over-literary speeches which even the best actor couldn't carry off' and 'set phrases' which, whilst reading well on the page, do not translate to the screen.[49] Chaparro Valderrama further criticises the film's use of commonplaces such as 'legendary widows' or the 'small provincial world of an imaginary town', indicating a dissatisfaction with what are now becoming the recurring stereotypes of García Márquez's tales.[50]

The most accomplished Garciamarquian adaptation of the 1990s – and, we may argue, of all the adaptations so far made – was to come in the last year of the decade: Arturo Ripstein's *El coronel no tiene quien le escriba* (*No One Writes to the Colonel* [1999]), which was shown at the Cannes Film Festival of that year. With high production values and a strong cast – including Spanish actress Marisa Paredes and Mexicans Fernando Luján and Salma Hayek – the film is atmospheric and captures well the tense, drawn-out sense of waiting that pervades the novella on which it is based. That said, fidelity to the original does not appear to be the overriding concern of the director, and, indeed, there are notable differences with García Márquez's original novella, the most obvious being the transposition of this very Colombian story into a Mexican setting. Minor references in the script are Mexicanised, where, for instance, we have mention of *sexenios,* the specifically Mexican term to relate to the six-year terms of the Mexican presidents (in Colombia, the presidential term is four years); similarly, references to the Republic which appear throughout the novella are here replaced by ones to the Revolution. Moreover, the entire driving force for the story – that the colonel is waiting for his pension which never arrives – has now been reworked in a Mexican context, since in the film, the Colonel fought in the Mexican *cristero* wars instead of the Colombian War of a Thousand Days. Whilst this transposition to a Mexican context may lose some of the specificity of the novella's political references, this transposition is used *strategically* to discuss the state of Mexico, its increasing bureaucracy and the abiding influence of the Church, amongst other issues. Thus, as Sally

Faulkner has reminded us in another context, when considering an adaptation it is not a question of assessing to what extent a film is 'faithful' to the text but the relationship between text and film in which neither is presumed to have hierarchy over the other.[51]

Moving into the twenty-first century, whilst several potentially interesting works are still in pre- or post-production, of those which have already been released, we can note Lisandro Duque Naranjo's *Los niños invisibles* (*The Invisible Children* [2001]), on which García Márquez collaborated on the screenplay, which is a charming little story about young boys growing up in 1950s Colombia. Also, Ruy Guerra's most recent Garciamarquian endeavour, *O veneno da madrugada* (*Dawn Poison*), an adaptation of *In Evil Hour,* came out in 2004 and is an interesting film, albeit with somewhat exaggerated characterisation in places.

Finally, one of the latest-released of Garciamarquian films, Mike Newell's *Love in the Time of Cholera* (2007), has proved somewhat of a disappointment for reviewers, with Javier Bardem's acting in particular being the subject of criticism.[52] Moreover, Newell does not appear to have given much thought to adaptation as an active, selective process and has tried to cram in too much from the lengthy novel. This results in an overlong film (139 minutes) and in characters who are never fully developed; the nuances and subtleties of the novel are skimmed over in an attempt to cover too many events. In this, *Love in the Time of Cholera* provides an interesting contrast to Ruy Guerra's *Fábula de la bella palomera* as discussed earlier: Guerra's film is based on the same source but takes only a short section from the novel as inspiration for an entire film. Here, the same event – the murder of the young Olimpia – appears in Newell's film but is passed over with such alacrity that the audience is never sure what purpose the episode has to play in the plot. Finally, the film also suffers from the same chronic problem of Garciamarquian portrayals of women and gender roles; whilst Florentino is allowed to, in Bradshaw's words, 'have his narrative cake and eat it', Fermina is shackled to a stifling marriage, and, moreover, the film is littered with gratuitous shots of the female breasts of Florentino's young conquests.[53] Overall, then, this latest endeavour fails to live up to the expectations generated by what would appear to be a strong combination of seasoned director, acclaimed actor and celebrated literary source.

García Márquez in other media

Whilst García Márquez's influence on the Seventh Art is the most notable, he has also been involved to a lesser extent with other media. In his early years in Mexico, he worked in advertising, and also in television, although the programmes on which he worked are virtually untraceable nowadays since his input was unaccredited. Later, he was involved in some adaptations for Colombian television, including a mini-series based on Jorge Isaac's classic novel *María,* whilst his own *In Evil Hour* was made into a mini-series for television in the late 1970s. His writing also generated another television series of six episodes based on the character from his short story 'Me alquilo para soñar' ('I Sell My Dreams') from the collection *Strange Pilgrims,* which was directed by Ruy Guerra and shown in 1992.

García Márquez has also made a brief foray into theatre, with his play, *Diatriba de amor contra un hombre sentado* (*Diatribe of Love against a Seated Man*), first published in 1994. A one-act monologue, this is García Márquez's only theatrical work to date, and, although not yet translated into English, it has been performed widely in Spain and Argentina. The play is set on the day that a couple celebrate their silver wedding anniversary and focuses on a wife's disillusionment and frustration after so many years of marriage. The wife's famous line 'there's nothing more like hell than a happy marriage' neatly sums up the play's central theme of bourgeois married life being one of disappointment and lack of love.

Despite these endeavours in other media, it is García Márquez's relationship with the cinema which has proved the most enduring, and, doubtless, his narrative works will continue tempting directors into the future.

NOTES

1. Gabriel García Márquez, 'La penumbra del escritor de cine', in Eduardo García Aguilar, *García Márquez: la tentación cinematográfica,* Mexico City: UNAM, 1985, pp. 97–105; p. 103. The translation is mine.
2. See, for example, 'La alta chismografía' in *Obra periodística,* edited and with an introduction by Jacques Gilard, 4 vols., Barcelona: Bruguera, 1981–3: vol. I: *Textos costeños (1948–1952),* pp. 539–41, a piece discussing Rita Hayworth's private life. See also 'Continúa la función' in *Textos costeños,* pp. 343–4, which relates the humorous consequences when an audience stands up to leave before the last reel of the film. See also *Textos costeños,* pp. 374–5 and pp. 295–6 respectively.
3. Eduardo García Aguilar, *García Márquez: la tentación cinematográfica,* Mexico City: UNAM, 1985, p. 31. This and all subsequent translations of García Aguilar are my own.
4. César Augusto Montoya, 'Gabriel García Márquez: el crítico de cine', *Kinetoscopio,* 38 (1996): 81–7; p. 82. This and subsequent translations of Montoya are my own.
5. See *Obra periodística,* vol. II: *Entre cachacos (1954–1955),* p. 388; pp. 174, 374, and 382; p. 341; and p. 332 respectively.
6. See *Entre cachacos,* pp. 338 and 227; pp. 309, 314, 348, 396 and 419; pp. 209 and 314; and pp. 340 and 389, respectively.

7. A. Paxman, 'On the Lot with García Márquez', *Variety* (26–31 March 1996), p. 55.
8. In interview in Miguel Fernández-Braso, *La soledad de Gabriel García Márquez (una conversación infinita)*, Barcelona: Planeta, 1972, pp. 61–2. This and subsequent translations of Fernández-Braso are my own.
9. Donald M. Morales, 'García Márquez and His Image of Women', *Contributions to the Study of World Literature*, 122 (2003): 333–42; p. 342.
10. Kathleen McNerney, *Understanding Gabriel García Márquez*, Columbia, SC: South Carolina University Press, 1989, p. 130.
11. García Aguilar, *García Márquez*, p. 22.
12. Montoya, 'Gabriel García Márquez: el crítico de cine', p. 86.
13. Matías Montes-Huidobro, 'From Hitchcock to García Márquez: The Methodology of Suspense', in Bradley Shaw and Nora Vera-Godwin, *Critical Perspectives on Gabriel García Márquez*, Lincoln, NE: Society for Spanish and Spanish American Studies, 1986, pp. 105–23.
14. Gabriel García Márquez, *No One Writes to the Colonel*, Harmondsworth: Penguin, 1974, trans. J. S. Bernstein, p. 1.
15. See David Bordwell and Kristin Thompson, *Film Art: An Introduction*, New York: McGraw Hill, 1997, who classify 'behaviour of figures' as one of the four pillars of *mise en scène*.
16. Cited in García Aguilar, *García Márquez*, p. 26.
17. In Fernández-Braso, *La soledad*, p. 62.
18. Cited in Montoya, 'Gabriel García Márquez', p. 87.
19. Álvaro Ramírez Ospina, 'García Márquez en el cine', *Kinetoscopio*, 38 (1996): 88–93; pp. 91 and 89. The translations are my own.
20. Ramírez Ospina, 'García Márquez en el cine', pp. 91 and 89.
21. Ramírez Ospina, 'García Márquez en el cine', pp. 91 and 89.
22. Julián David Correa, Lía Master and César Augusto Montoya, 'Gabriel García Márquez y el cine: los amores difíciles', *Entreextremos*, 2 (1997): 32–8; pp. 32–3. The translation is my own.
23. Cited in García Aguilar, *García Márquez*, p. 46.
24. Óscar Collazos, *García Márquez: la soledad y la gloria – Su vida y su obra*, Barcelona: Plaza y Janés, 1983, p. 92. ('México, publicidad, cine y supervivencia.')
25. Cited in García Aguilar, *García Márquez*, p. 47.
26. Orlando Mora, 'García Márquez visto por sus directores', *Kinetoscopio*, 38 (1996): 94–101; p. 96. The translation is my own.
27. García Aguilar, *García Márquez*, p. 47.
28. García Aguilar, *García Márquez*, p. 63.
29. Ramírez Ospina, 'García Márquez en el cine', p. 89. Eligio García Márquez, *La tercera muerte de Santiago Nasar: crónica de la crónica*, Madrid: Mondadori, 1987, p. 167. This and subsequent translations of Eligio García Márquez are my own.
30. García Aguilar, *García Márquez*, p. 53.
31. Cited in García Aguilar, *García Márquez*, p. 55.
32. Cited in García Aguilar, *García Márquez*, p. 56.
33. García Aguilar, *García Márquez*, p. 59.
34. Ramírez Ospina, 'García Márquez en el cine', p. 89.

35. McNerney, *Understanding Gabriel García Márquez,* p. 129. García Aguilar, *García Márquez,* p. 63.
36. In interview with Mora, 'García Márquez visto por sus directores', p. 99.
37. Ramírez Ospina, 'García Márquez en el cine', p. 91.
38. Gabriel García Márquez, *Innocent Eréndira and Other Stories,* trans. Gregory Rabassa, London: Jonathan Cape, 1979, p. 32.
39. Wendy B. Faris, *Ordinary Enchantments: Magical Realism and the Remystification of Narrative,* Nashville, TN: Vanderbilt, 2004, p. 7.
40. Ramírez Ospina, 'García Márquez en el cine', p. 89.
41. See S. Sabine Schlickers, *Verfilmtes Erzählen: Narratologisch-komparative Untersuchung zu* El beso de la mujer araña *(Manuel Puig/Héctor Babenco) und* Crónica de una muerte anunciada *(Gabriel García Márquez: Francesco Rosi),* Frankfurt: Vervuert, 1997, for a detailed analysis of the differences between the novel and the film.
42. Cited in Eligio García Márquez, *La tercera muerte,* p. 167.
43. In interview with Mora, 'García Márquez visto por sus directores', p. 97.
44. Susan Conde, 'Readerly and Writerly Letters from the Park', *Journal of Film and Video,* 44 (3–4) (1992–3): 105–18.
45. Morales, 'García Márquez and His Image of Women', p. 338.
46. Morales, 'García Márquez and His Image of Women', p. 333.
47. C. Cabezón Doty, 'Latinoamérica y Europa en diálogo intermedial: Gabriel García Márquez, Hanna Schygulla y Cesare Zavattini en *Amores difíciles*', *Taller de Letras,* 37 (2005): 23–50; p. 44.
48. Frank Ramírez is most famous for his role in Francisco Norden's *Cóndores no entierran todos los días* (*Condors Don't Die Every Day*) and *Man of Principle* of 1984, and was later to appear in such other modern Colombian classics as Camila Loboguerrero's biopic *María Cano* of 1990, and Sergio Cabrera's *La estrategia del caracol* (The Snail's Strategy) of 1993.
49. Hugo Chaparro Valderrama, '*Edipo alcalde,* de Jorge Alí Triana: cine vs. literatura', *Kinetoscopio,* 38 (1996): 3–6 (p. 4). The translation is mine.
50. Chaparro Valderrama, '*Edipo alcalde'*, p. 4.
51. Sally Faulkner, *Literary Adaptations in Spanish Cinema,* Woodbridge: Tamesis, 2004, p. 3.
52. See Peter Bradshaw, 'Review: *Love in the Time of Cholera*', *The Guardian,* 21 March 2008, who declares Bardem's acting in the film 'unbearably mannered and self-conscious'.
53. Bradshaw, 'Review.'

12

MICHAEL BELL

García Márquez, magical realism and world literature

It is often thought that Gabriel García Márquez was principally responsible for a worldwide popularity of the marvellous in late-twentieth-century fiction, but this claim, like the phrase 'magical realism' itself, now involves a measure of cliché and confusion. The most popular version of the story, the one that everyone 'knows', is that in the 1960s a generation of 'Boom' novelists in Latin America devised a mixture of 'magic' and 'realism' which subsequently extended to almost all parts of the globe. 'Magical realism' draws on pre-scientific folk belief to subvert the 'Western' commitment to scientific reason, itself associated with both imperialism and a history of realist representation so that the genre is intrinsically oppositional and progressive. Since García Márquez's *One Hundred Years of Solitude* (*Cien años de soledad* [1967]) was the most popular, substantial and summative work in this mode, it is the principal source from which magical realism became a dominant form in late-twentieth-century fiction worldwide. There is considerable truth in this story, and writers from around the world, such as Salman Rushdie, have acknowledged the importance of his example. Nonetheless, this broad-brush account obfuscates a number of important questions and may occlude a different story. The aim here is to highlight some less noticed aspects by considering more closely what 'world', 'literature' and the 'marvellous' might mean in García Márquez.[1]

As is noted elsewhere in this volume, García Márquez's long career as newspaper columnist, film critic and investigative journalist clearly influenced his fiction both in its subject matter and in its forms. It may be symptomatic that from his earliest journalistic writing he often used the common phrase 'in the world' with a range of meaning extending from purely emotional folk rhetoric, as in the expression 'the most beautiful girl in the world', to serious statistical or geopolitical references. In a column of April 1950 written for the local newspaper of Barranquilla, his home town in the Caribbean coastal region of Colombia, he reflected on the case of one Garry Davis who had rejected his American passport to declare himself a 'citizen of the world'.[2] The young García Márquez, who would one day become world famous for his 'magical' literalisation of metaphor, plays with the practical difficulties of the concept in order to celebrate the utopian impulse of this piece of performance art. Without recourse either to the supernatural or to the pre-modern folk imagination, indeed by literalising a cosmopolitan ideal stemming directly from Enlightenment universalism, García Márquez already creates the essential political dynamic commonly associated with 'magical realism'. But before developing that theme, I wish to note simply his abiding interest, both practical and utopian, both conscious and linguistically subtextual, in a world context. For García Márquez's literary career was to make him experience at a higher level the possibility and impossibility of being a citizen of the world. Since he began to publish, academic literary scholars, such as Franco Moretti, have increasingly argued the importance of reading all literature in a world context, or at least in an interrelated set of regional contexts, and García Márquez is one of many contemporary writers whose work has brought about this new consciousness in the Academy.[3] This important truth, enshrined in the familiar story, can be seen as an internal dynamic of García Márquez's oeuvre.

Pascale Casanova has analysed the literary economy of the 'world republic of letters' whereby some languages, and literary capitals, such as Paris and London, enjoy particular prestige and power.[4] In early modern times, for example, the vernacular languages of Europe had to assert, or more truly, to earn, a status equal to, and eventually surpassing, the learned and literary language of Latin. In the early twentieth century, Latin American Hispanic writers suffered a double occlusion: the regional reputation for provincial violence and instability was compounded by the relative decline of Spanish literary culture over the nineteenth century to a largely imitative status. Casanova points out that ever since the mid to late eighteenth century, when J. G. Herder did much to underpin the extraordinary rise of German to challenge French cultural hegemony, there has been an emphasis on the uniquely indigenous folk experience embodied in vernacular culture. As *One Hundred Years of Solitude* draws on local folk experience and sensibility, it builds into its narrative structure a reflection on the status and impact of its language by borrowing Cervantes's device of the foreign historian. Just as the local (hi)story of Don Quixote is 'translated' from the notional Arabic, a prestige language at the time, of the fictional historian, Cide Hamete Benengeli, so the Buendías' history is inscribed in a Sanskrit which they cannot understand. In Cervantes, the Arabic version is a mere trace within his Castilian masterpiece. In García Márquez's case, doubtless also influenced by Jorge Luis Borges, the Sanskrit chronicle of the world-travelled sage, Melquíades, written in a sacred but dead language, seems rather to enclose the Buendías in a further solitude; they are unknown even to themselves. The device images their linguistic solitude and links it to their lack of self-knowledge: it suggests some important truth at once apparent and inaccessible to them. One fine day, the Buendías must awake from their sleepwalking, and the deciphering of the Sanskrit is the image of such an awakening from what Joyce's Stephen Dedalus called the 'nightmare' of history in *A Portrait of the Artist as a Young Man*. Hence, despite the novel's concluding dictum that 'races condemned to one hundred years of solitude did not have a second opportunity on earth', the implosion of the family's foretold history has a positive potential which García Márquez strikingly affirmed by reversing this statement in his Nobel Prize acceptance speech.[5] The Buendías' historical equivalents can perhaps escape their 'fate' by awaking from fatalism. Between the apparent pessimism of the writing and the overt optimism of the prize speech lay more than the sudden world fame of the individual author: there was the new literary prestige of the language and the region. It seems not accidental that a structural condition of linguistic solitude should be central to this one pivotal work after which his longer fictions take on a different authority. While still intensely local, *Chronicle of a Death Foretold* (*Crónica de una muerte anunciada* [1981]), *Love in the Time of Cholera* (*El amor en los tiempos del cólera* [1985]) and *The General in His Labyrinth* (*El general en su laberinto* [1989]) seem to breathe in a different air from the emotional and cultural solipsism of *One Hundred Years of Solitude*.

García Márquez's contribution to this shift was no accident as his relation to world literature was always that of a geopolitical thinker, and he had to absorb much from the world's imaginative writing in order to give something to it. Although his acknowledged tendency to creative memory means that his memoirs in general must be approached with care, there seems no reason to doubt the striking impact of his early reading as recorded on various occasions. Or rather, if there is some post-facto mythologising of these moments of literary discovery, it only serves to confirm the admiration, or influence, in question. For example, he speaks of deciding to become a writer at the discovery of sheer imaginative possibility in first reading Kafka's *Metamorphosis*.[6] He says the kind of writer he became was affected by the uncanny perception of the aura and hollowness of power at the beginning of Virginia Woolf's *Mrs Dalloway* in which the present London scene is suddenly imagined as ruins seen from the retrospect of a distant future.[7] He recalls the entrancement of listening to another 'time' book, Thomas Mann's *The Magic Mountain*, read aloud in a school dormitory of senior boys.[8] He admires in William Faulkner the concentrated historical, mythic and realist creation of a local world.[9] And he reviews with intense admiration a work of Italian realist cinema, de Sica's *Umberto D*.[10] In retrospect, the potential outlines of his own creative territory can already be seen emerging from this combination of creative worlds: flights of fantasy, elisions and expansions of time and memory and the compulsion of local or family myth. But perhaps most importantly, all these are held in the tight discipline of a minimalist realism figuring the inescapable pressure of reality.

His own generation in Latin America achieved something comparable to these Anglo-American and European modernists but different because of its distinctive regional location and history, a difference that included an essential knowledge of the modernists themselves. But the other great difference commonly noted in this Latin American generation is its conscious recovery of the marvellous. The marvellous and the magical, with which García Márquez is now iconically associated, are significantly different from the turn to myth that characterised many of the modernists. But to appreciate the significance of this some further background is required.

To understand the wider recovery of the marvellous in world fiction it is first necessary to question the assumption of a mainly Latin American influence in the familiar account. The new sympathy for the marvellous has broader bases, and wider sources. As signs of a more general cultural change, for example, one might note over the same period a new interest in Shakespeare's late romances or the widened popularity of opera as a form. It may be, in other words, that García Márquez is less a cause than a harbinger of change. That would not, of course, reduce the interest of his case. To be the symptomatic index of a deep-lying cultural shift suggests a more profound order of significance than being the instigator of a literary fashion. Likewise, some of the conscious rationales of 'magical realism' may have an ex-post-facto aspect, and an ideological thrust, that miss some of its underlying cultural meaning.

We may approach this possibility by considering the unstable equilibrium in the very concept of 'magical realism'. It is often said that the *proprium* of the genre, in contradistinction to the fantastic, is that elements of the marvellous are naturalised, treated as unremarkable, in the narration.[11] But as some commentators have observed, it is often hard in practice to determine when this occurs; or if indeed it can truly be said to occur at all in respect of the reader's actual consciousness in absorbing even the most apparently naive narration. For even if neither characters nor narrator baulk at the marvels, the reader, by the very logic of the genre, must be aware of them. Not surprisingly, therefore, even Wendy Faris's classic study of the form serves partly to reveal its elusiveness.[12] Meanwhile, the phrase itself is as elusive as the genre it seeks to define. In oxymoronic formulations of this kind it is always a delicate matter to determine where the principal emphasis lies. To what extent is magical realism *opposed* to realism or a form *of* it? Much discussion of the genre emphasises, or assumes, the former while other commentators note the ultimate importance of the containing category of realism as it is expanded and enhanced, but not exploded, in this genre. That the tension between these emphases is particularly important for García Márquez is reflected in his oeuvre overall. As well as *One Hundred Years of Solitude* and several shorter works in the magical mode, there are works such as *No One Writes to the Colonel (El coronel no tiene quien le escriba,* [published 1961]) in which 'realism' is much more than a neutral convention. It is of the essence as the tale turns on the almost unbearable pressure of reality upon the central character. So too, what I take to be his last work of major and summative substance, *The General in His Labyrinth,* is a work of sober reflection on historical reality. Indeed, to think of García Márquez only, or primarily, as a magical realist is to occlude an important aspect, not just of his oeuvre but even of those works which are acknowledged to be in that mode.

It is also necessary to note here that the term 'magical realism', despite earlier usage in European art history, first came into general use as a literary generic term in the Latin American context where it was affected by the gravitational pull of a neighbouring phrase '*lo real maravilloso*' (the marvellous real, or reality). This was first expounded by Alejo Carpentier in the prologue to his 1949 novel *The Kingdom of This World* (*El reino de este mundo*). Carpentier records how on visiting Haiti after a decade in the Paris of the surrealists, he was overwhelmed by the 'surreal' quality of the Caribbean and Latin American landscape and history. Here the anti-rational devices of the surrealists were starkly revealed to him as formal games still essentially within the world of Western rationality. In being merely oppositional they were still defined by it. By contrast, the history of the slave uprisings inspired partly by African tribal beliefs or the story of Henri Christophe with his fantastic redoubt of Sans Souci, were marvels of reality. The phrase *lo real maravilloso,* therefore, refers to a *reality* whereas 'magical realism' refers to a literary *mode.* And 'marvel' similarly pertains to the natural just as 'magic' implies some departure from it. These expressions are, therefore, quite distinct in their meanings and claims, but Carpentier's argument, which was squarely based on a regional specificity, coloured the use of the English phrase so that it became a matter of debate whether an ethnographic exceptionalism is part of the meaning of the literary subgenre.

Perhaps one can say that 'magical realism' has acquired such a meaning de facto in so far as it has been widely thought of in this way, but there is no intrinsic connection of the genre per se with Latin America. At the same time, Carpentier's prologue, illuminating as it is for the creative impulse behind the book, is actually quite two-dimensional as compared to the work itself. *The Kingdom of This World* is a poetically concentrated meditation on history in which the experience of the marvellous is ethnographically relativised and is ultimately assimilated into the narrative as a form of artistically sustained mythopoeia.[13] However duplicitous the European category of the aesthetic is shown to be, it remains the basis of the book's own utopian affirmation. The book is consciously a work of *literature,* of literary *art.* Equally, while the book owes much of its local power to the communal imagination of the black slaves, it is squarely in the tradition of European Enlightenment in seeing slavery itself as an intrinsic, that is to say a universal, not a merely local and relative evil.

Once again, it is difficult, and perhaps unimportant, to determine how far Carpentier may have been conscious of a gap between the rousingly simple reality claim in his prologue and the literary complexity of his actual achievement. The gap itself matters, however, because it separates a direct claim about reality from the significance of an artistically created world. And that matters in turn because the claim of an ethnographically specific experience is a common rationale for valorising 'magical realism' as a challenge to 'Western' rationality. Such a claim, although offered as a compliment, actually makes such works vulnerable to the charge of unreflecting sentimentality. I say unreflecting because the rationality sometimes labelled 'Western', and thereby contaminated with imperialism and other evils, is also the very universalism on which the moral standpoint of the book is at the same time likely to depend. And I say 'sentimental' because such a viewpoint seeks to enjoy a moral high ground on a simplified basis. But that is what Carpentier, in this classic and founding instance, notably avoids. If his prologue comes close to making such an argument, the book itself does not.

The distinction made here is very relevant to García Márquez who has been a convinced Marxist throughout his mature life and therefore a child of the Enlightenment. The force of this may be obscured because, whereas in Carpentier the political themes are in the conscious foreground of the narrative, in García Márquez the political consciousness is typically more suffused into the action. But if he maintains the integrity of his fictional world with such rigour that his specific political commitments may be thought irrelevant to it, he nonetheless sustains the fictional world within a geopolitical standpoint that assumes an Enlightenment universalism. For García Márquez, just as much as Carpentier, therefore, it would be misleading to identify the presence of the magical or the marvellous too closely with an ethnographic or regional exceptionalism claimed by the book itself. In that respect, it is fruitful to take another hint from Carpentier and to stress the densely literary concentration of his narrative. To call Carpentier's method 'poetic' gives the wrong impression if that suggests a tendency to purple writing. It is a matter rather of focusing, with a near anthropological detachment, on metonymic moments which become radiantly iconic concentrations of historical experience.

In the light of this, we may return to the internal instability of the phrase 'magical realism' as reflecting an instability in the underlying notion of realism, an instability which the phrase both exacerbates and occludes. A common argument for magical realism is that it subverts or expands the protocols of a more traditional novelistic realism, itself associated with philosophical assumptions underwriting the political possession, and the scientific understanding, of the world. There is an important measure of truth in this. Several Hispanic writers of the region turned to the example of Cervantes who is commonly accredited with founding European novelistic realism on mocking the marvellous in the form of medieval romance but who, as Borges and others have insisted, rather found in *Don Quixote* a cunning means of indulging his affection for it. In this respect, Cervantes represents a route back to the pre-Cervantean marvellous, and Carpentier in his prologue comments on the cultural ambiguity of a Cervantean episode in precisely this spirit. But there repeatedly creeps into the rehearsals of this account an assumption that 'realism' is a naively mimetic form, seeking to encapsulate reality objectively in language. It is one thing for writers such as Borges, within his fictions, to promote such a reductive conception of realism, but others, whether scholars or general readers, should not be drawn into taking such ideas too literally. Of course, the reality effect is crucial to much nineteenth-century fiction, hence the term 'realism', but it is necessary every so often to remind some readers, including academics, that realism itself is only a literary convention. The great works of nineteenth-century realist art doubtless inform us about human experience, but, despite their occasional rhetoric or rationalisations as in Balzac's 'All is true', they do so, no less than Dante or Greek tragedy, through literary means.[14] All art affects us, in Nietzsche's words, as 'a concentrated image of the world'.[15] In this respect, the assumed internal polarity in the phrase 'magical realism' has to be significantly reconfigured. The 'magical' and the 'realist' are both equally literary. Hence, along with the notions of 'magical realism' as either critiquing or expanding realism, one can also see it as simply foregrounding the literariness of the narrative. 'Magical realism' has origins beyond the ethnographic, and in that respect it is highly suggestive that it should so often flaunt a literary pedigree.

This may initially seem a banal and circular reduction: literature is a minimal and empty category as compared to magic and realism. But it is sometimes the obvious that is most overlooked. In the late twentieth century, despite the de-facto popularity of literature, and specifically of fiction, it became a deeply problematic category, and especially under the pressure of political thinking on a geopolitical scale. In a pedagogical volume entitled *Literature in the Modern World,* designed to introduce students to advanced, globally conscious thinking about literature at the end of the twentieth century, the editor includes an excerpt from Terry Eagleton arguing the ideologically oriented arbitrariness of literary judgements. Literature, Eagleton suggests, is merely what a given set of people at a particular time find valuable or judge to be fine writing, and the supposed specialness of literature is a mystification.[16] His argument has a structural similarity to the notorious statement of former British Prime Minister Margaret Thatcher that there is no such thing as society. Many observers saw this as a wicked dishonesty because it used the literal truth that there is indeed no such *thing* as 'society' to obfuscate the fact that every one born onto the planet is governed by a network of socio-economic relations which are man-made and a matter of political responsibility. As a popularising Marxist, Eagleton summarises with unusual candour the deconstructive pressure to which the category of the literary has been widely subjected. Although literary fiction remains buoyant in so far as it continues to sell and is popular across a wide spectrum of readers, there is a question as to *how* it is read or what it is read *as*.

Literature has been a threatened category, if not at the level of practice then at the level of understanding, and the notion that nineteenth-century realist writers practised a naive literalism is itself a symptom of this general occlusion of the literary. Imaginative writers such as Carpentier and García Márquez, who have strong political and historical views, are for that very reason impelled to create a literary density within their fiction which is why it may be an important underlying impulse of 'magical realism' more generally to foreground and affirm the literary as such. To take the subgenre in this way is to deflect its meaning from pre-modern ethnographic exceptionalism and to see it rather as the expression of a highly sophisticated universality. García Márquez's own remarkable novels written after *One Hundred Years of Solitude,* including *The Autumn of the Patriarch (El otoño del patriarca* [1975]), which he long considered his masterpiece, are not magical but they are highly, and consciously, literary. That also explains why 'magical realism' has characterised widely different writers around the world, irrespective of influence from a single regional centre.

In this respect, for example, Mikhail Bulgakov's *The Master and Margarita* provides an illuminating comparison. First published with the Kruschev thaw in 1966 from a manuscript which had survived the author's death in Stalinist Russia in 1941, its publication is almost contemporary with *One Hundred Years of Solitude* yet its particular brand of 'magical realism' emerged from a completely different history, both literary and political. Both works use the Bible as a significant structural model within which to mobilise magically realist effects. Indeed, on a world-historical scale, the most influential work of 'magical realism' in a colonial context is the Bible, although this fact is commonly overlooked for the very feature that makes it so interesting a case: its peculiar status of having survived into modernity with a large readership for whom the magical elements are a matter of literal faith. The novels of Bulgakov and García Márquez exploit this fact in different ways, but in both cases it ultimately serves to foreground the meaning of their own literariness.

Several chapters of Bulgakov's novel consist of the Master's novel, which he has actually burned, telling the story of Christ and the imperial official, Pontius Pilate. Whereas James Joyce's fictional inauguration of the twentieth century took a Jew as its everyman figure, Bulgakov, in the latter half of the century, made Pilate the modern archetype. Pilate, the hand-washer, if not the moral centre of the book, is the centre of its moral significance. Unlike many of the real functionaries or bystanders in twentieth-century history, this Pilate is subsequently tortured by the thought of his missed opportunity. And Pilate's failure is central because it figures forth the responsibility of the Master, who has imagined him, and through that of the writer as such. But, although the Master has destroyed his own work, in the magical world of this fiction 'Manuscripts don't burn', and the work survives the personal weakness of its creator.[17] Moreover, the work which survives is specifically a literary one in multiple contrast to the familiar biblical story. Not only is the Master's novel narrated from Pilate's rather than Christ's viewpoint and the characters given unfamiliar names, but Christ, known as Yeshua ha-Nosri, is presented in entirely secular terms. Yeshua repeatedly warns his disciple, Matthu Levi, the Evangelist Matthew, that he misunderstands and misrepresents his master. The proverbial value of the phrase 'Gospel truth' is inverted by an alternative history envisaged through the literary imagination. Meanwhile, the entirely secular conception of Yeshua/Christ in the Master's novel is in ironic contrast with the story of modern atheistic Moscow in which it is embedded for this relates the grotesque mayhem created by a group of supernatural demons. Here again, however, the devils are deflected from traditional Christian figures and have an essentially literary provenance. Indeed, the whole Moscow story is both a homage to, and a putting-to-use of, the moral imagination of the nineteenth-century Russian novel. It is not only strewn with allusions from Pushkin to Tolstoy, it also uses the grotesquerie of Gogol and the psychological imagery of Dostoevsky to explode the spiritual vacuity of Soviet Russia. If it drew on a literal religious faith, the effect would be more narrowly reliant on this. As it is, the literary imagination is felt as a spiritual power and a historical resource.

To be sure, *One Hundred Years of Solitude* draws more evidently on the folk imagination for its mediation of biblical motifs, but that mediation too is through explicitly literary means: Cervantes's signature device of the foreign historian. The final discovery that the chronicle has already been written by Melquíades gives the whole narrative a Proustian doubleness requiring us to reread its story of lost time in the light of this knowledge. But the significance of the doubled text is already cunningly implanted within it, for another Proustian dimension of the narration is its local distraction of the reader when major links are being forged so that what seems on first reading to be a randomly associative process proves on the second to have a tautly constructed logic. A major episode in the story of Macondo is the memory sickness which may be thought of as the moment in which the communal memory becomes dependent on writing. The townsfolk initially seek to stay the loss of memory by the mechanical means of putting name labels and instructions on everyday items, and then they start to produce an 'imaginary reality, one invented by themselves, which was less practical for them, but more comforting'.[18] After these rather desperate veerings between mechanical records and flights of imagination, José Arcadio starts to construct a memory machine: a wheel turning thousands of cards reminiscent of a 1960s computer. But just as José Arcadio has written some 14,000 cards it is rendered redundant by the arrival of a mysterious, decrepit old man who eventually proves to be Melquíades. The focus veers in mid-sentence, and the memory machine itself quickly fades from the memory of most readers as the narrative goes on to tell how Melquíades cures the memory sickness with his magic potion.

Only at the end of the novel does the conjunction of Melquíades and the memory machine become significant. For Melquíades's true remedy for the memory sickness is the written narrative he produces in the timeless zone of the chamber to which he retires. The timeless room figures both a Nietzschean superhistoricism, the capacity to escape 'presentist' illusions and the traditional 'Once upon a time' of fiction.[19] So too, within the world of the novel, Melquíades's manuscript may be seen as a chronicle, the simplest and most factual form of history, yet within the novel which we read *as* a novel, it is the purest fiction. As an internal image of the novel itself, therefore, it preserves all the ambiguities signalled at the moment of its birth. If the novel itself is a memory machine, how should this be understood? Is it a reductive image of the genre, exposing its limitations, or is it a contrastive image suggesting how it transcends the mechanical dimension of its medium? The chronicle within the novel is an image of the novel's ambiguous status as history and fiction in which its considerable power as each is inseparable from the other. Most notably, the memory of the massacre, echoing the memory sickness, disappears from the official history, and even from collective memory, but is revived, in a more mythic than historically accurate form, by virtue of García Márquez's fiction. Fiction need not be a deviation from history but a concentration of it as meaning. As such, it may not be transparent, and interpretation, or a lived experience of history, may be necessary before its meaning can be appreciated. In that respect, the final deciphering only when the experience has been lived is a resonant symbol, in Michael Wood's words, of what literature knows.[20] It knows in a mode of the open secret, both transparent and opaque. In this respect, the populist literary charm of the book is itself part of the seductive illusion from which the Buendías need to awake in their sleepwalking through history. Literary formal self-consciousness is the figure, and the means, of historical awareness.

At this point, we may recollect, too, that the memory sickness, in its conjunction of insomnia and amnesia, is effectively a reworking of Borges's philosophical fable 'Funes, the Memorious' ('Funes el memorioso'), which also exalts the oneiric transformations of literature over any merely literal or mechanical recall, however stupendous that may be.[21] Thomas Mann once saw the twentieth century under the gaze of a Don Quixote with Nietzsche's features.[22] Unlike Mann, García Márquez does not think creatively through discursive or philosophical reflection: his imagination expresses itself through the elusive concreteness of characterisation, action, iconic images and genealogical connections. But Borges had provided for García Márquez's generation a highly suggestive assimilation of a Nietzschean outlook into literary images that were formally teasing, imaginatively compelling and regionally specific. Borges, for example, speaks of the Cervantean vertigo created by the play within the play in *Hamlet*. In truth, *The Murder of Gonzago,* unlike comparable moments in *The Tempest,* is a fully embedded and motivated plot device that hardly arouses the metafictional and metaphysical response Borges rather forces upon it unless one puts it beside Nietzsche's remarks in *The Birth of Tragedy* on Hamlet as the Dionysian hero who feels, with superhistorical insight, the nausea of existence behind the phenomenal world of appearances in which the action of the play takes place.[23] Such a Nietzschean/Borgesian implication is enacted in the metafictional exposure of Melquíades's manuscript at the end of *One Hundred Years of Solitude.* The personal illusions of the characters, and of the Buendías collectively, may be understood within a more encompassing sense of the presentist illusions that make up history at any time. For all three, the difficult art is to live not without illusion but within it, while in García Márquez's case the fictional enclosure also suggests the national and regional condition from which the characters must escape.

Perhaps the single most classic work of magical realism in the postcolonial vein is Salman Rushdie's *Midnight's Children* (1982) but, like *The Master and Margarita*, this has other sources antedating the popularity of García Márquez. Günter Grass's *The Tin Drum* (1959), for example, is a major structural and thematic influence and is itself a book of dense literary-historical allusion. Rushdie's novel creates a formal self-consciousness designed, in his case, to negotiate the problematic nature of representation in both its mimetic and its political senses. The narrator, Saleem Sinai, is constantly cast, by himself, by others and by circumstances, as a representative of the collective Indian experience after Independence. Yet his capacity to embody the national history is continually ridiculed, and his magical property of being able to enter telepathically the consciousness of individuals all over India gives him what is referred to as the 'illusion of the artist'.[24] In so far as this is specifically the Balzacian artist whose dramatic narrative can express the national experience, the comparison is ambiguous. Does it mean that India cannot be represented as nineteenth-century France could? Or does it mean that, to the eye of a late-twentieth-century, postmodern and postcolonial consciousness, this was always an impossible ambition even in Balzac's time? No doubt both implications are in varying measure present and are made equally irrelevant because the narrative uses the incapacity of Saleem to achieve more implicitly the representativeness that is apparently denied. The overt literariness of the work pre-empts the literalistic objections to which it could be vulnerable at the level of history while constantly putting into imaginative orbit highly concentrated iconic foci of the national experience. Once again, it is specifically as literature that the text is able to embody a history, or to become what Fredric Jameson calls a 'national allegory'.[25]

Like García Márquez, Rushdie holds the formal and the substantive, the historical weight and the fictional fantasy, in a testing tension. Although the present essay has focused on *One Hundred Years of Solitude* because of its evident relation to the genre of magical realism, this literary tension between the utopian and the real is the more essential dynamic that pervades García Márquez's oeuvre at large. *Love in the Time of Cholera* creates an intertextual relation with Flaubert to reflect on the place of romantic love in human life and literature. *The General in His Labyrinth* meditates on the apparently necessary solitude of Simón Bolívar and his failure to achieve the regional union of Latin America which had been his political ambition. The novel has a contemporary resonance, and, in so far as its utopian motive belongs equally to the literary and the political imagination, the doubleness of García Márquez's appreciation perhaps reflects his loyal friendship with Fidel Castro long after other progressive writers had become disenchanted with the Cuban leader's regime. The tension between literature and life is always vital, but magical realism is peculiarly susceptible to short-circuiting the relationship and slipping into coyness or sentimentality – and especially when it is deemed to privilege an exceptional viewpoint. García Márquez saw this danger in *One Hundred Years of Solitude* even after its success.[26] Exceptionalism may be ideological rather than ethnographic. Isabel Allende's *The House of the Spirits* (1982), Laura Esquivel's *Like Water for Chocolate* (1993) or Angela Carter's *Nights at the Circus* (1984) express a female sensibility with a view, in Allende and Carter especially, to critiquing the feminine from within. Allende is critical of magical sentimentality and discards the magic in her book as history closes in on her characters. Rather differently, Louis de Bernière's *Captain Corelli's Mandolin* (1994) takes up the romantic and regional charm of García Márquez without the internal tension. It belongs to a late-twentieth-century subgenre of romance set in times of violence in which the two elements achieve sentimental contrast rather than the thematic interrelation of Tolstoy's *War and Peace*. In whatever mode the work is disposed formally, the discipline of the real is vital, and, no doubt for that reason, it continues at all times to take the traditional form of realism. Indeed, it is important to recollect that over the same period in which magical realism has flourished, there have been writers of equal if not greater power, such as Anita Desai, on India, and John McGahern and William Trevor from Ireland, whose works have achieved the enigmatic transparency of literary transformation the more effectively for observing the protocols of realism. In this respect, a writer of singular power to compare with García Márquez is another Nobel Prize-winner, the South African novelist, J. M. Coetzee.

Until his relatively late novels, *Elizabeth Costello* (2003) and *Slow Man* (2005), Coetzee's fiction had stayed principally within the protocols of realism, yet his work is saturated with a metafictional concern for the modes of meaning and responsibility peculiar to imaginative literature. Coetzee thinks of major historical questions but does so strictly within, or through, the category of literature. He repeatedly refuses to translate the moral substance dramatised in his work into general discursive opinion. But just as *Foe* (1986) and *The Master of Petersburg* (1994) reflect respectively on the tortuous truth conditions of imaginative writing and the dark sources of creativity, so his works concerning the woman novelist alter ego, Elizabeth Costello, begin to take leave of the realist frame under the same pressure of concern about the responsibilities of fiction. Hence, although we may properly think of them generally as inhabiting different fictional universes, García Márquez and Coetzee have a deeper commonality. The vital, peculiar and untranslatable mode of meaning known as literature is made richly self-conscious in them both.

Comparison with Coetzee suggests more specific and political reasons why a globally conscious, post-colonial fiction in the late twentieth century should wish to emphasise its own literariness. The early twentieth-century generation of European modernist writers, most of them in some sense post-Nietzschean, frequently turned to myth as a mode not just of literary organisation but of metaphysical meaningfulness. Although a pre-modern mythopoeic sensibility was no longer possible, it was thought to have a functional counterpart in imaginative literature. The aesthetic is modernity's equivalent of the mythic world-making.[27] Such a privileging of myth was largely progressive in spirit: Joyce and Mann especially exposed the arbitrariness of all philosophical systems and accepted the universalistic implications of late Victorian anthropology as a way of cutting through the divisions of class and nation. But to a later generation around the world the universalistic claims of these writers seemed Eurocentric, and it became more urgent, while recognising the mythic nature of every world-view, both individual and cultural, to question the hegemonic power of myth. If human beings are indeed mythopoeic animals, they have to adopt a more relativistic, quizzical and postmodern relation to myth. As the francophone Caribbean novelist, Edouard Glissant, put it in 1973: 'The main difficulty facing national literatures today ... is that they must combine mythification with demystification, this primal innocence with a learned craftiness.'[28] The difference in spirit is strikingly evident in comparing D. H. Lawrence's *The Rainbow* (1915) with *One Hundred Years of Solitude*. Both invoke Genesis to tell a modern regional history through a generational family saga, but Lawrence's high seriousness contrasts sharply with García Márquez's playful populism. García Márquez draws on a folk imagination without that imagination being sentimentally endorsed.

In this respect, the fictional marvellous is importantly distinct from the mythopoeia with which, because literature is their common term, it may be confused. The difference can be focused through Nietzsche's remarks on literary response in *The Birth of Tragedy:*

> Whoever wishes to test rigorously to what extent he is related to the true aesthetic listener ... needs only to examine sincerely the feeling with which he accepts miracles represented on stage: whether he feels his historical sense, which insists on strict psychological causality, insulted by them, whether he makes a benevolent concession and admits the miracle as a phenomenon intelligible to childhood but alien to him, or whether he experiences anything else. For in this way he will be able to determine to what extent he is capable of understanding myth as a concentrated image of the world that, as a condensation of experience, cannot dispense with miracles.[29]

Nietzsche instances the marvellous in fiction as an index of the aesthetic response through which modern man comes closest to the experience of myth. But miracle in itself is not myth in this aesthetic sense: the person who literally believed in the miracle would be as far removed as the scientific positivist from a properly aesthetic response. The miracle occurs in an aesthetic realm equally separate both from the spectator's life world and from ethnographic identification. But whereas Nietzsche, as a proto-modernist, wished to recover the mythopoeic *through* literature, the magical realist like García Márquez is seeking to deconstruct the mythopoeic *as* literature. Both are internal transformations of Enlightenment.

In this, as in other ways, *One Hundred Years of Solitude* is a highly positive exemplar of features which are widely evident but not always so richly successful in other late-twentieth-century fiction. It truly dissolves the 'great divide' between elite and popular culture which modernism, despite its demotic aspirations, generally did not achieve.[30] Likewise, the growing distrust of the novel form itself as an encompassing vision of the world, and the corresponding turn to oral narration as a model, are formally incorporated into the narration.[31] As Glissant says, 'The marvellous is first and foremost an oral phenomenon', but when García Márquez said he got the clue to writing the work in realising he must tell it in the manner of his grandmother who told of marvels as everyday events, he affirmed a local value but he also created a voice which could have no authority but a literary one.[32] Even as it may assert an ethnographic challenge to hegemonic world-views, the narrative incorporates a radically literary self-positing. *One Hundred Years of Solitude* remains exemplary for its subtle combination of historical *gravitas* and popular humour and for the moral and philosophical pregnancy of its fictional self-consciousness. This may be partly because of the literary sources on which it drew for its own inspiration, and it is an index of its achievement that the work has had in its turn such a widespread influence while eluding any simple account of the 'magical realism' with which it is now indissolubly identified. Edward Braithwaite, the narrator of Julian Barnes's *Flaubert's Parrot,* speaks scathingly of South American 'magical realism' but in truth it is the degeneration into clichéd formula that excites his boredom, while Barnes's book is itself a celebration of the literary imagination.[33]

Western literature has a long tradition of Gothic and romantic writing that critiques internally the cultural tendency to instrumental reason, and magical realism can be seen as a contemporary manifestation of the same internal balancing. But the most radical critique has always been that of the literary imagination itself for which the implication of Wendy Faris's phrase 'ordinary enchantments' could be reversed. Enchantment can indeed become ordinary, and magical realism may eventually offer a too-ready short cut to it, but it is the *proprium* of the literary imagination to achieve enchantment within the ordinary. In his radical attempt to get beneath the habits of modern Western thought and to recover an originary relation to being such as he saw in pre-Socratic Greek culture, Martin Heidegger remarked that 'the uncanny, or the extraordinary, shines through the familiar ambit of things we deal with and know, beings we call ordinary.'[34] Taken in that sense, magical realism is a definition of literature as such, and would notably apply to the whole of García Márquez's oeuvre.

NOTES

1. See Wendy B. Faris, *Ordinary Enchantments: Magical Realism and the Remystification of Narrative,* Nashville, TN: Vanderbilt University Press, 2004; Wendy B. Faris and Lois Parkinson Zamora (eds.), *Magical Realism: Theory, History, Community,* Durham, NC: Duke University Press, 1995; Stephen M. Hart and Wen-chin Ouyang (eds.), *A Companion to Magical Realism,* Woodbridge: Tamesis, 2005. Also useful is Wendy B. Faris and Lois Porkinson Zamora (eds.), *Magical Realism: Theory, History, Community,* Durham, NC: Duke University Press, 1995.
2. Gabriel García Márquez, *Obra Periodística,* 4 vols., Barcelona: Bruguera, 1981–3, vol. I: *Textos Costeños,* pp. 258–9.
3. Franco Moretti, *Modern Epic: The World System from Goethe to García Márquez,* London: Verso, 1996.
4. Pascale Casanova, *The World Republic of Letters,* trans. M. B. DeDevoise, Cambridge, MA: Harvard University Press, 2004.
5. Gabriel García Márquez, *One Hundred Years of Solitude,* London: Picador, 1978, p. 335.
6. Gabriel García Márquez, *Living to Tell the Tale,* trans. Edith Grossman, London: Jonathan Cape, 2003, pp. 247–8.
7. Gabriel García Márquez, *Obra Periodística,* vol. IV: *De Europa y America,* p. 414.
8. García Márquez, *Living to Tell the Tale,* pp. 196–7.
9. See Gabriel García Márquez, *The Fragrance of the Guava: Conversations with Plinio Apuleyo Mendoza,* London: Faber, 1988, p. 47.
10. García Márquez, *Obra Periodística,* vol. II: *Entre Cachacos,* pp. 475–6.
11. Amaryll Chanady, *Magical Realism and the Fantastic,* New York: Garland, 1985.
12. Faris, *Ordinary Enchantments.*
13. For a discussion of this, see Michael Bell, *Literature, Modernism and Myth,* Cambridge: Cambridge University Press, 1997.
14. The phrase occurs at the opening of *Le Père Goriot* (1835).
15. Friedrich Nietzsche, *The Birth of Tragedy,* trans. Walter Kaufmann, New York: Random House, 1967, p. 135.
16. Dennis Walder (ed.), *Literature in the Modern World,* 2nd edn, Oxford: Oxford University Press, 2004, pp. 31–2.
17. Mikhail Bulgakov, *The Master and Margarita,* trans. Mirra Ginsburg, London: Picador, 1989, p. 300.

18. Gabriel García Márquez, *One Hundred Years of Solitude,* trans. Gregory Rabassa, New York: Harper, 1970, p. 46; *Cien Años de Soledad,* Buenos Aires: Sudamericana, 1967, p. 124.
19. This notion was developed in Friedrich Nietzsche, *The Uses and Disadvantages of History for Life* (1874).
20. Michael Wood, *Literature and the Taste of Knowledge,* Cambridge: Cambridge University Press, 2005.
21. Jorge Luis Borges, 'Funes, the Memorious', in *Labyrinths,* trans. Donald A. Yates and James E. Irby, Harmondsworth: Penguin, 1970, pp. 87–95.
22. Thomas Mann, *Essays of Three Decades,* trans. H. T. Lowe-Porter, London: Secker & Warburg, 1947, p. 438.
23. Nietzsche, *The Birth of Tragedy,* p. 60.
24. Salman Rushdie, *Midnight's Children,* London: Pan, 1982, p. 174.
25. Fredric Jameson, 'Third World Literature in the Age of Multinational Capitalism', *Social Text,* 15 (autumn 1986): 65–88.
26. García Márquez, *The Fragrance of the Guava,* pp. 26–30.
27. See Bell, *Literature, Modernism and Myth.*
28. Edouard Glissant, *Caribbean Discourse: Selected Essays,* trans. J. Michael Dash, Charlottesville, VA: University of Virginia Press, 1989, p. 100.
29. Nietzsche, *The Birth of Tragedy,* p. 135.
30. See Andreas Huyssen, *After the Great Divide: Modernism, Mass Culture, Postmodernism,* Bloomington, IN: Indiana University Press, 1986.
31. See as a portent of this, Walter Benjamin, 'The Storyteller', in *Illuminations,* trans. Harry Zohn, London: Fontana, 1973, pp. 82–108. I discuss the theme in Bell, *Literature, Modernism and Myth,* pp. 175–81.
32. Glissant, *Caribbean Discourse,* pp. 156, 30, 74.
33. Julian Barnes, *Flaubert's Parrot,* London: Jonathan Cape, 1984, p. 99.
34. Martin Heidegger, *Parmenides,* Bloomington, IN: Indiana University Press, 1992, p. 105.

FURTHER READING

Compiled by Pascale Baker

Major published works

La Hojarasca, Bogotá: Sipa, 1955.
El coronel no tiene quien le escriba, Medellin: Aguirre, 1961.
Los funerales de la mamá grande, Xalapa: Universidad Veracruzana, 1962.
La mala hora, Madrid: Talleres de Gráficas Luis Pérez, 1962. (García Márquez distanced himself from this heavily edited version of his work, and the novel was republished in Mexico by Era in1966 with the full endorsement of the author.)
Cien años de soledad, Buenos Aires: Sudamericana, 1967.
Isabel viendo llover en Macondo, Buenos Aires: Estuario, 1967.
La novela en América Latina (diálogo), with Mario Vargas Llosa, Lima: Carlos Milla Batres, 1968.
Relato de un náufrago, Barcelona: Tusquets, 1970. (First published in *El Espectador* newspaper, 1955, then later as a short story.)
La increíble y triste historia de la cándida Eréndira y de su abuela desalmada, Barcelona: Barral, 1972.
Ojos de perro azul: nueve cuentos desconocidos, Rosario: Equiseditorial, 1972.
El otoño del patriarca, Barcelona: Plaza and Janés, 1975.
Todos los cuentos de Gabriel García Márquez (1947–1972), Barcelona: Plaza y Janés, 1975.
De viaje por los países socialistas: 90 días en la 'Cortina de Hierro', Cali: Ediciones Macondo, 1978.
Crónica de una muerte anunciada, Bogotá: Oveja Negra, 1981.
Obra periodística, edited and with an introduction by Jacques Gilard, 4 vols., Barcelona: Bruguera, 1981–3: (I) *Textos costeños (1948–1952);* (II) *Entre cachacos I;* (III) *Entre cachacos II;* (IV) *De Europa y América (1955–1960).*
El olor de la guayaba, conversations with Plinio Apuleyo Mendoza, Barcelona: Bruguera, 1982.
El rastro de tu sangre en la nieve: El verano feliz de la señora Forbes, Bogotá: William Dampier, 1982.
El amor en los tiempos del cólera, Bogotá, Oveja Negra, 1985.
La aventura de Miguel Littín clandestino en Chile, Madrid: El País, 1986.
El general en su laberinto, Madrid: Mondadori, 1989.
Notas de Prensa, 1980–1984, Madrid: Mondadori, 1991.

Doce cuentos peregrinos, Madrid: Mondadori, 1992.
Del amor y otros demonios, Barcelona: Mondadori, 1994.
Noticia de un secuestro, Barcelona: Mondadori, 1996.
Obra periodística, vol. v *(1974–1995): Por la libre,* Barcelona: Mondadori, 1999.
Vivir para contarla, Barcelona: Mondadori, 2002.
Memoria de mis putas tristes, Barcelona: Mondadori, 2004.

Translations into English

One Hundred Years of Solitude, trans. Gregory Rabassa, London: Picador, 1970.
Leaf Storm and Other Stories, trans. Gregory Rabassa, New York: Harper & Row, 1972.
No One Writes to the Colonel, trans. J. S. Bernstein, Harmondsworth: Penguin, 1974.
The Autumn of the Patriarch, trans. Gregory Rabassa, London: Jonathan Cape, 1977.
Innocent Eréndira and Other Stories, trans. Gregory Rabassa, New York: Harper & Row, 1978.
Chronicle of a Death Foretold, trans. Gregory Rabassa, New York: Knopf, 1983.
The Fragrance of Guava, trans. Ann Wright, London: Verso, 1983.
Collected Stories, trans. Gregory Rabassa and J. S. Bernstein, New York: Harper & Row, 1984.
The Story of a Shipwrecked Sailor, trans. Randolph Hogan, New York: Vintage, 1986.
Clandestine in Chile: The Adventures of Miguel Littín, trans. Asa Zatz, New York: Henry Holt, 1987.
Love in the Time of Cholera, trans. Edith Grossman, London: Jonathan Cape, 1988.
The General in His Labyrinth, trans. Edith Grossman, Harmondsworth: Penguin, 1991.
Strange Pilgrims: Twelve Stories, trans. Edith Grossman, London: Jonathan Cape, 1993.
Of Love and Other Demons, trans. Edith Grossman, New York: Knopf, 1995.
In Evil Hour, trans. Gregory Rabassa, Harmondsworth: Penguin, 1996.
News of a Kidnapping, trans. Edith Grossman, New York: Penguin, 1998.
Living to Tell the Tale, trans. Edith Grossman, New York: Vintage, 2004.
Memories of My Melancholy Whores, trans. Edith Grossman, New York: Knopf, 2005.

Selected criticism

Amestoy, Lida Aronne, *El mito contra el mito: narración e ideografía en* El otoño del patriarca, *Revista Iberoamericana*, 52 (135–6) (1986): 521–30.
Arnau, Carmen, *El mundo mítico de Gabriel García Márquez*, Barcelona: Península, 1971.
Bell, Michael, *Gabriel García Márquez: Solitude and Solidarity*, London: Macmillan, 1993.
Bell-Villada, Gene H., *Gabriel García Márquez: The Man and His Work*, Chapel Hill, NC: University of North Carolina Press, 1990.

(ed). *Gabriel García Márquez's* One Hundred Years of Solitude: *A Casebook*, Oxford: Oxford University Press, 2002.

Benedetti, Mario, *Nueve asedios a García Márquez*, Santiago de Chile: Editora Universitaria, 1969.

Bhalla, Alok (ed.), *García Márquez and Latin America*, New York: Envoy, 1987.

Bloom, Harold, *Gabriel García Márquez*, New York and Philadelphia, PA: Chelsea House Publications, 2007.

(ed.), *Gabriel García Márquez's* Love in the Time of Cholera, New York: Chelsea House, 2005.

Bloom, Harold and Welsch, Gabriel (eds.), *Gabriel García Márquez's* One Hundred Years of Solitude, New York: Chelsea House, 2006.

Carreras González, Olga, *El mundo de Macondo en la obra de Gabriel García Márquez*, Miami, FL: Ediciones Universal, 1974.

Carrillo, Germán, *La narrativa de Gabriel García Márquez*, Madrid: Castalia, 1975.

Cobo Borda, Juan and García Nuñez, Luis (eds.), *Repertorio crítico sobre Gabriel García Márquez*, 2 vols., Bogotá: Instituto Caro y Cuervo, 1995.

Collazos, Oscar, *García Márquez: la soledad y la gloria – Su vida y su obra*, Barcelona: Plaza y Janés, 1983.

Corrales, Pascual M. (ed.), *Lectura de García Márquez (doce estudios)*, Quito: Centro de Publicaciones de la Pontífica Universidad Católica del Ecuador, 1975.

Corwin Jay, *La transposición de fuentes indígenas en* Cien años de soledad, Oxford, MS: University of Mississippi, 1997.

Detjens, Wilma Else, *Home as Creation: The Influence of Early Childhood Experience in the Literary Creation of Gabriel García Márquez, Agustín Yáñez and Juan Rulfo*, New York: Peter Lang, 1993.

Dolan, Sean, *Gabriel García Márquez*, New York: Chelsea House, 1994.

Fahy, Thomas, *Gabriel García Márquez's* Love in the Time of Cholera*: A Reader's Guide*, New York: Continuum, 2003.

Fernández Braso, Miguel, *La soledad de Gabriel García Márquez (una conversación infinita)*, Barcelona: Planeta, 1972.

Fiddian, Robin (ed.), *García Márquez*, London and New York: Longman, 1995.

García Márquez: Los funerales de la mamá grande, London: Grant & Cutler, 2006.

Fox, Geoffrey E., *Gabriel García Márquez's* One Hundred Years of Solitude: *A Critical Commentary*, New York: Monarch, 1987.

Giacoman, Helmy F., *Homenaje a Gabriel García Márquez*, New York: Las Américas, 1972.

González, Nelly Sfeir, *Bibliographic Guide to Gabriel García Márquez, 1992–2002*, Westport, CT: Praeger, 2003.

Gullón, Ricardo, *García Márquez o el olvidado arte de contar*, Madrid: Taurus, 1970.

Hann, Hannelore, *The Influence of Franz Kafka on Three Novels by Gabriel García Márquez*, New York: Peter Lang, 1993.

Hart, Stephen M., *Gabriel García Márquez*, Crónica de una muerte anunciada, London: Grant & Cutler, 1994.

Hart, Stephen M. and Ouyang, Wen-Chin (eds.), *A Companion to Magical Realism*, Woodbridge: Tamesis, 2005.

Ínsula 723 (March 2007), special edition on García Márquez, 'Ciento cuarenta años de soledad y ochenta de vida'.
Janes, Regina, *Gabriel García Márquez: Revolutions in Wonderland*, Columbia, MO: University of Missouri Press, 1981.
One Hundred Years of Solitude: *Modes of Reading*, Boston, MA: Twayne, 1991.
Jara Cuadra, René and Mejía Duque, Jaime, *Las claves del mito en García Márquez*, Valparaíso: Ediciones Universitarias, 1972.
Joset, Jacques, *Gabriel García Márquez: Coetáneo de la eternidad*, Amsterdam: Rodopi, 1984.
Kline, Carmenza, *Fiction and Reality in the Works of Gabriel García Márquez*, Salamanca: Universidad de Salamanca, 2002.
Violencia en Macondo: Tema recurrente en la obra de García Marquéz, Bogotá: Universidad de Salamanca, Sede Colombia, 2002.
Levine, Suzanne J., *El espejo hablado: Un estudio de* Cien años de soledad, Caracas: Monte Ávila, 1975.
Martin, Gerald, *Gabriel García Márquez: A Life*, London: Bloomsbury, 2008.
Martínez, Pedro S., *Recopilación de textos sobre Gabriel García Márquez*, 2nd edn, Havana: Casa de las Américas, 1971.
McGuirk, Bernard and Cardwell, Richard (eds.), *Gabriel García Márquez: New Readings*, Cambridge: Cambridge University Press, 1987.
McMurray, George, *Gabriel García Márquez*, New York: Frederick Ungar, 1977.
(ed.), *Critical Essays on Gabriel García Márquez*, Boston, MA: G. K. Hall, 1987.
Gabriel García Márquez: Life, Work and Criticism, Fredericton, New Brunswick, NJ: York Press, 1987.
McNerney, Kathleen, *Understanding Gabriel García Márquez*, Columbia, SC: South Carolina University Press, 1989.
Mejía Duque, Jaime, *Mito y realidad en Gabriel García Márquez*, Bogotá: Prisma, 1970.
Mellen, Joan, *Literary Masters: Gabriel García Márquez*, Farmington Hills, MI: Thomson Gale, 2000.
Minta, Stephen, *Gabriel García Márquez: Writer of Colombia*, London: Jonathan Cape, 1987.
Molina Fernández, Carolina, *Gabriel García Márquez: crónica y novela*, Cáceres: Universidad de Extremadura, 2006.
Mose, Kenrick, *Defamiliarization in the Work of Gabriel García Márquez*, Lewiston, NY: Edwin Mellen Press, 1989.
Muaddi Darraj, Susan, *Gabriel García Márquez: The Great Hispanic Heritage*, New York: Chelsea House Publications, 2006.
Oberhelman, Harley D., *Gabriel García Márquez: A Study of the Short Fiction*, Boston, MA: Twayne, 1991.
The Presence of Hemingway in the Short Fiction of Gabriel García Márquez, Fredericton, New Brunswick, NJ: York Press, 1994.
García Márquez and Cuba: A Study of its Presence in His Fiction, Journalism, and Cinema, Fredericton, New Brunswick, NJ: York Press, 1995.
The Autumn of the patriarch: Text and Culture, in Robin Fiddian (ed.), *Garcia Márquez*, London and New york: Longman, 1995, 121–43.
Ortega, Julio (ed.) with Elliot, Claudia (assistant editor), *Gabriel García Márquez and the Powers of Fiction*, Austin, TX: University of Texas Press, 1988.

(ed.), *Gaborio: Artes de releer a Gabriel García Márquez*, Mexico City: Jorale, 2003.
Oyarzún, Kemy and Megenney, William W. (eds.), *Essays on Gabriel García Márquez*, Riverside, CA: University of California, 1984.
Palencia-Roth, Michael, *Gabriel García Márquez: La línea, el círculo y las metamorfosis del mito*, Madrid: Gredos, 1983.
Pelayo, Ruben, *Gabriel García Márquez: A Critical Companion*, Westport, CT: Greenwood Press, 2001.
Penuel, Arnold M., *Intertextuality in García Márquez*, York, SC: Spanish Literature Publications Company, 1994.
Rodríguez Vergara, Isabel, *El mundo satírico de Gabriel García Márquez*, Madrid: Pliegos, 1991.
Haunting Demons: Critical Essays on the Works of García Márquez, Washington: CIDI, 1998.
Saldívar, Dasso, *García Márquez: El viaje a la semilla – La biografía*, Madrid: Alfaguara, 1997.
Scherman Filer, Jorge, *La parodia del poder: Carpentier y García Márquez: Desafiando el mito sobre el dictador latinoamericano*, Santiago de Chile: Cuarto Propio, 2003.
Segui, Agustín, *La verdadera historia de Macondo*, Frankfurt: Vervuert Verlag, 1994.
Shaw, Bradley and Vera-Godwin, Nora, *Critical Perspectives on Gabriel García Márquez*, Lincoln, NE: Society for Spanish and Spanish American Studies, 1986.
Sims, Robert L., *The Evolution of Myth in Gabriel García Márquez from* La hojarasca *to* Cien años de soledad, Miami, FL: Universal, 1981.
The First García Márquez: A Study of his Journalistic Writing from 1948 to 1955, Lanham, MD: University Press of America, 1992.
Sorela, Pedro, *El otro García Márquez: los años difíciles*, Madrid: Mondadori, 1981.
Swanson, Philip, *Cómo leer a Gabriel García Márquez*, Madrid: Júcar, 1991.
Torres, Benjamín, *Gabriel García Márquez o la alquimia del incesto*, Madrid: Playor, 1987.
Vargas Llosa, Mario, *García Márquez: Historia de un deicidio*, Barcelona and Caracas: Seix Barral and Monte Avila, 1971.
Waters Hood, Edward, *La ficción de Gabriel García Márquez: Repetición e intertextualidad*, New York: Peter Lang, 1993.
Williams, Raymond L. *Gabriel García Márquez*, Boston, MA: Twayne, 1984.
Wood, Michael, *Gabriel García Márquez:* One Hundred Years of Solitude, Cambridge: Cambridge University Press, 1990.
Zuluaga, Osorio C. (ed.), *Anthropos*, 187: 1999. A special edition on García Márquez.

INDEX

Note: GM = García Márquez

absurd humour, 131, 139
adolescent girls, 127
Aguilar, García, 163
Agustín (*No One Writes to the Colonel*), 47, 48, 49
Ali, Tariq, 108
Allende, Isabel, 191
Almodóvar, Pedro, 171
Amador, Pepe (*In Evil Hour*), 52, 53
ambiguity in GM's fiction, 50, 75
América (*Love in the Time of Cholera*), 120–1
the Americas
anachronic techniques, 86
anality, 89
Andean Colombia, 8
Anderson, John Lee, 90
Angel, Padre (*In Evil Hour*), 53
Angela (*Chronicle of a Death Foretold*), 113, 114–16
animal imagery, 73, 82
'Another Story' column (*El Universal*),
Antigone (Sophocles), 43
Aracataca, Colombia, 156
Aragonés, Patricio (*The Autumn of the Patriarch*), 88
archetypal narratives, 44, 48
Arnau, Carmen, 30
As I Lay Dying (Faulkner), 43
Asturias, Miguel Angel, 81, 100
Aureliano (*One Hundred Years of Solitude*), 60, 130
autobiography, 154–8
The Autumn of the Patriarch, 17, 78–91, 95, 100

banana workers' strike, 60, 71, 155
Barcelona, 16
Barcha, Mercedes, 8, 13, 14
Barnes, Julian, 193
Bayardo (*Chronicle of a Death Foretold*), 115
Beckett, Samuel, 134
Bell, Michael, 33, 79
biblical motifs, 61
  see also Christian themes
'Big Mama's Funeral' (short story), 41, 99, 137–8
The Birth of Tragedy (Nietzsche)
'Bitterness for Three Sleepwalkers' (short story), 132
The Blue Lobster (film),
Bogotá, Colombia, 9
Bolívar, Simón, 19, 102–11
book title formulas, 23
the Boom,
Borges, Jorge Luis, 70
brothels, 114, 124
Buell, Lawrence, 64
Buendía, Colonel Aureliano, *see* Aureliano (*One Hundred Years of Solitude*)
Buendía, José Arcadio, *see* José (*One Hundred Years of Solitude*)
Bulgakov, Mikhail, 186–7
burial theme, 97–102, 111, 131

cachacos, 9, 106
capitalism, 71, 130
Carballo, Emanuel, 26
Caribbean Colombia, 9, 10, 72, 74, 107
Carmichael (*In Evil Hour*), 53–4
Carpentier, Alejo, 58, 82, 183–5
Carrillo, Germán, 31
Cartagena, 21

Casanova, Pascale, 180
Casares, Adolfo Bioy, 70
Castro, Fidel, 90, 103
Cayetano (*Of Love and Other Demons*), 121–4
Carlos ('Tuesday Siesta'), 43
Cepeda Samudio, Alvaro, 71
Cervantes, Miguel de, 185
César (*In Evil Hour*), 52
Chaparro Valderrama, Hugo, 174
characters, naming of, 156
Chávarri, Jaime, 172
Chile, 149
'The Chocó Ignored by Colombia' (*El Espectador*),
cholera, 117
Christian themes, 30–1, 48, 49, 50
  see also biblical motifs
Chronicle of a Death Foretold, 18, 96, 100
  film, 170–1
  love theme, 113–16
  the Church, intolerance of,
cinema, 160–76
  adaptations of GM's works, 165–75
  GM's criticism, 160–2
  script-writing, 13, 19, 162–3
  writing style influence, 163–5
circus motifs, 49, 60
Clandestine in Chile: the Adventures of Miguel Littín, 149–51, 161
classical myths, 43–4
climate, 64
Clinton, Bill, 18
cock-fighting motif, 48, 69, 167, 170
Coetzee, J. M., 191
Collazos, Oscar, 28
Colombia, 96
  civil conflict, 10
  geography, 8–9
  history, 105–11
  kidnapping, 20, 151–4
  nature writings, 66–7
  newspapers, 145
colonialism, 60, 61, 73, 138
Columbus, Christopher, 82–3, 90
Communist Party, Colombia, 135
Conde, Susan, 172
consciousness, 131
Correa, Julián David, 166
Cortázar, Julio, 71
cosmopolitanism, 180
Cosmos (Humboldt), 67
costeños (coastal-dwellers), 9, 106
Cova (*The Vortex*), 69–70
criollista texts, 68–70
critical overview of GM's fiction, 25–36
Cruz Konfly, Fernando, 104
Cuba, 13, 21, 135
current affairs, 51

Dangerous Loves (films), 19, 171–4
Darío, Rubén, 78, 89–90
Dawn Poison (film), 175
de Bernières, Louis, 191
de Sica, Vittorio, 181
death theme, 95, 97–102, 111, 131, 138
decolonisation, 51
Defoe, Daniel, 168
Delgadina (*Memories of My Melancholy Whores*), 125–6
dialogue, 129, 131, 132, 133, 139
'Dialogue with the Mirror' (short story), 132
A Diatribe of Love against a Seated Man (play), 176
dictatorship theme, 78–91, 100
dictionaries, 157
Difficult Loves (films), 171–4
Dominican Republic, 85
double narration, 149–51
dreams, 51
drug trafficking, 20, 153
Duque, Lisando, 173

Eagleton, Terry, 186
early fiction of GM, 41–55
eco-criticism, *One Hundred Years of Solitude*, 64–75
Ecuador, 107
Efraín (*María*), 67–8
Eliécer Gaitán, Jorge, 10, 106
Eligio García, Gabriel, 7–8
enchantment, 193
endings in GM's fiction, 97–102
environmentalism, 66
Eréndira (film), 169–70
'Eréndira' (short story), 16, 139–41
Escobar, Pablo, 21
Escuela Internacional de Cine y Televisión, 21, 162
El Espectador, 10, 11, 144, 145–9
Estrada Cabrera, Manuel, 85
European travels, 12, 16
'Eva Is Inside Her Cat' (short story), 10, 131

'Evaluation and Reconstruction of the Catastrophe in Antioquia' (*El Espectador*),
Everett, Rupert, 171
exceptionalism, 191
excrement motif, 79, 89, 99
exile, 151
exorcism, 124
expletives, 50
'Eyes of a Blue Dog' (short story), 11, 132

Fable of the Beautiful Pigeon Fancier (film), 172
the family,
Faulkner, William, 11, 41, 43, 181
female objectification, 121, 123, 125, 127
Fermina (*Love in the Time of Cholera*), 116, 117–20
film, 160–76
  adaptations of GM's works, 165–75
  GM's criticism, 160–2
  script-writing, 13, 19, 162–3
Flaubert's Parrot (Barnes), 193
Florentino (*Love in the Time of Cholera*), 116–21, 124
flowers motif, 138
follow-up stories, 144, 146–58
foreign historian device, 180, 188–9
Franco, Francisco, 85
Fuentes, Carlos, 26, 29, 84, 90, 166

García Márquez, Gabriel (Gabo)
  biography, 7–23
  character in *One Hundred Years of Solitude*,
  cinema, 160–76
  critical overview
  early fiction, 10, 11, 35, 41–55
  early years, 7–9
  illness, 22
  influences, 41, 43, 52, 97, 181
  journalism, 12, 17, 20, 21, 144–54
  law studies, 9
  Nobel Prize, 18
  parents, 7–8
  politics, 17
  wife, 8, 13, 14
The General in his Labyrinth, 94, 102–11, 190
ghosts, 134
'The Giraffe' column (*El Heraldo*), 145
Glissant, Edouard, 192
The Golden Cockerel (film), 166
Gómez, Juan Vicente, 85
Grass, Günter, 190
Greene, Graham, 103
Guerra, Ruy, 169, 172, 175
Gullón, Ricardo, 27
Gutiérrez Alea, Tomás, 172

hallucinations, 51
Hamlet (Shakespeare), 189
Happy Sunday (film), 173
Harss, Luis, 25–6
Heidegger, Martin, 194
Hemingway, Ernest, 41
El Heraldo, 11, 145
Hermosillo, Jaime Humberto, 168
historical novels, 82, 108
history
  The Autumn of the Patriarch, 84–6
  The General in the Labyrinth, 102–11
  One Hundred Years of Solitude, 155
Hitchcock, Alfred, 163
hoax message, 22
Hopscotch (Cortázar), 71
The House, 11
How to Tell a Story: Gabriel García Márquez's Scriptwriting Workshop, 163
Humboldt, Alexander von, 66–7
humour, 131, 139

I the Supreme (Roa Bastos), 82
I'm the One You're Looking For (film), 171
illness of GM, 22
imperialism, 82, 86
In Evil Hour, 13, 41, 51–5
incest theme, 61–2
'The Incredible and Sad Tale of Innocent Eréndira and Her Heartless Grandmother' (short story), 16
India, 190
Indians, 69, 83, 90
internet hoax message, 22
intertextuality, 82
Into the Mainstream (Harss), 25–6
investigative journalism, 146–54
The Invisible Children (film), 175
Isaac, Alberto, 167
Isaacs, Jorge, 67–8, 71
Isabel (*Leaf Storm*), 45

José Aracadio (*One Hundred Years of Solitude*), 73

journalism, 12, 17, 20, 21, 144–54
justice themes, 43, 48
Juvenal (*Love in the Time of Cholera*), 118–19

Kafka, Franz, 131, 181
kidnapping, 21, 151–4
The Kingdom of This World (Carpentier), 183
Kline, Carmenza, 32

La casa grande (Cepeda Samudio), 71
Labanyi, Jo, 80
Latin America
  colonialism, 138
  history, 105–11
  nature writings, 66–7
  novelists, 14
Leaf Storm, 11, 41, 42–6, 98
Letters from the Park (film), 172
letter-writing motif, 117
Liberal Party, Colombia, 10, 105
literalism, 186
Littín, Miguel, 149–51, 161, 168
Living to Tell the Tale, 22, 154–8
Love in the Time of *Cholera*, 18, 96, 101–2
  film, 175
  love theme, 116–21
love themes, 18, 20, 22, 36, 96, 113–27
  Chronicle of a Death Foretold, 113–16
  Love in the Time of Cholera, 116–21
  Memories of My Melancholy Whores, 124–7
  Of Love and Other Demons, 121–4
Loveluck, Juan, 25
Ludmer, Josefina, 32
Lukács, Georg, 108

machismo, 170
Macondo, 26, 156
  in *Leaf Storm*, 98
  in *One Hundred Years of Solitude*, 188
magical realism, 15–16, 23, 58–9, 74, 129, 132, 134, 139, 179–94
male desire, 121, 123, 127
Mama Grande (*Big Mama's Funeral*), 137
Mann, Thomas, 181
María (Isaacs), 67–8, 71
Márquez, Gabriel García *see* García Márquez, Gabriel
Márquez, Nicolás, 7, 157
marriage, 114, 115, 176
Martin, Gerald, 59, 79
Martínez, Tomás Eloy, 26
martyrdom, 48, 49
the marvellous, 182, 183, 185, 192, 193
Marxist criticism, 29
Mary My Dearest (film), 168
masculinity, 67, 170
massacre of strikers, 60, 71, 155
The Master and Margarita (Bulgakov), 186–7
Maturo, Graciela, 30
mayor (*In Evil Hour*), 52, 54
McMurray, George, 33, 64
melodrama, 101, 167
Melquíades (*One Hundred Years of Solitude*), 188
memoirs, 22, 154–8
Memories of My Melancholy Whores, 22, 97, 99, 124–7
memory, 156, 188
Mena, Lucila, 31
Méndez, José Luis, 32
Menton, Seymour, 82
metafiction, 72
Mexico, 13, 15, 17, 162, 174
Mexico City, 13, 17
Midnight's Children (Rushdie), 190
Minta, Stephen, 130, 135
Miracle in Rome (film), 173–4
modernism, 193
modernistas, 68
modernisation, 71
Momento (magazine), 12
'Monologue of Isabel Watching it Rain in Macondo' (short story), 41
monologues, 19
Montaner, Maria E., 32
Montero, César (*In Evil Hour*), 52
Montiel's Widow (film), 168
Morales, Donald M., 172
morality themes, 43, 54, 55
movies *see* cinema
Munday, Jeremy, 33
Mutis, Alvaro, 104
mythic themes, 30–1, 43

narrative techniques, 29, 30, 147, 148–51
  see also cinema, writing style influence
narrator-reader complicity, 58
nature, 65–6, 71–5
Neruda, Pablo, 88
New Journalism, 146
New Novel genre, 57, 82
Newell, Mike, 175

News of a Kidnapping, 21, 151–4
Nietzsche, Friedrich, 189, 192–3
'The Night of the Curlews' (short story), 136
No One Writes to the Colonel, 13, 41, 46–51, 98, 109, 163–4, 183
film, 174–5
Nobel Prize, 18, 81
non-fiction works, 21, 144–58
see also journalism
North American United Fruit Company, 60
novel titles, 23
novela policial, 54
see also political themes
el nueve de abril, 10

obsessive love theme, 116–21
Oedipus Mayor (film), 174
Of Love and Other Demons, 20
Ohana, Claudia, 172
One Hundred Years of Solitude, 14, 15–16, 57–75, 95, 100, 130, 155, 179, 193
'anti-cinematic' style, 164
criticism, 26, 27, 29–35
an eco-critical reading, 64–75
foreign historian device, 180, 188–9
sources, 72–5
'One of These Days' (short story), 136
one-liners, 132–3
Ong, Walter, 72
oral cultures, 72–5, 193
orality, 89
Ortega, Julio, 139
Ospina, Ramírez, 165, 167, 169, 171
'The Other Side of Death' (short story), 131

Pachón, Maruja, 151, 152–3
paedophilia, 79, 120, 126, 127
Paris, 12
passionate love theme, 121–4, 125
Pastor (*In Evil Hour*), 52, 53
Patricio (*The Autumn of the Patriarch*), 88
Pedro Páramo (Rulfo), 16
Pepe (*In Evil Hour*), 52, 53
Pérez Jiménez, Marcos, 135
Pinochet, General Augusto, 96, 149, 151
playfulness in GM's fiction, 57
plays, 19, 176
political themes,, 54, 60
Portent (film), 168
power theme, 95, 104
prediction motif, 87
Prensa Latina, 13, 135
prequels, 55, 80
Prieto, René, 50
prolepsis, 87
prostitution, 114, 124, 140
'The Puppet' (hoax internet message), 22

Quiroga, Facundo, 81

racism, 13
Rama, Angel, 28, 136
reader – narrator complicity, 58
realism, 182, 185, 191
reality, representation of, 58–9
Reasons of State (Carpentier), 82
refritos (follow-up stories), 144, 146–58
Reina ('The Woman Who Came at Six O'Clock'), 133
Remedios la bella (*One Hundred Years of Solitude*), 71, 73
Rivera, José Eustasio, 68–70
Roa Bastos, Augusto, 82
Rodríguez Monegal, Emir, 27
Rodríguez, Emir, 27
Rodríguez, Ileana, 29
romance genre, 116
Romanticism, 67, 68
roses motif, 138
Rosi, Francesco, 170, 171
Rulfo, Juan, 16
Rushdie, Salman, 190

Santander, Francisco de Paula, 105
Santiaga Márquez, Luisa, 7–8
Santiago (*Chronicle of a Death Foretold*), 113–15
Santos, Francisco (Pacho), 153
Sarmiento, Domingo Faustino, 81, 107
'The Sea of Lost Time' (short story), 138
El Señor Presidente (Asturias), 81
sexuality, 65, 89, 114, 119, 124
short stories, 10, 11, 16, 20, 41, 129–41, 144
Sierva María (*Of Love and Other Demons*), 121–4
social context in GM's fiction, 32, 34, 45
society, 186
solipsistic love theme, 125
solitude theme, 95, 96, 109, 117, 124
'Someone Has Been Disarranging These Roses' (short story), 134–5
Sophocles, 43, 174
Sorela, Pedro, 147
Soriano, Osvaldo, 109
Soviet Union, 187

Spain, 16, 28, 180
Spanish American authors, 14
Spanish literary culture, 180
specularisation, 149
The Story of a Shipwrecked Sailor, 12, 147–9
Strange Pilgrims, 20
Struebig, Patricia, 65
Sucre, Colombia, 8
The Summer of Miss Forbes (film), 173
superstition, 123
surrealism, 183
Swanson, Philip, 34

Taylor, Anna Marie, 30
technology, 73, 74
television, 171, 176
temporality in GM's fiction, 84, 86, 129, 133–5
theatre, 176
There Are No Thieves in This Village (film), 167
'The Third Resignation' (short story), 10, 97–8, 111, 130
The Thousand and One Nights, 157
time themes, 45
  see also temporality in GM's fiction
Time to Die (film), 167–8, 170
Tobin, Patricia, 79
Torrijos, Oscar, 90
Triana, Jorge Alí, 170, 174
Trujillo, Rafael, 85, 86
'Tuesday Siesta' (short story), 43

United States, 22, 82, 86
Ursula (*One Hundred Years of Solitude*), 61, 73, 74

Vargas Llosa, Mario, 27, 29, 30, 57
Velasco, Luis Alejandro, 147
Venezuela, 12, 106, 107
Vinyes, Ramón, 10
el violencia (the violence), 10, 52, 101, 104
virginity, 114, 115
Volkening, E., 25
The Vortex (Rivera), 68–70

waiting motif, 107
weather, 65
whodunnit device, 52, 54
Williamson, Edwin, 34, 59, 61
'Winter' (short story)', 41
'The Woman Who Came at Six O'Clock' (short story), 133–4
women, 157, 172
Woolf, Virginia, 181
world literature, and magical realism, 179–94

The Year of the Plague (film), 168

Zalamea, Jorge, 81

Cambridge Companions To ...

AUTHORS

Edward Albee *edited by Stephen J. Bottoms*

Margaret Atwood *edited by Coral Ann Howells*

W. H. Auden *edited by Stan Smith*

Jane Austen *edited by Edward Copeland and Juliet McMaster*

Beckett *edited by John Pilling*

Bede *edited by Scott DeGregorio*

Aphra Behn *edited by Derek Hughes and Janet Todd*

Walter Benjamin *edited by David S. Ferris*

William Blake *edited by Morris Eaves*

Brecht *edited by Peter Thomson and Glendyr Sacks* (second edition)

The Brontës *edited by Heather Glen*

Frances Burney *edited by Peter Sabor*

Byron *edited by Drummond Bone*

Albert Camus *edited by Edward J. Hughes*

Willa Cather *edited by Marilee Lindemann*

Cervantes *edited by Anthony J. Cascardi*

Chaucer *edited by Piero Boitani and Jill Mann* (second edition)

Chekhov *edited by Vera Gottlieb and Paul Allain*

Kate Chopin *edited by Janet Beer*

Caryl Churchill *edited by Elaine Aston and Elin Diamond*

Coleridge *edited by Lucy Newlyn*

Wilkie Collins *edited by Jenny Bourne Taylor*

Joseph Conrad *edited by J. H. Stape*

Dante *edited by Rachel Jacoff* (second edition)

Daniel Defoe *edited by John Richetti*

Don DeLillo *edited by John N. Duvall*

Charles Dickens *edited by John O. Jordan*

Emily Dickinson *edited by Wendy Martin*

John Donne *edited by Achsah Guibbory*

Dostoevskii *edited by W. J. Leatherbarrow*

Theodore Dreiser *edited by Leonard Cassuto and Claire Virginia Eby*

John Dryden *edited by Steven N. Zwicker*

W. E. B. Du Bois *edited by Shamoon Zamir*

George Eliot *edited by George Levine*

T. S. Eliot *edited by A. David Moody*

Ralph Ellison *edited by Ross Posnock*

Ralph Waldo Emerson *edited by Joel Porte and Saundra Morris*

William Faulkner *edited by Philip M. Weinstein*

Henry Fielding *edited by Claude Rawson*

F. Scott Fitzgerald *edited by Ruth Prigozy*

Flaubert *edited by Timothy Unwin*

E. M. Forster *edited by David Bradshaw*

Benjamin Franklin *edited by Carla Mulford*

Brian Friel *edited by Anthony Roche*

Robert Frost *edited by Robert Faggen*

Gabriel García Márquez *edited by Philip Swanson*

Elizabeth Gaskell *edited by Jill L. Matus*

Goethe *edited by Lesley Sharpe*

Günter Grass *edited by Stuart Taberner*

Thomas Hardy *edited by Dale Kramer*

David Hare *edited by Richard Boon*

Nathaniel Hawthorne *edited by Richard Millington*

Seamus Heaney *edited by Bernard O'Donoghue*

Ernest Hemingway *edited by Scott Donaldson*

Homer *edited by Robert Fowler*

Horace *edited by Stephen Harrison*

Ibsen *edited by James McFarlane*

Henry James *edited by Jonathan Freedman*

Samuel Johnson *edited by Greg Clingham*

Ben Jonson *edited by Richard Harp and Stanley Stewart*

James Joyce *edited by Derek Attridge* (second edition)

Kafka *edited by Julian Preece*

Keats *edited by Susan J. Wolfson*

Lacan *edited by Jean-Michel Rabaté*

D. H. Lawrence *edited by Anne Fernihough*

Primo Levi *edited by Robert Gordon*

Lucretius *edited by Stuart Gillespie and Philip Hardie*

David Mamet *edited by Christopher Bigsby*

Thomas Mann *edited by Ritchie Robertson*

Christopher Marlowe *edited by Patrick Cheney*

Herman Melville *edited by Robert S. Levine*

Arthur Miller *edited by Christopher Bigsby* (second edition)

Milton *edited by Dennis Danielson* (second edition)

Molière *edited by David Bradby and Andrew Calder*

Toni Morrison *edited by Justine Tally*

Nabokov *edited by Julian W. Connolly*

Eugene O'Neill *edited by Michael Manheim*

George Orwell *edited by John Rodden*

Ovid *edited by Philip Hardie*

Harold Pinter *edited by Peter Raby* (second edition)

Sylvia Plath *edited by Jo Gill*

Edgar Allan Poe *edited by Kevin J. Hayes*

Alexander Pope *edited by Pat Rogers*

Ezra Pound *edited by Ira B. Nadel*

Proust *edited by Richard Bales*

Pushkin *edited by Andrew Kahn*

Rabelais *edited by John O'Brien*

Rilke *edited by Karen Leeder and Robert Vilain*

Philip Roth *edited by Timothy Parrish*

Salman Rushdie *edited by Abdulrazak Gurnah*

Shakespeare *edited by Margareta de Grazia and Stanley Wells* (second edition)

Shakespearean Comedy *edited by Alexander Leggatt*

Shakespeare on Film *edited by Russell Jackson* (second edition)

Shakespeare's History Plays *edited by Michael Hattaway*

Shakespeare's Last Plays *edited by Catherine M. S. Alexander*

Shakespeare's Poetry *edited by Patrick Cheney*

Shakespeare and Popular Culture *edited by Robert Shaughnessy*

Shakespeare on Stage *edited by Stanley Wells and Sarah Stanton*

Shakespearean Tragedy *edited by Claire McEachern*

George Bernard Shaw *edited by Christopher Innes*

Shelley *edited by Timothy Morton*

Mary Shelley *edited by Esther Schor*

Sam Shepard *edited by Matthew C. Roudané*

Spenser *edited by Andrew Hadfield*

Laurence Sterne *edited by Thomas Keymer*

Wallace Stevens *edited by John N. Serio*

Tom Stoppard *edited by Katherine E. Kelly*

Harriet Beecher Stowe *edited by Cindy Weinstein*

August Strindberg *edited by Michael Robinson*

Jonathan Swift *edited by Christopher Fox*

J. M. Synge *edited by P. J. Mathews*

Tacitus *edited by A. J. Woodman*

Henry David Thoreau *edited by Joel Myerson*

Tolstoy *edited by Donna Tussing Orwin*

Mark Twain *edited by Forrest G. Robinson*

Virgil *edited by Charles Martindale*

Voltaire *edited by Nicholas Cronk*

Edith Wharton *edited by Millicent Bell*

Walt Whitman *edited by Ezra Greenspan*

Oscar Wilde *edited by Peter Raby*

Tennessee Williams *edited by Matthew C. Roudané*

August Wilson *edited by Christopher Bigsby*

Mary Wollstonecraft *edited by Claudia L. Johnson*

Virginia Woolf *edited by Susan Sellers* (second edition)

Wordsworth *edited by Stephen Gill*

W. B. Yeats *edited by Marjorie Howes and John Kelly*

Zola *edited by Brian Nelson*

TOPICS

The Actress *edited by Maggie B. Gale and John Stokes*

The African American Novel *edited by Maryemma Graham*

The African American Slave Narrative *edited by Audrey A. Fisch*

Allegory *edited by Rita Copeland and Peter Struck*

American Modernism *edited by Walter Kalaidjian*

American Realism and Naturalism *edited by Donald Pizer*

American Travel Writing *edited by Alfred Bendixen and Judith Hamera*

American Women Playwrights *edited by Brenda Murphy*

Ancient Rhetoric *edited by Erik Gunderson*

Arthurian Legend *edited by Elizabeth Archibald and Ad Putter*

Australian Literature *edited by Elizabeth Webby*

British Romanticism (second edition) *edited by Stuart Curran*

British Romantic Poetry *edited by James Chandler and Maureen N. McLane*

British Theatre, 1730–1830, *edited by Jane Moody and Daniel O'Quinn*

Canadian Literature *edited by Eva-Marie Kröller*

Children's Literature *edited by M. O. Grenby and Andrea Immel*

The Classic Russian Novel *edited by Malcolm V. Jones and Robin Feuer Miller*

Contemporary Irish Poetry *edited by Matthew Campbell*

Crime Fiction *edited by Martin Priestman*

Early Modern Women's Writing *edited by Laura Lunger Knoppers*

The Eighteenth-Century Novel *edited by John Richetti*

Eighteenth-Century Poetry *edited by John Sitter*

English Literature, 1500–1600 *edited by Arthur F. Kinney*

English Literature, 1650–1740 *edited by Steven N. Zwicker*

English Literature, 1740–1830 *edited by Thomas Keymer and Jon Mee*

English Literature, 1830–1914 *edited by Joanne Shattock*

English Novelists *edited by Adrian Poole*

English Poets *edited by Claude Rawson*

English Poetry, Donne to Marvell *edited by Thomas N. Corns*

English Renaissance Drama, second edition *edited by A. R. Braunmuller and Michael Hattaway*

English Renaissance Tragedy *edited by Emma Smith and Garrett A. Sullivan Jr.*

English Restoration Theatre *edited by Deborah C. Payne Fisk*

The Epic *edited by Catherine Bates*

Feminist Literary Theory *edited by Ellen Rooney*

Fiction in the Romantic Period *edited by Richard Maxwell and Katie Trumpener*

The Fin de Siècle *edited by Gail Marshall*

The French Novel: from 1800 to the Present *edited by Timothy Unwin*

German Romanticism *edited by Nicholas Saul*

Gothic Fiction *edited by Jerrold E. Hogle*

The Greek and Roman Novel *edited by Tim Whitmarsh*

Greek and Roman Theatre *edited by Marianne McDonald and J. Michael Walton*

Greek Lyric *edited by Felix Budelmann*

Greek Mythology *edited by Roger D. Woodard*

Greek Tragedy *edited by P. E. Easterling*

The Harlem Renaissance *edited by George Hutchinson*

The Irish Novel *edited by John Wilson Foster*

The Italian Novel *edited by Peter Bondanella and Andrea Ciccarelli*

Jewish American Literature *edited by Hana Wirth-Nesher and Michael P. Kramer*

The Latin American Novel *edited by Efraín Kristal*

The Literature of Los Angeles *edited by Kevin R. McNamara*

The Literature of New York *edited by Cyrus Patell and Bryan Waterman*

The Literature of the First World War *edited by Vincent Sherry*

The Literature of World War II *edited by Marina MacKay*

Literature on Screen *edited by Deborah Cartmell and Imelda Whelehan*

Medieval English Literature *edited by Larry Scanlon*

Medieval English Theatre *edited by Richard Beadle and Alan J. Fletcher* (second edition)

Medieval French Literature *edited by Simon Gaunt and Sarah Kay*

Medieval Romance *edited by Roberta L. Krueger*

Medieval Women's Writing *edited by Carolyn Dinshaw and David Wallace*

Modern American Culture *edited by Christopher Bigsby*

Modern British Women Playwrights *edited by Elaine Aston and Janelle Reinelt*

Modern French Culture *edited by Nicholas Hewitt*

Modern German Culture *edited by Eva Kolinsky and Wilfried van der Will*

The Modern German Novel *edited by Graham Bartram*

Modern Irish Culture *edited by Joe Cleary and Claire Connolly*

Modern Italian Culture *edited by Zygmunt G. Baranski and Rebecca J. West*

Modern Latin American Culture *edited by John King*

Modern Russian Culture *edited by Nicholas Rzhevsky*

Modern Spanish Culture *edited by David T. Gies*

Modernism *edited by Michael Levenson*

The Modernist Novel *edited by Morag Shiach*

Modernist Poetry *edited by Alex Davis and Lee M. Jenkins*

Narrative *edited by David Herman*

Native American Literature *edited by Joy Porter and Kenneth M. Roemer*

Nineteenth-Century American Women's Writing *edited by Dale M. Bauer and Philip Gould*

Old English Literature *edited by Malcolm Godden and Michael Lapidge*

Performance Studies *edited by Tracy C. Davis*

Postcolonial Literary Studies *edited by Neil Lazarus*

Postmodernism *edited by Steven Connor*

Renaissance Humanism *edited by Jill Kraye*

Roman Satire *edited by Kirk Freudenburg*

The Roman Historians *edited by Andrew Feldherr*

The Spanish Novel: From 1600 to the Present *edited by Harriet Turner and Adelaida López de Martínez*

Travel Writing *edited by Peter Hulme and Tim Youngs*

Twentieth-Century Irish Drama *edited by Shaun Richards*

The Twentieth-Century English Novel *edited by Robert L. Caserio*

Twentieth-Century English Poetry *edited by Neil Corcoran*

Victorian and Edwardian Theatre *edited by Kerry Powell*

The Victorian Novel *edited by Deirdre David*

Victorian Poetry *edited by Joseph Bristow*

War Writing *edited by Kate McLoughlin*

Writing of the English Revolution *edited by N. H. Keeble*